International Environmental Externalities
and the Double Dividend

NEW HORIZONS IN ENVIRONMENTAL ECONOMICS

General Editors: Wallace E. Oates, *Professor of Economics, University of Maryland, USA* and Henk Folmer, *Professor of General Economics, Wageningen University and Professor of Environmental Economics, Tilburg University, The Netherlands*

This important series is designed to make a significant contribution to the development of the principles and practices of environmental economics. It includes both theoretical and empirical work. International in scope, it addresses issues of current and future concern in both East and West and in developed and developing countries.

The main purpose of the series is to create a forum for the publication of high quality work and to show how economic analysis can make a contribution to understanding and resolving the environmental problems confronting the world in the twenty-first century.

Recent titles in the series include:

Designing International Environmental Agreements
Incentive Compatible Strategies for Cost-Effective Cooperation
Carsten Schmidt

Spatial Environmental and Resource Economics
The Selected Essays of Charles D. Kolstad
Charles D. Kolstad

Economic Theories of International Environmental Cooperation
Carsten Helm

Negotiating Environmental Quality
Policy Implementation in Germany and the United States
Markus A. Lehmann

Game Theory and International Environmental Cooperation
Michael Finus

Sustainable Small-scale Forestry
Socio-economic Analysis and Policy
Edited by S.R. Harrison, J.L. Herbohn and K.F. Herbohn

Environmental Economics and Public Policy
Selected Papers of Robert N. Stavins, 1988-1999
Robert N. Stavins

International Environmental Externalities and the Double Dividend
Sebastian Killinger

Global Emissions Trading
Key Issues for Industrialized Countries
Edited by Suzi Kerr

The Choice Modelling Approach to Environmental Valuation
Edited by Jeff Bennett and Russell Blamey

Uncertainty and the Environment
Implications for Decision Making and Environmental Policy
Richard A. Young

International Environmental Externalities and the Double Dividend

Sebastian Killinger

Inhouse Consultant, DG BANK AG, Germany

NEW HORIZONS IN ENVIRONMENTAL ECONOMICS

Edward Elgar

Cheltenham, UK • Northampton, MA, USA

Published by
Edward Elgar Publishing Limited
Glensanda House
Montpellier Parade
Cheltenham
Glos GL50 1UA
UK

Edward Elgar Publishing, Inc.
136 West Street
Suite 202
Northampton
Massachusetts 01060
USA

A catalogue record for this book
is available from the British Library

Library of Congress Cataloguing in Publication Data

Killinger, Sebastian, 1967–
International environmental externalities and the double dividend / Sebastian Killinger.
    p. cm. — (New horizons in environmental economics)
    Includes bibliographical references and index.
    1. Environmental impact charges. 2. Externalities (Economics) 3. International economic integration. 4. Environmental policy. I. Title. II. Series.

HJ5316.K55 2001
333.7—dc21

00–055114

ISBN 1 84064 493 1

Printed and bound in Great Britain by MPG Books Ltd, Bodmin, Cornwall

Contents

List of Figures

List of Tables

Acknowledgements

This book was mainly written while I was a member of the long-term research programme *Internationalization of the Economy* (*Sonderforschungsbereich 178*) at the University of Konstanz. Intense cooperation with both members of the research programme as well as the faculty has contributed to the shape of the present study.

I owe sincere thanks to my academic teacher, Bernd Genser, who constantly supported this work with both general advice and detailed comments, and who created a stimulating and cooperative environment within his research unit. I am also indebted to Hans-Jürgen Vosgerau for having been second supervisor of my thesis as well as for his successful efforts in creating favourable working conditions in the *Sonderforschungsbereich 178*.

I have further benefited from helpful discussions with and suggestions received from Lucas Bretschger, Stefan Felder, Andreas Haufler, Frank Hettich, Christoph John, Jürgen Meckl, Michael Pflüger, Shannon Ragland, Michael Rauscher, Carsten Schmidt, Ronnie Schöb, Günther Schulze and some anonymous referees. Special thanks are due to Max Albert and Nadine Leiner-Killinger. I am very grateful to Johannes Leiner for carefully correcting the language mistakes in the manuscript.

Finally, I wish to thank my parents and my wife for their invaluable support.

Chapter 1

Introduction

Chapter 1

Introduction

Environmental destruction caused by human beings is manifold and can be observed at all stages of economic activities – from the individual to the global. In general, it does not result from destructiveness, but from economic activities – i.e. consumption and production – which satisfy human needs. The extent of human impact on ecological systems and the complexity of its consequences represent a considerable potential danger for the welfare of future generations. Neoclassical economic theory explains that environmental resources are used excessively because of negative external effects. For a correction of this allocative market failure, the ecopolitical decision-maker has to consider two interdependent aspects: the first concerns the optimal level of exploiting environmental resources; the second deals with the right choice of instruments that have to be used in order to realize this desired level.

Traditional analysis in the field of environmental economics is implicitly based on assumptions such as for instance that the sphere of governmental competence coincides with the radius of action of the externality or that the externality is the only distortion within the economic system. However, reality shows that such idealized conditions are not met. Instead, national environmental policy takes place in a context where the respective country is highly integrated into the world economy and where further distortions prevail apart from the environmental one.

The actual ecopolitical debate in Germany exactly reflects these circumstances. The intensively discussed idea is to reap a so-called double dividend from an ecological tax reform. The twin benefits of improving environmental quality and of reducing tax distortions simultaneously through the recycling of environmental tax proceeds is an attractive policy objective.[1] In the literature, the evaluation of whether a double dividend exists is based on different concepts. For a critical analysis of the proposed ecological tax reform scenarios a thorough analysis of the underlying concepts is necessary.

A different aspect covered by the ecopolitical discussion is whether environmental policy should be implemented unilaterally or in cooperation with other countries. Although various multinational environmental agreements have been signed in the past, their relevance is rather limited because an agreement has to satisfy the need of incentive compatibility in order to cope with free-rider incentives. The likely consequence is that commitments are not very ambitious. Therefore, unilateral policy actions are also an important policy strategy – especially in the case of cross-border externalities.

The aim of this book is to thoroughly analyse unilateral environmental policy measures and to elaborate under which conditions a double dividend can be achieved. The analysis is undertaken in the context of international capital mobility and cross-border externalities. Although international integration progresses steadily as international capital mobility increases, the literature on ecological tax reforms has not given enough weight to this aspect. So far, the double-dividend issue of ecological tax reforms has not been analysed in depth for large open economies. Nor have strategic actions and transborder externalities been taken into consideration in this context. This investigation tries to fill this gap. Accordingly, a theoretical platform is provided which makes it possible to work with the above-mentioned different double-dividend concepts.

Chapter 2 starts with the presentation of an empirically relevant example for Germany, namely the proposal of the *Deutsches Institut*

---

[1]On 1 April 1999, an environmental tax reform was implemented in Germany. It is designed so that energy-intensive industries are to a great extent exempt from tax payments. The general aim of compensating the production sector as a whole for the additional tax burden is pursued by earmarking tax proceeds for a reduction of social security contributions, which constitute part of the wage costs.

für Wirtschaftsforschung[2] (DIW) for an environmental tax reform (see DIW 1994). The report is criticized with respect to the underlying methodology.

Chapter 3 then focuses on the deviations of the DIW proposal from the normative guidelines that economic theory offers for dealing with the problem of externalities. Shortcomings especially concern international repercussions of national environmental policy. Also in order to classify the fiscal policy issues that will be analysed in Chapters 4 and 5, Chapter 3 gives a broad survey of various aspects of environmental policy. In particular, cooperative policy measures are contrasted with unilateral options for national environmental policy in the presence of local or transboundary environmental externalities when a country is highly integrated into the world economy. In most contributions to the literature, these two options are dealt with only in an isolated manner, if not ignored. Thus, once the main deficiencies of the DIW proposal in particular and economic literature in general have been highlighted , the reader can assess the basis of the theoretical analysis in Chapters 4 and 5.

Chapter 4 analyses the central idea of the DIW tax reform scenario, namely the double-dividend aspect. This conceptual approach is needed as the double-dividend discussion, although very popular in the theoretical as well as the political field, suffers from a certain diffuseness of terminology. Therefore, the two main double-dividend concepts are formalized within the same trade model. It is shown that the coexistence of both concepts in the literature is due to differing interpretations of the first-best Pigou analysis, which is introduced as a benchmark. The direct comparison allows a discussion of the (very often only implicitly made) assumptions connected to the concepts with respect to the likelihood that a double dividend can be reaped and to information requirements. Finally, a relationship is established between both concepts and the second-best optimal environmental tax rate. It becomes apparent that, in contradiction to the literature, an optimal tax rate higher than the marginal environmental damage is not tantamount to a double dividend according to either concept.

---

[2]German Institute for Economic Research.

In Chapter 5 the discussion is extended to another important subject left aside by the DIW report, namely international mobility of pollution, goods and factors. The analysis concentrates on internationally migrating capital and considers an externality that has a global effect. It is assumed that there is no international cooperation regulating the joint internalization of the externality. The analysis deals with gradual national environmental policy steps and additionally derives nationally optimal tax structures which directly and indirectly internalize the cross-border externalities. In the presence of lump-sum taxes both pollution taxes and capital taxes serve to internalize the externalities and strategically to influence the price of capital on the world capital market. Where lump-sum taxes are not available, the existence of a double dividend arising from the implementation of pollution taxes is evaluated by applying the concepts that have been introduced in Chapter 4. Conditions are listed under which either of both dividends or a double dividend results from the implementation of an ecological tax reform. It is shown that in a capital-importing country there is greater harmony of policy objectives than in a capital-exporting country.

Finally, Chapter 6 draws conclusions and suggests further fields of research.

By presenting a critical discussion of the two often-used double-dividend concepts and by applying them to capital mobility and transborder externalities, this book contributes to a more critical evaluation of ecological tax reforms.

Chapter 2

The DIW report: an empirical example

2.1 INTRODUCTION

As a starting point in this chapter the well-known DIW report (Bach et al. 1994) will be presented as an example of a possible ecological tax reform in Germany.[1] The report was the first rigorous econometric analysis in this field. The chapter proceeds as follows.

Section 2.2 will briefly present the design of the proposed tax reform, the methodology that underlies the econometric analysis as well as the main results of the report. In section 2.3 the report is critically discussed with respect to methodological aspects. Section 2.4 concludes. The normative aspects of the DIW tax reform proposal, i.e. aspects that refer to the design of the tax reform, are dealt with extensively in Chapter 3.

2.2 THE REPORT

Against the background of the 1990 environmental summit in Rio de Janeiro the German government committed itself to reduce German CO_2 emissions by 25 per cent to 30 per cent by the year 2005 with

---

[1]The presentation is mainly based on Hettich et al. (1997).

1987 as reference year. The report of the DIW is based on this commitment (Bach et al. 1994, pp. 14–15). The instrument chosen is an energy tax, and its proceeds are redistributed to firms via a reduction in employers' social security contributions and to households via per capita lump-sum payments. The overall economic effects are simulated in a macro econometric model over the period from 1995 to 2010. The model disaggregates total demand in private and public consumption, capital expenditure on plant and building, and in exports. Production factors explicitly modelled are capital and labour. More disaggregated submodels are used for an estimation of the development in energy demand and for an estimation of price effects resulting from the energy tax.

2.2.1   The Design of the Tax Reform

The energy tax in the DIW report is designed as follows. The use of various sources of energy is subject to taxation. The energy content is supposed to be an approximate criterion for different kinds of environmental pollution consisting of, for instance, climatically relevant CO_2 emissions or the risk and the decontamination costs of nuclear energy use. In order to cope with the problem of imports of secondary sources of energy, not only is there a general energy tax on primary sources of energy, such as hard coal, brown coal, peat and natural gas, a differing tax rate is also levied on secondary sources of energy like electricity and oil products. This rate is derived from an implicit tax burden on the primary energy basis which is identical to the tax rate on primary energy. Double taxation is avoided since tax payments on primary inputs can be deducted. Existing tax exemptions for oil products, particularly for air traffic, are abolished and renewable sources of energy, energy from refuse incineration and waste heat from production plants, are excluded from the tax base.

The DIW proposes a linearly increasing specific tax that leads to a rise in the price of energy input by 7 per cent each year. This is equivalent to 0.63 DM/gigajoule (GJ) in the first year, 1995, and to 15.83 DM/GJ in 2010, measured in 1990 prices and assuming an initial price for each unit of energy content of 9 DM/GJ in 1995. The estimated income from the energy tax for the whole of Germany is approximately DM 8574 m.

in 1995 and approximately DM 205 593 m. in the year 2010 (Bach et al. 1994, p. 126).

Since the reform is supposed to be revenue-neutral, the concept includes a proposal on how the tax proceeds, increasing in the course of time, should be redistributed to taxpayers. Both the production and household sector, are supposed to get back their shares in tax revenue, which means that approximately 70 per cent is transferred to the production sector. There will be no discrimination between the various production sectors, though. The reimbursement to the production side is realized by means of a reduction in the employers' social security contributions and for the household sector through a lump-sum per capita bonus (called an eco-bonus). The environmental tax reform thus pursues two aims simultaneously: positive effects on the environment, and a positive impact on employment by means of reducing the non-wage labour costs.

2.2.2 Methodology

The proposed reform of the tax system is expected not only to have a direct effect on primary energy use but also to bring in its wake several indirect effects. The induced adaptations of the price system will lead to a sectoral reorganization of the economy, to a change in production technologies and in the composition of foreign trade, and to a new growth and employment path. Many of these effects can be analysed separately but also jointly with respect to their overall impact on the primary objective, i.e. the reduction of environmental depletion, or with respect to other key economic variables. In order to be able to make quantitative statements, model estimations are indispensable. The DIW study is one of the so far rare examples of a comprehensive model-based simulation in this area.[2] It is, however, not based on a complete sectoral econometric model for Germany, but estimates the effects on the basis of three separate model calculations that to some extent apply only to West Germany:

1. a prediction of the development of energy consumption;

---

[2]For other studies see Bovenberg and Goulder (1996) and Oepping (1995).

2. an estimation of sectoral price effects;
3. the simulation of a macroeconomic model of the business cycle.

In the first step the DIW estimates the development of energy consumption in response to the proposed ecological tax reform within a partial equilibrium model. The assumptions concerning the overall economic, sectoral and structural development, including technical factors that have an impact on the energy intensity of production, have primarily been taken from studies by the Prognos Institute (Prognos 1991 and 1993; see also Enquête-Kommission 1990 and 1993).

A second model evaluates how the increase in energy prices as well as the redistribution of tax revenues is shifted on to final demand prices across different sectors. This is accomplished by means of a static input–output table with a Leontief production structure, estimated for the year 1988 and for the old *Bundesländer*.

Finally, in the third step of the analysis, an econometric macro-model is used. The overall economic effects of the tax reform are determined by means of a deterministic *ex post* simulation. The econometric model is dynamically simulated first for a benchmark scenario without tax reform and then for the tax reform scenario with error terms equal to zero. The model, which is tailored for West Germany for the time period from 1983 to 1992, contains central components of the national income accounting and also equations for the job market and the receipts and expenses of the public sector.

The DIW tries to bring the separate model parts in line by feeding the macro-model with the results of the first two models. This input is exogenous to the business cycle model. The tax revenue determined in the energy model raises nominal income of private households and simultaneously reduces unit labour costs of firms. Aggregate price effects from the input–output table which are already adjusted for compensatory payments to firms have an exogenous impact on relative prices of consumption, capital goods, government consumption, buildings and exports, and therefore on final demand for these components.

2.2.3   Results of the DIW Report

The primary objective of the proposed ecological tax reform is a considerable reduction of greenhouse gas emissions. Compared to the base year 1987, the reduction of primary energy use in the year 2010 is forecast at 23.5 per cent and that of CO_2 emissions at 24.8 per cent (Bach et al. 1994, p. 121). Despite the introduction of the stepwise rising pollution tax, even by the year 2010 the political target for 2005 will hence not be met.

The main merit of the DIW report is to provide a quantitative evaluation of a green tax reform. Table 2.1 shows the relative deviation of some key variables, accumulated over ten years, from those resulting from the business-as-usual scenario, i.e. without a green tax reform. For the basic scenario the DIW assumes constant real interest rates and

Table 2.1: Economic effects of an ecological tax reform: deviations from benchmark scenario in %, accumulated over ten years

	Basic scenario	Variant I	Variant IV	Variant V
Employed population	2.1	2.2	1.1	2.8
GDP (real)	−2.2	−2.3	−1.0	−1.1
Prices (GNP)	1.5	1.2	0.9	3.8
Standard wages (hrs.)	0.2	−0.4	0.7	2.9
Non-wage labour costs	−4.8	−4.9	−4.7	−4.4
Unit labour costs	−2.2	−2.6	−3.0	−0.7

Source: Bach et al. (1994), p. 11*; own calculations.

a constant real foreign value of the D-Mark as well as no changes in wage setting and fiscal behaviour. Variant I accounts for changes in the real exchange rate of the D-Mark, which means that the exchange rate does not completely neutralize the rise in domestic prices. This variant is more appropriate for capturing repercussions on international competitiveness. The authors suspect that their econometric business cycle model overestimates the elasticity of employment with respect to labour costs and therefore halve it in variant IV. In variant V they allow for compensatory fiscal policy measures, i.e. increased public investments in regions that are severely hit by the induced structural changes.

The simulation results for the basic scenario indicate a reduction in annual GDP growth by 0.22 per cent compared to the benchmark. Second, apart from the reduction in CO_2 emissions, the DIW forecasts a positive employment effect of 300 000 to 800 000 additional jobs over the ten-year period. Regions with a predominance of energy-intensive industries perform significantly below average, whereas those regions whose industries are mainly energy-extensive will achieve a rise in employment above average. The qualitative results were confirmed in the other scenarios. However, variant IV reveals the dependence of the employment effects on the wage elasticity of labour demand.

2.3   CRITIQUE

As already mentioned, the DIW estimation of a green tax reform is based on three separate models. Our critique will deal with each individual step of the analysis separately.

2.3.1   Development of Energy Consumption

As long as energy consumption exhibits at least some elasticity with respect to energy prices, an energy tax will reduce energy demand as well as the input of primary resources. In the first step of the report energy savings induced by the energy tax are determined for each sector. The evaluation of this direct impact does not stem, however, from an explicit modelling but falls back on other studies. The estimated effects on energy consumption are therefore exclusively founded on forecasts of changes in the specific energy input in production at the sectoral level. The DIW model is hence not appropriate to determine the general equilibrium repercussions on energy consumption resulting from adaptations in technology and in the sectoral structure (Bach et al. 1994, p. 85).

The DIW has been criticized for systematically overestimating the fall in energy demand since price-elasticities in other studies were significantly lower (EU-Commission, International Energy Agency; see BDI 1994, pp. 16–17, and Böhringer et al. 1994, p. 623). The DIW, on the other hand, believes that the results are rather conservative. It presumes that this would take account of the relatively short estimation period, the only gradual increase in the energy prices as well as the manifold obstacles to implementing energy-saving methods and a substitution of sources of energy. The relatively low energy savings in other studies can be explained by lower energy tax rates and elasticities derived from historical data. But there has never before been a comparably persisting and foreseeable change in energy prices of the proposed dimension (see Bach et al. 1995, pp. 248–249). Therefore, the elasticities of the other studies do not include the additional positive impact on technological progress that is likely to emerge. Even if energy demand is inelastic in the short run, the increase in energy prices will entail considerably higher demand elasticities in the long run.[3] The relevance of such effects for the assumed documentation period of only 15 years has to be evaluated by means of a more thorough analysis.

The energy-saving effects in the household sector, especially for heating, are not realistic since the landlords of flats or houses (with 65 per cent of actual housing being rented) do not have any incentive to invest in thermal insulation or improved heating systems – especially in view of the existing excess demand for housing. The consequences of a misinterpretation are considerable since more than three-quarters of final energy demand falls on heating, which is equivalent to 18 per cent of total final energy demand in Germany in 1990 (see Bach et al. 1994, p. 107). Although the DIW is aware of this investor–user dilemma and therefore pleads for supporting legal measures (see Bach et al. 1994, ch. 8.3.4.), it expects energy savings which are up to 30 per cent higher than those of the benchmark scenario of Prognos (1991).

2.3.2 Input–Output Approach

To determine the price effects of the energy tax, the DIW uses an input–output table that is based on a Leontief production structure and the supply system of the year 1988. Since intersectoral flows of goods and intermediate inputs remain constant over time in such an input–output

---

[3]See Mauch et al. (1992, part I, ch. 6), for a valuation of long-term elasticities for fuels.

table, substitution effects in the production and demand structure across inputs, intermediates and consumption goods are disregarded at this stage of analysis. By relying on an input–output table, the DIW implicitly assumes that it is possible to shift the energy tax burden to final demand components, which implies perfect competition in all markets and constant economies of scale in production. Since there was no close correlation between GDP and primary energy consumption in Germany after the two oil crises (see Münch and Böttcher 1995, p. 11), it can be expected that the energy tax will cause considerable changes in production technology, energy consumption and in the intersectoral structure. But customary or additionally induced process innovations cannot be depicted within the chosen framework. This seems to be true even though the oil crises, different from the green tax reform, had a global impact and energy-saving potentials were developed worldwide. An opposing argument supporting the expectation is that a national energy tax as analysed by the DIW with its gradually increasing tax rate ensures certainty for planning, which was not the case with the oil crises.

Price effects in this segment of modelling are caused by taxation of energy as well as by redistribution of tax proceeds. Due to the neglected substitution effects and process innovations, price effects on consumption goods induced by the energy tax will generally be overestimated. But in contrast to the assessment by the DIW (Bach et al. 1994, p. 127), this partial price effect does not necessarily represent the upper limit of the general equilibrium effect, which is due to the fact that changes in factor demand remain unconsidered. Overestimation of prices as well as disregard of the delocation of production to foreign countries carry over into energy tax revenues which are too high, resulting in too high compensatory payments. This in turn counteracts the immediate effect.[4] The total effect on prices of final consumption goods can hence be expected to be conservative for labour-intensive sectors and overestimated for energy-intensive sectors. The abstraction from sectoral adaptations and technological developments fundamentally distorts the price effects shown, which are therefore of only indicative relevance.

---

[4]For the aspect of a delocation of industries see also Münch and Böttcher (1995, p. 10).

2.3.3   Econometric Macro-model

The third part of the analysis uses an econometric macro-model which contains 49 stochastic equations and 26 exogenous variables. It is based on quarterly data of the national income accounting for the years 1983 to 1992 for West Germany. This general equilibrium approach has to be approved since analysis of ecologically motivated policy measures have so far only been undertaken within partial equilibrium frameworks.

By including the results of the other two models discussed above as exogenous inputs, the insufficiencies already mentioned are introduced into the macro-model. The price distortions of the input–output table should be mitigated through the aggregation, though. All effects derived from the aggregate model result from changes in the relative prices of final demand components (which primarily favour public consumption and investment), and from a shifting of the tax burden from labour to consumption (see Bach et al. 1994, p. 158).

The business cycle model is not sufficiently disaggregated to allow for a separation between labour, capital and energy as factors of production. It therefore neglects direct substitution possibilities between these inputs so that changes in factor input shares are left as an open question.[5]

Criticism can furthermore be levelled against the assumptions in the monetary sector (see Böhringer et al. 1994, p. 623). The constant real interest rate in the basic scenario is unrealistic because the effects of higher investment demand for energy-saving measures and of induced structural changes are disregarded. In this respect it would of course be useful to endogenize exchange rates and interest rates. But at least the endogenization of interest rates in an econometric model seems to be a largely unsolved problem. From that point of view the simulation of different scenarios with respect to the development of exchange rates and interest rates as done by the DIW appears to be more practicable, especially because one gets a feeling for the sensitivity of the results with respect to the assumptions.

More critical are the assumptions relating to wage settlements and

---

[5]Böhringer et al. (1994, p. 623), discuss the case of energy and labour being complements when the rise in energy prices would induce a fall in employment (see also BDI 1994, p. 16).

the resulting employment effects: the wage fixing of bargaining agents is based on expected prices, labour productivity, and the level of unemployment. In the basic scenario it is additionally assumed that wage settlements are not influenced by compensatory payments to the firms or price increments on the consumption side. Variant III even supposes that income effects due to the redistribution of tax proceeds to the household sector lead to lower wage claims than in the basic scenario. But a faster rise in wages due to the compensation payments to firms as well as the price effects are just as plausible (see Council of Economic Advisors 1994, pp. 211–212). Furthermore, effects on employment do not only depend on variations in wages; what also matters, for instance, is the actual unemployment regime. And the extent to which production technologies in the various sectors will be adapted to price changes is determined by structural features.

Another weakness of the DIW report is that Germany's integration into the world economy and subsequently the possibility of a delocation of production is not sufficiently taken into consideration (Böhringer et al. 1994, p. 624, and BDI 1994, p. 16). The consideration of international integration is carried out by means of an import and an export function that mainly depend on prices of domestic goods. With the help of these functions the model captures the international repercussions of tax reform on employment, international competitiveness, consumption and implicitly also on the possibility of a delocation of industries abroad (see Bach et al. 1995, p. 248). It is plausible to expect that there is a connection between import and export demand on the one hand and the locational choice of firms on the other. A *ceteris paribus* rise in imports in one sector may be due to the fact that there have been domestic investments abroad. But a correlation between exports and foreign direct investment is plausible as well, since increased exports need a more elaborated sales system. From these reflections it becomes evident that location decisions of firms cannot be modelled solely by means of import and export demand functions.

The estimation of the business cycle model covers the period from the third quarter of 1983 to the second quarter of 1992. It would have been interesting to extend the estimation period for one variant in order to include the oil crises in the seventies. Then profound energy price changes would have been incorporated, which of course occurred abruptly and had not been anticipated.

2.3.4   Summary of the Critique

Due to various interdependencies, the repercussions of a substantial green tax reform can be evaluated only with the help of a sufficiently disaggregated econometric model. Hence the study of the DIW can only be regarded as a first – though very welcome – step of analysis. The results of the study have to be interpreted against the background of the methodological deficiencies mentioned above. The effects not, or not sufficiently, considered are, above all, induced technical progress, possible delocations of industries abroad, repercussions between the three separate model parts, and substitutability between the primary factors of production as energy, capital and labour. These weaknesses considerably reduce the reliability of the quantitative results regarding the effects on employment, growth and other economic features that are gained from the business cycle model. A question mark has also to be put against the qualitative conclusion that the targeted reduction of CO_2 emissions can be reached by the proposed instrument without creating a macroeconomic shock. Therefore, the simulation results do not allow the conclusion that the ecological tax reform represents the ideal way of earning a double dividend, i.e. less pollution and more jobs.

2.4   CONCLUSIONS

In this chapter, the DIW report as an often-cited model with ecological taxes was presented and critically discussed in order to demonstrate the relevance and importance of environmental policy in general and ecological tax reforms in particular. The theoretical framework to be developed below avoids three critical deficiencies of the DIW model:

1. The inadequate design of an ecological tax reform. Chapter 3 questions whether the DIW scenario is in accordance with the normative basis of economic theory.

2. It includes international aspects, i.e. the mobility of goods, factors and pollution.
3. It explicitly includes revenue effects that allow us to focus on the possibility of a double dividend.

These issues constitute the focal points of the subsequent chapters.

Chapter 3

National environmental policies and international integration

3.1 INTRODUCTION

This chapter surveys the international dimension of environmental problems and discusses the scope for national environmental policy. The critical discussion of the DIW report in Chapter 2 has shown that a thorough analysis of normative fundamentals is indispensable for environmental policy design. The challenges for normative economic theory increase if environmental policy is assessed against the background of additional distortions apart from the environmental one and if national competence does not cover the whole radius of action of the externality. The overview is primarily motivated by the fact that most environmental problems are not restricted to national territories but affect several countries, sometimes even the whole world. International environmental policy in the sense of a joint internalization of cross-border environmental externalities by means of a supranational authority is – at least at present – not a real option. Therefore, all environmental initiatives, including the internationally coordinated ones, are determined by national considerations. But for local or national externalities it must also be taken into account that national policies are limited by the growing integration of the world economy. Especially when additional distortions prevail in an economy, international repercussions may be substantial. They have to be borne in mind when environmental decisions are made.

Environmental policies differ with respect to whether they internalize national or cross-border externalities. They also vary with respect to the extent to which they interact with policies of other countries. Figure 3.1 schematizes this distinction and serves as a basis for the structure of this chapter.

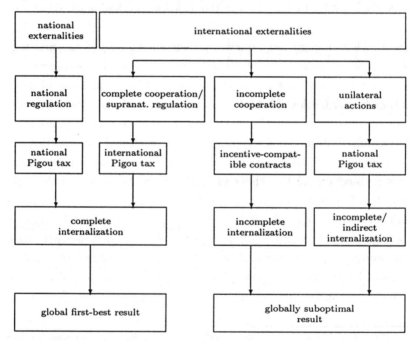

Note: Pigou taxes in this presentation are used in place of all market internalization instruments.

Figure 3.1: National environmental policy in the presence of national and international externalities

Section 3.2 starts the discussion of normative issues by assessing the allocative aspects of ecological tax reforms in general and the DIW tax scenario in particular in model frameworks, with the externality representing the sole distortion of the economic system.

The subsequent survey in sections 3.3 and 3.4 integrates different kinds of additional distortions and restrictions that have to be considered for environmental policy design.[1] Political-economy considerations of environmental policy, aspects of sustainable growth or empirical questions (apart from the DIW report) remain excluded from the discussion.[2] Section 3.3 first analyses the case of purely national externalities in a setting where economies are closely integrated, for instance via trade, and where the political decision-maker is confronted with additional distortions through, e.g., tariffs or other taxes or restrictions like public budgetary needs. In this context the aspects of a double dividend arising from ecological tax reforms will be outlined. As will be seen, Figure 3.1 (left branch) only shows the benchmark case of the first-best scenario for national externalities with no lack of policy instruments. In section 3.4 environmental policies are analysed in the presence of international externalities. If there is no supranational institution with the necessary tax competence for an efficient internalization policy, two main decentralized strategies for coping with international externalities can be identified: (i) incomplete environmental cooperation between countries (subsection 3.4.1) – this case is shown in the middle of the right branch of Figure 3.1 and is concerned with aspects of incentive compatibility (see Heister et al. 1995); (ii) unilateral actions (on the right of the right branch) mainly include aspects of an indirect internalization (subsection 3.4.2). As the analysis will show, the possibility of complete cooperation leading to a global first-best result (on the left of the right branch) can again only be regarded as a benchmark case. Section 3.5

---

[1]The survey is based on Killinger and Schmidt (1998). In other contributions these additional aspects that also include questions arising from cooperation or non-cooperation are dealt with only in an isolated manner or are ignored. See e.g. Baumol and Oates (1988) for a general introduction to the theory of environmental economics, Mäler (1990) for a categorization of international environmental problems and the problems of international cooperation, and Dean (1992) for aspects of trade and environment. A new and applied analysis of global environmental problems is provided by Sandler (1997).

[2]See Schulze and Ursprung (2000) for political-economy analyses of national and international environmental policies, Smulders (1995) and Hettich (2000) for dynamic aspects, and Cropper and Oates (1992) for an ecological cost–benefit analysis.

concludes.

With the overview in this chapter the ground is laid for the subsequent formal analyses in Chapters 4 and 5 that specify two core aspects of an ecological tax reform hardly addressed in the DIW report: (i) the interpretation of the double-dividend characteristic of environmental tax reforms and (ii) the welfare effects for unilaterally acting countries highly integrated into the world economy; these welfare effects can result from an international reallocation of factors, production and pollution.

3.2   NORMATIVE BASIS

The economic analysis of environmental problems is based on the theory of externalities. Textbook economics distinguishes between pecuniary and technological external effects.[3]

Pecuniary externalities are changes in market prices caused by the activity of an economic agent. But the shift in prices leads neither to a shift in the production possibility locus nor to a falling-apart of the marginal rate of transformation and the social marginal rate of substitution.[4] This means that in the new equilibrium, incomes could be redistributed so as to make sure that all agents suffering from income losses due to the pecuniary externalities are compensated. Furthermore, a pecuniary externality does not enter the utility functions of the affected agents, so that social and private marginal rates of substitution do not deviate from each other. Since pecuniary externalities do not drive a wedge between private and social marginal rates of substitution or transformation, the set of marginal conditions of the market equilibrium corresponds to that of a Pareto optimum. The new equilibrium again is Pareto-efficient. Therefore, with respect to allocative efficiency there is no need to call for government intervention in the presence of pecuniary externalities.[5]

---

[3]See for the following Cropper and Oates (1992, pp. 678–681), Laffont (1988, pp. 6–10), Cornes and Sandler (1986, pp. 29–66), Smith (1992, pp. 23–25), and Baumol and Oates (1988, ch. 2).

[4]*Social* marginal rates of substitution account for external effects; *private* do not.

[5]The remarks on pecuniary externalities refer to a Arrow–Debreu model framework of a perfect market system without information asymmetries. If this model

Technological externalities on the other hand cause a shift of such functions that set up a relationship between resources (as independent variables) and output or utility levels (as dependent variables) (Baumol and Oates 1988, p. 30). Technically speaking, a technological externality is present whenever some economic agent's welfare (utility or profit) includes real variables whose values are chosen by others without particular attention to the effect upon the welfare of the other agents they affect. This means that linkages via the externality result in the optimal choice of each agent being dependent upon the actions of others. Depending on where they are caused, one distinguishes between production and consumption externalities. The conveyance of the external effect does not take place by means of the market process and is therefore not reflected by the price system. It is precisely the non-existence of functioning markets for external effects that leads them to be classified as externalities. Missing competitive markets are most likely due to incomplete or even undefined property rights, and can be traced to the following reasons (Cornes and Sandler 1986, pp. 31–32; Myles 1995, pp. 323–326):

- the assignment and enforcement of property rights is either not possible or too costly;
- the costs connected with transactions on a market are too high;
- costs which are too high during the setting up of a market may mean that the convexity conditions for the existence of an equilibrium and the consistency of a Pareto optimum are no longer fulfilled in a decentralized market system;
- too few market participants.

Missing or imperfect markets imply that gains from trade between economic agents remain unexploited. The costs or benefits imposed on others through an externality are hence not taken into consideration when the agent determines her or his activity level in production or con-

---

framework is left, prices not only serve the purpose of adjusting demand and supply; they are also used to convey information (for example risk). The resulting interactions can lead to efficiency problems. This is because the activity of an economic agent which induces a price change will lead to a modification of expectations and hence the expected utility of other individuals (see Laffont 1988, pp. 30–31). In the present analysis, this additional aspect of pecuniary externalities will not be further discussed.

sumption. Instead, the only decision variables are her or his utility gains and private costs, the latter differing from social costs by exactly the externality.

In the case of a negative environmental externality, from a Pareto perspective the efficient level of an activity is achieved if the marginal cost of abatement corresponds to the social marginal environmental damage. Therefore, in a competitive equilibrium, activities with a negative external effect are pursued generally at a level which is too high from the social point of view; those with a positive externality at a level which is too low. An externality is illustrated and graphically explained with the help of Figure 3.2. Here, it is assumed that there is a resource which is in the public domain: the figure depicts the functions relevant

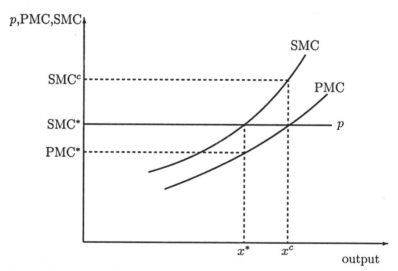

Source: Boadway and Bruce (1984), p. 111.

Figure 3.2: Impact of an externality

for production of the good for which the publicly accessible resource is used. As an example, one could think of a fishing ground. Access to this resource is free for producers. The stock or population within the fishing ground is assumed to be exogenously given so that the resource is a scarce economic good. Because of free access to the resource as well as its free use, the production activity is extended up to level x^c, the competitive output level, at which the price of the produced good equals private marginal costs of production (PMC). The opportunity cost of the fixed-factor fishing ground, namely the disadvantage of a reduced population affecting also the other fishermen, is not, however, taken into consideration. The social marginal cost curve (SMC) on the contrary represents the complete marginal cost of additional output, i.e. including the marginal scarcity rent of the fishing ground. The gap between the social and private cost curves hence corresponds to the external costs that are imposed on other economic agents if output is expanded. The optimal output level is x^*, where the price equals marginal social cost. At this output the difference between SMC* and PMC* represents the level of marginal external costs imposed on other fishermen when one fisherman produces one extra unit in the social optimum. The competitive output level x^c hence lies above the optimal level (Boadway and Bruce 1984, pp. 110–112).

The various types of technological externalities can roughly be classified into three main categories:

- *Externalities between producers*
  These are generated in the production process; can affect another producer positively or negatively; and may be correlated with the output level and the kind, the amount or the composition of the employed factors of production, or with joint products. An example would be water pollution by a steel-works that affects a downstream laundry.
- *Externalities between consumers*
  Consumption of one individual has an impact on the utility of another, as for example in the case of smoking.
- *Externalities between consumers and producers*
  Production activities affect the utility of a consumer, or the production possibilities of a firm are affected by the consumption activities of an individual. One could think of noise disturbance or road congestion, respectively.

Externalities frequently show the character of a public good. This means that (i) they enter every utility or production function equally and that

(ii) the individual perception of the externality level is independent of the degree to which other consumers or firms are affected. An example of such a non-exhaustible externality in the international context is greenhouse gas emissions, which are regarded as a cause of global warming (see, for example, Enquête-Kommission 1992). If however the degree to which one individual is affected does influence that of others, an externality is called private or exhaustible. Hence there is rivalry in consumption. An example of this kind of externality at the international level is acid rain (see Freeman 1984). In the case of an aggregate externality the contribution of each single polluter is negligible; only by cumulation of individual activity levels is an externality generated. The individual polluter does not take her or his own contribution to the externality level into consideration. An example would be a street that will be congested if it is used by too many cars. This kind of externality can be regarded as the most relevant one, especially at the international level. An aggregate externality – e.g. global warming – can have the above-mentioned characteristics of a public good. For this type Meade (1952) introduced the notion *additive atmosphere externality*. Specific to the externality-generating process is that the marginal contribution of each individual to the total is identical.

This distinction between different kinds of externalities with their respective characteristics will be of great importance when the analysis shifts from the national to the international level.

Internalization

The internalization of externalities can be accomplished with the help of command and control, or market-compatible, instruments, both of which can theoretically safeguard an efficient internalization; the marginal cost of abatement in the case of a negative environmental externality must be identical for all polluters.[6] For an efficient allocation, the use of command and control measures requires complete information about

---

[6]The discussion of internalization possibilities is restricted to allocative aspects. Fiscal and distributional targets with respect to the DIW scenario or in general are not dealt with here. For fiscal issues see Linscheidt and Truger (1994 and 1995, respectively), and Hettich et al. (1997, p. 217), and for distributional aspects Bach et al. (1994, p. 16*), DIW (1994, p. 403), and Hettich et al. (1997, p. 218).

abatement cost curves for each single polluter in order to be able to prescribe optimal individual reduction rates. For market instruments the economically efficient target connected with the socially lowest cost is – in the case of perfect markets – reached through the market process itself. Compared to command and control instruments, market instruments have the essential advantage of being dynamically efficient since the additional cost they impose on polluters induces incentives to develop clean technologies. An internalization of external effects can be realized for instance by means of Pigou taxes (see Pigou 1932) if the tax directly assesses the externality-generating activity and if tax rates equal the aggregate marginal external cost each individual imposes on others in the optimum (Figure 3.1, left branch). This means that in general Pigou taxes have to be differentiated across individuals. Thus the informational requirement for optimally designed market-compatible internalization instruments is also very large. Only if the optimal tax is represented by uniform tax rates across all individuals, as is the case when all individuals are identical or when the externality is of the aggregate and pure public-good type (i.e. Meade's additive atmosphere externality), do information hurdles diminish considerably (see Myles 1995, ch. 10, sec. 6). If marginal external costs are negative, and, accordingly, the externality is positive, the Pigou tax consequently is negative, i.e. a subsidy. In Figure 3.2 the optimal tax rate for each fisherman corresponds to the distance between the social and private marginal cost curves at the optimal activity level x^*. The tax is successful in including the generation of an external effect into a polluter's optimization calculus.

Apart from Pigou taxes, Pigou subsidies are also suitable for guaranteeing the marginal conditions for a Pareto optimum in a decentralized market system, even in the case of a negative externality.[7] Here again, an individual subsidy amounting to the aggregate external effect the respective economic agent imposes on others in the optimum would have to be granted for every unit of emissions she or he avoids. Producers or consumers have an incentive to reduce pollution by adapting their

---

[7]From now on, the case of a negative environmental externality will exclusively be dealt with.

marginal cost of abatement to the marginal subsidy. As in the case of Pigou taxes, the externality level in equilibrium will be Pareto-efficient. However, compared to taxes, subsidies have some disadvantages when used for the internalization of negative external effects: on account of the subsidy, enterprises which would otherwise be forced to leave the market can possibly survive. The increased number of market participants will work against the reduction of the externality-generating activity due to the subsidy and may even cause a rise. Additionally, there is an incentive strategically to raise own externality generation before the rate of the specific subsidy is determined so as to increase the subsidy payments (see Smith 1992, p. 29; Cropper and Oates 1992, p. 681; Baumol and Oates 1988, ch. 14).

The first-order conditions for a Pareto optimum can under certain circumstances also be met without the introduction of taxes or subsidies in competitive equilibria – even if competitive markets for external effects do not exist. This requires that the parties involved in an externality enter into voluntary negotiations in order to be able to realize gains from trade. A precondition for this case described by Coase (Coase 1960), however, is a limited number of polluters and of those affected by the externality.[8] Property rights have to be assigned, and transaction costs combined with the negotiations must not be high (actually zero); those affected by pollution need to know the polluter as well as the extent of the damage. If a negotiated solution can be reached in such an environment, the introduction of Pigou taxes may even hinder attaining a Pareto optimum. In Figure 3.3 line JK exhibits the marginal environmental damage (MED_B) of an individual B that suffers from pollution generated by an activity of individual A (for instance smoking). Marginal utility of the emission-generating activity or, equivalently, marginal cost of abatement for individual A is represented by the MCA_A curve. This curve is defined so as to depict marginal utility net of the price which individual A has to pay for the activity (in this example the price of a cigarette). Without an agreement between the two parties, individual A increases her activity level up to point D, where net marginal utility is equal to zero. Socially optimal on the other hand would be activity

---

[8]See for a rigorous analysis of the Coase theorem Myles (1995), ch. 10, sec. 4.

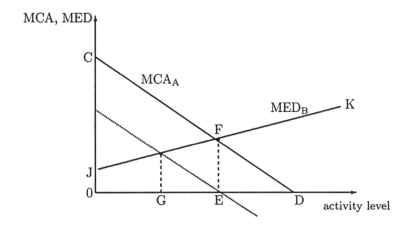

Source: Baumol and Oates (1988), p. 33.

Figure 3.3: Pigou tax in a Coase environment

level E, where MCA_A corresponds to MED_B. In a Coase situation, this Pareto-efficient level is achieved by voluntary negotiations. Individual B, for example, would agree to compensate individual A for utility losses suffered from reducing her activity level until the marginal compensatory payment just corresponds to marginal utility from reduced pollution. It is equally conceivable that individual A pays B in order to compensate her for the suffered damages. Under these circumstances, the efficient activity level would be achieved as well. The direction of compensation payments exclusively depends on how property rights are assigned to both individuals.[9] If, however, a Pigou tax is raised from individual A at a rate that corresponds to MED_B in the social optimum (EF), the MCA_A curve will shift leftward. Without negotiations, this tax will bring forth the social optimum as explained before. If an internalization of the external effects has already been reached by means of negotiation, the implementation of a Pigou tax leads to a suboptimal allocation. Instead of the socially optimal activity level E, the inefficient level G would

---

[9]This result corresponds to that of the Lindahl equilibrium with personalized prices that can decentralize the optimum level of public goods provision (see Myles 1995, pp. 336–337).

be chosen. In a Coase, setting Pigou taxes are consequently allocation-distorting.

A Coase setting in this understanding is reflected by a situation where external effects are traded, but where thinness of the market undermines the assumption of competitive behaviour that can support the efficiency hypothesis. Such bargaining or trading between two agents, with approved strategic behaviour of the actors, can be interpreted as taking the form of a non-cooperative game with complete information.[10] In this case the Coase result no longer holds because the incentive for each agent to exploit her or his private information prevents all the gains from trade being exhausted. Consequently, asymmetric information leads to inefficiency in the outcome of bargaining (see Myles 1995, pp. 327–330). With incomplete information, the introduction of a Pigou tax is more likely to guarantee a Pareto-efficient result, even in the case of only a small number of people involved. However, in the case of only a few individuals involved, the Pigou tax may also be subject to manipulation through strategic behaviour. If polluters or pollutees do not take the level of marginal damage as given (as it has been assumed so far), but have the possibility of exerting an influence, the Pigou tax may by mistake be determined at an inefficient level due to strategic behaviour. In this case a taxation even of those hurt by pollution can at least theoretically be advisable (Baumol and Oates 1988, p. 35). Coase calls for a taxation of the victims not only in the case of few people involved but also generally (Coase 1960, p. 42). In the literature, however, a compensation of the victims of an externality is often demanded.[11] But it can be shown that both compensating and taxing those affected by an externality is not compatible with a Pareto optimum, at least as long as lump-sum payments are not available (see Baumol and Oates 1988, ch. 4) – a result that will be of importance when aspects of an ecological tax reform are dealt with below.

---

[10]The alternative interpretation of a cooperative game between agents, i.e. a Nash bargaining solution, is critical since there the bargains over compensation payments are assumed to be placed in front of an external arbitrator. This, however, is not what is envisaged in the Coase theorem, which focuses on the actions of markets free of any regulation (see Myles 1995, pp. 326–327).

[11]A discussion of both points of view can be found in Baumol and Oates (1988), pp. 23–24.

As demonstrated, an efficient allocation can be produced by means of an environmental tax, provided that the tax is being levied at rates that equal the social marginal environmental damage an individual imposes on others in the optimum. In the setting assumed so far, where pollution represents the unique distortion within the economy, this so-called Pigou tax produces a first-best result. Reality, however, is characterized by incomplete information and many distortions. Presumably, the greatest difficulty of implementing a Pigou tax according to its theoretical design is the very huge information requirements. In order to determine social marginal environmental damage caused by each economic agent, an aggregation over all people affected is necessary. This means that individual preferences need to be revealed, which is especially difficult. Individuals themselves are very often unable to evaluate the damage they are exposed to. Furthermore, the individual tax rate should not reflect social marginal environmental damage at the time of its introduction, but rather at the optimal externality level. Consequently, knowledge of the existing marginal environmental damage is not sufficient. The functions of aggregate marginal environmental damage each individual causes, as well as the respective functions for the marginal cost of abatement, need to be derived over a certain range of externality levels. The information costs remain considerable even if the externality is of Meade's additive atmosphere externality type or if individuals are identical – in these cases the optimal environmental tax rate is uniform across all individuals. The determination of the social marginal environmental damage curve and the marginal cost of abatement curve also poses severe problems in this less complicated scenario. What indeed appears to be easier is to pursue an iterative adaptation process to the efficient tax level. But this for its part brings in its wake uncertainty for enterprises and therefore imposes additional costs on the production side.[12]

An additional problem of the Pigou tax is that concavity and convexity features may break down if a specific externality level is exceeded. In the analytical derivation of the tax, this aspect is excluded by assumption. If second-order conditions are not met, there may in fact exist

---

[12]For aspects of a gradual approximation to the optimal environmental tax see Baumol and Oates (1988, ch. 7). However, it is controversial whether an iterative process can achieve an optimal level.

a great number of local maxima which would considerably complicate the determination of the first-best result. Equilibrium prices no longer allow a statement concerning the efficiency of an existing output level, and the direction of an improvement cannot be determined (Baumol and Bradford 1972).

In consideration of the difficulty of correctly determining marginal environmental damage in the optimum (a problem which becomes even more severe if additional distortions exist) and therefore to be able to realize the optimal pollution level, the standard-price approach pursues the concept of imposing a specific *ad hoc* standard. This standard should of course not be chosen arbitrarily but can for example be based on scientific findings or can be motivated politically. Baumol and Oates (1971, p. 46) have shown that such an exogenously determined standard can be realized at least social cost again by means of a tax; this would lead to a second-best result. The energy tax proposed by the DIW can be interpreted as an implementation of the standard-price approach since it is based on Germany's self-commitment with regard to CO_2 emissions. As a market-consistent instrument it is superior to command and control instruments which have predominated in Germany up to now. As an alternative to a tax solution it would be equally efficient to regulate emissions directly, e.g. by means of tradable emission permits – a market instrument which has been subject to intensive theoretical analysis but which in practice has so far been largely neglected due to implementation problems.[13] Since there is only one price for emission permits that are being traded on competitive markets, the analogy with taxes as an internalization instrument refers only to cases where the externality is of Meade's additive atmosphere type or where individuals are identical. If these conditions do not prevail, however, taxes that can be differentiated between economic agents are the more flexible instrument and hence are superior from the allocational point of view. Furthermore, the state would receive regular proceeds from emission permits only in the case of recurring auction procedures. Another difference between these market instruments, apart from flexibility and revenue aspects, becomes

---

[13]Throughout the analysis the main emphasis will be on taxes. Permits and sometimes command and control instruments will be considered only for comparison purposes.

relevant in the case of uncertainty. The choice of tradable permits as an internalization instrument may incur immense costs, whereas taxes involve the danger that ecological targets may be missed by far – an aspect that is taken up again when the aptitude of both instruments at the international level is discussed.

In order to avoid unintended incentives in the case of taxes and, consequently, efficiency losses, it is crucial to choose the right tax base; accordingly, a detailed list of targets needs to be determined. The DIW report, however, is not based on such a list, since energy use is assumed to represent only an approximate value for different environmental pollutions. If the objective was restricted to limiting the anthropogenic greenhouse effect, the planned energy tax would for several reasons be afflicted with inefficiencies. An efficient climate policy needs to assess the various greenhouse gas emissions directly at the source. This, if at all technically feasible, will, however, result in high administrative costs due to the diverse and often mobile sources of pollution. A complementary taxation of fossil sources of energy according to their carbon content serves as a pragmatic alternative to a CO_2 tax since carbon content and released CO_2 emissions are proportional.[14] The energy tax proposed by the DIW assesses the various fossil sources of energy uniformly, without differentiating the tax burden according to the specific carbon content. This means that there exists no incentive to substitute CO_2-intensive sources of energy for CO_2-extensive ones. Due to unexploited substitution possibilities, the social costs of an energy tax are higher than those of a CO_2 tax. Abatement costs could be further reduced if other important greenhouse gases in addition to CO_2 were included in the internalization strategy (see Michaelis 1994*a,b* for an estimation).[15] The report, however, does not find appreciable differences in the macroeconomic effects of the energy tax and the CO_2 tax concept (Bach et al. 1994, p. 57). This

---

[14]The disadvantage of a complementary taxation is that it carries no incentive to modify the relation between pollution and the underlying tax base through technological innovations as, for example, end-of-pipe technologies. However, such a technology in connection with CO_2 is not conceivable with present know-how.

[15]An exclusive taxation of greenhouse gases favours atomic energy which, however, is connected with the problem of nuclear waste dumping, in addition to the potential dangers of released radioactivity. Therefore, its price should reflect the actual social costs as well.

result is not suprising since substitution effects are in any case excluded from the model due to the assumed limitational production function.

In the case of a national single-handed policy effort, imports that use energy inputs intensively receive – at constant exchange rates – a price advantage in the domestic market.[16] For imports of secondary energy, such as electricity or oil products, this problem of so-called grey energy is bypassed in the DIW scenario since the tax is proposed to assess not only primary but also secondary sources of energy. The tax, however, provides no additional incentive to producers of secondary energy to increase the efficiency of energy transformation since it is not imposed on the input factors for energy generation, namely the primary sources of energy.[17] Instead, it is the average implicit tax burden contained in the price of domestically produced secondary energy in respect of primary energy input taxation which determines the tax on secondary sources of energy.

Owing to the undifferentiated effects, the energy tax proposed by the DIW has to be rejected from an allocative point of view. The discussion will now be extended so as to include aspects that arise when an economy is seen within an open setting, i.e. the analysis is shifted on to the international level. The question will be raised as to how far international economic integration has an impact on the possibilities of autonomous (environmental) policies. As the first step, the following section starts the analysis by surveying aspects of national environmental policy design in respect of international flows of goods and factors, but where externalities are assumed to be purely national. In the second step, in section 3.4, international externalities will also be allowed for.

3.3 NATIONAL EXTERNALITIES

The following considerations will again begin with the closed-economy case. In the preceding section, it was shown that negative external effects, for example pollution, are distorting since they drive a wedge be-

---

[16] A discrimination between imports is not possible due to international trade rules (GATT/WTO and EU treaty).

[17] This is mistakenly claimed differently in Bach et al. (1994), p. 401, and DIW (1994, p. 119).

tween the private and social marginal cost of an activity associated with externalities. In a first-best framework, an internalization is efficient if in the equilibrium the aggregate marginal utility from reduced pollution exactly balances the individual marginal cost of further abatement. If the internalization is achieved with the help of an environmental tax levied on the externality-generating activity, the efficient tax level for each individual exactly corresponds to the aggregate marginal environmental damage an economic agent imposes on others in the optimum. This – as already pointed out – is the so-called Pigou tax (Figure 3.1, left branch).[18] If the externality is of Meade's additive atmosphere externality type, where the individual contribution to the overall externality level is negligible, the pollution tax level determines the marginal cost of abatement. In this case, the marginal cost of abatement can alternatively be interpreted as the marginal loss in tax proceeds that results from the erosion of the pollution tax base, the latter reflecting the corrective effect of a marginal increase in the pollution tax rate.[19] Income from such a corrective tax under efficiency considerations is to be redistributed as a lump sum to economic agents. A compensation of those affected by an externality is – as already mentioned – not efficient since it would induce undesired behavioural changes due to strategic considerations (see Baumol and Oates 1988, pp. 23–24).

The analysis of an optimal environmental policy becomes more complicated if not only one but several distortions prevail within a system. In the case of monopolies where output is inefficiently low due to profit maximization, the introduction of a Pigou tax can entail a reduction in welfare instead of an increase. The positive aspect of a reduction of the externality level is faced by a detrimental additional cut in output. The total welfare effect is not clear (see Buchanan 1969). Apart from monopolies, reality is characterized by the existence of many other

---

[18] The notion 'Pigou tax' will in the following generally be taken as a tax that equals the aggregate marginal environmental damage that an economic agent imposes on others in an equilibrium, which is the shadow price of the environment. There will hence be no distinction between first-best and second-best analyses.

[19] The result that the marginal cost of abatement can be interpreted as the marginal loss in tax proceeds resulting from the erosion of the pollution tax base holds globally if the marginal cost of abatement is defined as needing to be corrected for negative effects on utility that result from own pollution.

incompletenesses of the market system which are in contrast to the idealized assumptions of the model analysis. For instance, a great number of
different environmental externalities under allocational aspects require
the introduction of just as many specific and individually differentiated
environmental taxes at the level of aggregate marginal environmental
damage of each externality in the optimum. Owing to the additional
distortions in other markets, a partial equilibrium analysis is no longer
sufficient for deriving an internalization strategy. If the optimality conditions are approximated in only one market, the repercussions of the
remaining distortions can be negative, so that positive welfare effects in
the considered market may even be overcompensated. This argumentation reflects the traditional findings of second-best theory. In a general
equilibrium analysis the result can be derived that in the face of several
environmental externalities a proportional decrease in all distortions towards the first-best optimum generally leads to an increase but never to
a decline in welfare (see Copeland 1994, pp. 50–51).

The following discussion refers to the extent to which national policy rules vary with regard to environmental control if the economies are
internationally interconnected. The first case considered is a small open
economy for which prices on international markets are fixed. For reasons of simplification it is assumed that there is only one representative
individual living in the economy. Internationally mobile goods or factors
have no influence on the sufficient conditions for welfare gains resulting
from a marginal increase in environmental taxes, provided that there
do not exist additional distortions apart from the environmental ones in
the initial equilibrium (see Copeland 1994, p. 62). Also in this case the
above-characterized Pigou tax – which is now uniform across all economic
agents since they are identical – is the suitable instrument in order to
achieve a first-best result. However, it is now assumed that there do exist
additional distortions in the initial equilibrium in the form of tariffs. The
sufficient condition for a welfare gain (or at least no welfare loss) from
a marginal tax reform is that both tax and environmental distortions
should be reduced proportionally: the environmental distortions again
proportional to the difference between aggregate marginal environmental damage and the specific environmental tax rate, the tariff distortions

proportional to the specific tariff rate (see Copeland 1994, p. 51).[20] First-order conditions for an optimal allocation demand levying no tariffs and fixing the environmental tax at aggregate marginal environmental damage of the respective externality in the optimum (Figure 3.1, left branch; see OECD 1994, p. 26).

The analysis of national environmental policy becomes more complex if a marginal environmental tax reform is not embedded in a concerted tax reform approach that aims at alleviating all distortions existing in a system simultaneously but is initiated in isolation. Such a second-best situation, where the number of instruments is smaller than that of the existing distortions in a system, may for instance result from political restrictions. In this case, the sufficient conditions for a marginal environmental tax reform that is welfare-increasing also account for the spill-over effects of pollution tax changes on the other distortions in the system: in the above example the tariff distortions. An equiproportional reduction of the distortions from all externalities in this case only represents a sufficient condition for a welfare increase (or at least no decrease) if the existing tariffs are exclusively import duties or export subsidies, and, moreover, if the industries being protected by the tariffs produce pollution intensively on average. The intuition behind this is that, due to the modification of the price vector in the economy associated with an increase in the environmental tax rate, some industries shrink, whereas others grow. The industries affected most severely by a tightening of environmental policy will be those producing pollution intensively. If these industries in the initial equilibrium are protected by import duties, their output is too high from a welfare point of view. Therefore, the spill-over effect on the tariff distortion caused by the rise in the environmental tax would be positive, and the environmental tax reform serves the additional objective of partially reducing the existing tariff distortions (see Copeland 1994, p. 55). Corresponding sufficient conditions can also be derived for an isolated reform of the tariff system.[21] Accordingly, each of the two policy instruments (tariffs and environmental taxes, respec-

---

[20] This result is derived generally, that is for distortions of every kind, by e.g. Dixit (1975).

[21] In this case the spill-over effects of the tariff reform would have partially to internalize the environmental externalities (see Copeland 1994, pp. 53–54).

tively) can under certain conditions also have a positive indirect effect on other economic objectives.

If the analysis is extended to the case of a large country, strategic considerations must also be borne in mind. A national first-best policy is still possible provided that there is an identical number of targets and instruments. In a pure trade model without international factor mobility, an optimal environmental tax would have to be determined according to the Pigou criterion and the tariff rate according to the theory of optimal tariffs (Krutilla 1991, p. 139). If national optimization is restricted to only one of the two policy instruments, the first-order conditions for a nationally optimal policy simultaneously take into consideration environmental and strategic aspects as well as possible repercussions. The analysis is similar to that for small countries.[22]

The above comments have illustrated that the introduction or increase of an environmental tax induces repercussions with other distortions prevailing in a system. Due to these interactions, an environmental tax – in contradiction to the Pigou idea – is a distorting tax. If repercussions are negative, not only direct abatement costs but also welfare losses on account of amplified other distortions need to be weighed within a cost–benefit analysis against social utility gains from a cleaner environment. If, however, interactions are positive, an additional benefit emerges from the environmental tax reform in addition to the improvement of the environment. It can then be spoken of as a double dividend resulting from a marginal rise in environmental taxes.

The literature and the political discussion, however, use the technical term 'double dividend' in a broader context. In the above models, it is implicitly assumed that the entire endogenous environmental tax income is redistributed to households in a lump-sum fashion. If distorting taxes – tariffs, for example, in an open economy – are needed to finance a governmental budget, the analysis receives an additional facet since further interactions result. The allocative distortions caused by fiscal taxes are the starting point for the consideration that a double dividend can be reaped through an environmental tax reform. The basic idea is to

---

[22]The case of large countries will be covered more fully in subsection 3.4.2, when the analysis takes place against the background of international externalities.

reduce the marginal tax rates of the distorting fiscal taxes by means of environmental tax proceeds (the so-called revenue-recycling effect) and thereby not only improving the environmental situation but at the same time reducing the excess burden of the existing tax system. This is a proposition which is being and has been discussed controversially at the economic level and which has been named 'ecological tax reform'. Dealing with this issue is in a way a return to the starting point, the DIW report, which in effect is based on this idea of an ecological tax reform. The discussion in this subsection, however, focuses on the theoretical basics underlying the issues raised in the report. The revenue-recycling effect that reduces distortions is accompanied by the effects of the environmental tax on its own tax base: at least, as long as economic agents are not completely inelastic, the environmental tax increase will lead to behavioural changes away from environment-degrading activities, which is tantamount to an erosion of the environmental tax base. For an effective pollution tax this so-called tax base erosion effect will hence always be welfare-reducing.[23] In a second-best setting, however, the tax base erosion effect not only becomes directly welfare-effective, but simultaneously reduces the possibility for revenue recycling. The combination of the Ramsey and Pigou objectives of taxation that underlies the idea of an ecological tax reform was first addressed by Diamond (1973) and Sandmo (1975). With the growing awareness of environmental depletion in the last few years, the discussion was taken up again for instance by Pearce (1991) and Oates (1993). But, since their contributions were restricted to partial analytical considerations, interdependencies of pollution taxes with other taxes were neglected. General equilibrium analyses of distorted economies show that in addition to these two effects, i.e. (i) the revenue-recycling effect and (ii) the tax base erosion effect, and in contrast to the expectations in the first euphoria of the discussion of ecological tax reforms, interactions with the tax bases of the fiscal taxes discussed before also occur. In the literature, these interactions are named the tax interaction effect.[24] This effect likewise not only affects

---

[23]The tax base erosion effect can be observed also in a first-best framework. For Meade's additive atmosphere externality it corresponds – as already mentioned – to marginal cost of abatement.

[24]See Bovenberg and de Mooij (1994*a*) and (1994*c*) or Parry (1995) for basic con-

welfare directly via an impact on existing distortions but also influences the possibilities of revenue recycling.

As already demonstrated, the interaction effect can be negative or positive. Goulder established definitions for a double dividend in the weak, middle and strong sense. His strong form (Goulder 1995, p. 159) requires that an ecological tax reform has to be welfare-increasing (fiscal dividend) even if the utility gain from an improved environmental situation (ecological dividend), which is difficult to evaluate, remains unconsidered. Goulder's idea is to implement a criterion which concentrates on measurable effects united within the fiscal dividend and thereby involves relatively low information hurdles. This double-dividend definition is taken as a basis for the more general comments within this section. Chapter 4 will go one step further by putting Goulder's concept on the test-bench and comparing it to a different concept within an analytically founded framework.

Figure 3.4 implicitly assumes an exogenous governmental budget, an economy consisting of only one representative individual, and an externality of Meade's additive atmosphere externality type. The figure shows the marginal cost of abatement associated with different abatement levels (MCA curve) *vis-à-vis* social marginal environmental damage (MED curve) that can be realized as a benefit from an improvement in environmental quality. Different from the partial equilibrium model, the marginal cost of abatement not only includes the effects of the environmental tax on its own base, but also accounts for the general equilibrium effects on the pollution tax base resulting from an endogenous adaptation of the remaining tax rates considered. The difference between marginal environmental damage and marginal cost of abatement is represented by the net marginal environmental damage curve (NMED). In order to demonstrate the interactions with distortions prevailing within a second-best framework, the TIE curves – TIE stands for 'tax interaction effect' – reflect different marginal changes in the cost of public funds with respect to all taxes apart from the environmental tax (i.e. net of direct internalization costs being reflected by the marginal cost of abatement). They correspond to the total effect on the tax base of taxes to be substituted.

tributions in the field of ecological tax reform analysis.

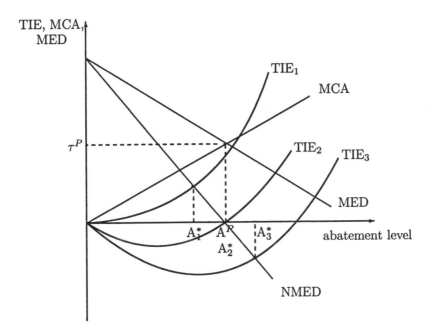

Source: Own presentation.

Figure 3.4: Internalization within a second-best framework

In the case of the TIE_1 curve the marginal increase in an environmental tax shows no positive repercussions from fiscal taxes over the entire abatement range. Rather, the environmental tax increase leads to an improvement of the environmental situation at the cost of enlarged pre-existing distortions. The Goulder concept of a double dividend in the strong form requires that the tax interaction effect be negative (i.e. that the TIE curve lies below the abscissa) or equivalently that the interactions with the remaining taxes be positive. Moreover, tax interactions must even be large enough to overcompensate the direct marginal costs of abatement (represented by the MCA curve) which take the form of general equilibrium erosion effects on the pollution tax base. The sum of the marginal cost of abatement and the marginal tax interaction effect – which is not made explicit in Figure 3.4 – corresponds to the change in the excess burden of the tax system being induced by an ecological tax reform. The result derived by Bovenberg and de Mooij from their models is that

> environmental taxes typically render the tax structure a less efficient instrument for raising revenue and, therefore, increase the welfare costs of financing public spending. The additional costs of environmental taxes due to less efficient revenue-raising are likely to be especially high if the marginal efficiency costs of the existing tax system are substantial

(Bovenberg and de Mooij 1994c, p. 677).

But when concentrating on the TIE_1 curve in Figure 3.4, it can also be seen for this case, where no double dividend can be realized, that a marginal ecological tax reform is welfare-increasing as long as the abatement level A_1^* is not reached, i.e. as long as NMED $> TIE_1$. The TIE_2 curve reflects a situation where the marginal increase in the environmental tax at a low level has a positive general equilibrium effect on the bases of the fiscal taxes up to an abatement level A^P. The same applies to the TIE_3 curve, for which the corresponding abatement level is even higher. All three TIE curves have in common that the effects of the ecological tax reform on the bases of the other taxes (i.e. tax interaction) are more negative the higher the initial level of the pollution tax rate or equivalently the initial abatement level is. A^P is the so-called Pigou level where marginal cost of abatement and social marginal environmental damage exactly balance, so that net marginal environmental damage is zero. The second-best optimal abatement levels A_1^*, A_2^* and A_3^* lie at the intersections of the respective TIE curves with the NMED curve.[25]

Bovenberg and de Mooij (1994a,c, resp.) examine an ecological tax reform in a simple model with a clean and a polluting consumption good, with proceeds from the pollution tax used to reduce a distorting tax on labour. Unemployment is only voluntary. The spill-over effect in this model consists of the fact that not only the wage tax but also (implicitly) the environmental tax on the dirty good affects labour supply via a change in real wages. Due to the assumption that utility is weakly separable between leisure and the consumption of private and

---

[25] At A_2^* the second-best optimal abatement level incidentally coincides with the Pigou level.

public goods, the discriminating taxation of goods associated with the environmental tax is less efficient under welfare aspects than a flat tax on all goods, or equivalently in this model, an explicit wage tax. In this case not only the erosion effect on the own tax base (marginal cost of abatement) is negative, but also the tax interaction effect (as it is the case for the TIE_1 curve in Figure 3.4 over the whole range). Independent of the level of the environmental tax in the initial equilibrium, the recycling of its marginal proceeds does not suffice to reduce the other taxes enough to mitigate the fiscal distortions of the tax system as a whole. Therefore a double dividend in the strong form is not achievable. However, this result hinges on the specification of the individual utility function. In the case of a non-separable utility function, a wage tax (or equivalently a flat commodity tax) is no more optimal from the fiscal stance, that is disregarding welfare-reducing environmental pollution. Instead, the Corlett–Hague rule of Ramsey taxation would have to be applied, which demands that the optimal tax rate on each commodity depends on its substitution elasticity with respect to leisure, which cannot be taxed directly. Provided that leisure and pollution are complements, the environmental tax, that discriminates between commodities, charges labour more efficiently than the explicit wage tax (i.e. a flat commodity tax).

In order to turn to the aspects of an ecological tax reform in an integrated economy, a switch is made to a different framework used by Bovenberg and de Mooij (1996). They analyse such a policy intervention in the context of internationally mobile capital. They consider a small open economy that is confronted with fixed prices on international markets. Environmental pollution this time arises on the production side due to the use of environmental resources as production inputs. The representative household receives its income from the net-of-tax returns on the factors labour, capital and the environment. Utility is optimized with respect to leisure and consumption, while the level of the public good provided by the government is exogenous. The government finances its exogenous budget through factor taxes on labour, the environment and capital (as a source tax). In an initial tax system which is optimal under fiscal aspects (that is without considering the negative environmental externalities), the pollution tax rate as well as the capital tax rate are zero (Bovenberg and de Mooij 1996, p. 18). A marginal tax reform in the course of which environmental tax earnings are used for reducing labour taxes has no first-order effect on wages. The labour supply decision of households and therefore the labour tax base are not affected by the change in the environmental tax; the second of Goulder's dividends is equal to zero. In a fiscally suboptimal tax system, where the capital tax rate in the initial equilibrium is still zero, but the environmental tax rate is positive, an analogous ecological tax reform results in decreasing wages. The part of welfare which stems from private consumption (i.e. without taking account of changes in environmental quality) decreases. The economic reason is that the environmental tax is less efficient in revenue generation than the tax on labour. On account of the infinitely high supply elasticity of the factors environment and capital, taxes levied on these factors are finally also borne by labour. Moreover, due again to a separability assumption between environmental quality and the remaining arguments of the utility function, there exists an asymmetry: the environmental tax indeed has a negative impact on labour supply, whereas an improved environmental situation leaves it unchanged. Consequently, the fiscal dividend is negative while the first one, resulting from the improvement in environmental quality, is positive; hence there exists no double dividend according to Goulder's definition.

The peculiarity of Bovenberg and de Mooij's models is that from a fiscal point of view the second-best optimal pollution tax is always zero. If on the other hand the authors had analysed a consumption tax instead of a labour tax, the second-best optimal total tax burden on the dirty good would have a non-environmental component equal to the tax burden on all other consumption goods. This is because the optimal consumption tax from a fiscal point of view would be a uniform tax across all commodities. Therefore, starting the analysis from a tax burden on the dirty good lower than the fiscally optimal one, a green tax reform would not only improve the environment but would also reduce the excess burden of the tax system.[26]

---

[26]These considerations are also part of a normalization issue raised by Fullerton (1997), Schöb (1997), and Bovenberg and de Mooij (1997). A very illuminating decomposition of the total tax burden on the dirty commodity in its fiscal and its corrective components can be found in Sandmo (1975, p. 92). Fullerton and Wolver-

Strictly speaking, the analysis of an environmental tax reform within a tax system that deviates from the Ramsey rule must be separated from the welfare-theoretical discussion of a double dividend. In this case, the introduction of an environmental tax possibly serves as a lever in order to reduce existing and for instance politically motivated inefficiencies of a tax system.[27] Subsuming these effects under the notion 'double dividend' is problematic, since welfare gains could already be achieved by a restructuring of the existing tax system: they are not specific to the introduction or increase of an environmental tax. However, it is clear that a marginal ecological tax reform can never yield a double dividend in Goulder's definition, provided that the initial tax system is second-best optimal from the fiscal point of view. The fiscal dividend in this case must always be equal to zero. However, it is conceivable that the tax system in the initial equilibrium is indeed fiscally optimal, but that there is not a sufficient number of instruments available to achieve the second-best optimal allocation. If the environmental tax, in addition to its corrective effect, makes a new tax base accessible, then it provides an independent contribution as a fiscal instrument and can – even though the ecological dividend is not considered – be different from zero in the fiscal optimum. Under these circumstances, a double dividend is also possible in Goulder's restrictive definition.

Whether a country, be it large or small, can achieve a double dividend or not crucially depends on the kind of international integration, on the specifics of factor and commodity substitution as well as on the available set of tax instruments. However, it is obvious that the 'double dividend' has no economic relevance if the government has full information. In this case, the government is always able to evaluate the net welfare gain from an environmental tax reform, and the decomposition of the total effect into different dividends is of merely theoretical interest. The double dividend becomes a relevant policy issue only if policy-makers are confronted with incomplete information, for example with regard to the

---

ton (1997) present an application of the normalization issue. They show that a tax–subsidy combination may be superior to a Pigou tax with respect to practical considerations, but still equivalent with respect to the allocational impact, by forcing the market to recognize the social cost of disposal.

[27] Bovenberg and de Mooij (1996) designate this the 'tax shifting effect'.

social marginal environmental damage function.[28] The information issue in the context of different double-dividend concepts will be dealt with in detail in the following chapter.

In the DIW report, the resulting positive employment effect is designated as a second dividend. In the full employment frameworks discussed above, a decrease in voluntary unemployment would be possible if the distortion in the consumers' work–leisure decision caused by a wage tax could be reduced by partially replacing it with an environmental tax. This employment effect would be accompanied by a positive welfare effect. In the literature, however – and the examples listed above are representative in this respect – this effect is judged as most doubtful and improbable for an ecological tax reform in the course of which environmental taxes are supposed to substitute for wage taxes. Therefore a double dividend can generally only be indentified in Goulder's weak form: the use of pollution tax earnings for financing the state budget, associated with corresponding less reliance on other financing instruments, is to be preferred to a lump-sum redistribution of the funds to households (Goulder 1995, p. 159). The German tax system studied in the DIW report is certainly far from optimal. Moreover, on account of the high level of involuntary unemployment it is – in contrast to the previous theoretical reflections – rather a distortion of the labour demand decision due to high labour costs which is relevant here. The predicted employment effects must therefore be attributed to the circumstance that the labour cost is reduced through a redistribution of energy tax proceeds to the firm sector, which is part of the tax reform. Moreover, if an ecological tax reform is oriented at the standard-price approach, revenue from the pollution tax is not endogenous but rather determined right from the beginning. In this case, investigations have to be focused on determining the most suitable way to recycle the funds. Even if the actual tax system in Germany deviates from an ideal one, the result is still valid that generally those taxes should be reduced which – considering all interactions – produce the highest marginal welfare loss. A more efficient design of the tax system combined with positive employment effects is equivalent to an improvement in welfare.[29] Therefore, the payment of a lump-sum

---

[28] This point is also made by Ruocco and Wiegard (1997).

[29] Positive employment effects do not necessarily mean a welfare increase. Welfare

eco-bonus to households as proposed by the DIW cannot be justified on allocative grounds. In its report the DIW alternatively addresses a reduction of VAT (DIW 1994, p. 397). Although the administrative costs of such a measure would be relatively low, VAT is certainly not the most distortive tax in the German tax system. Furthermore, lowering it would not be politically feasible on account of harmonization agreements within the EU. For the firm side, the DIW proposes a reduction of the employer contributions to social security. However, these contain strong equivalence components and therefore to a certain extent have to be considered as wage components (which are not market-clearing). On the other hand, equivalence of a compulsory insurance applies at best on aggregate so that distortions at the individual level can still exist.[30] The most serious distortions with respect to non-wage labour cost refer to insurance benefits extrinsic to the insurance, but which are bankrolled from the social security system, as well as to ranges in which the equivalence principle is likewise not valid, as for instance health insurance. Alternative to social security, it would be possible to use the environmental tax proceeds for reducing corporate taxes, which could result in positive employment effects, too. Faced with imperfect capital markets due to incomplete information, it could be useful to earmark part of the environmental tax proceeds for venture capital funds to support energy-saving investments.[31] However, the difficulty adhering to such a method is that suitable evaluation criteria have to be defined for the projects to be supported. Whether larger marginal welfare gains can be obtained by reducing the tax burden on the factors capital or labour or through a more efficient provision of venture capital can only be evaluated by means of econometric analysis.

A rational national economic policy in a first-best framework will always strive for a complete internalization of national external effects since social welfare (at least from the allocation point of view) can be increased in this manner. If every country pursues such a policy, the

---

effects of lowering the tax burden on the factor labour are negative if the reform causes the tax system gradually to drift away from its second-best optimal shape.

[30] In the case of demographic changes, the equivalence principle is no longer valid even on aggregate but is limited to an associated equivalence.

[31] For credit rationing of enterprises, see Winker (1996).

allocation of goods and factors will be globally efficient. If certain policy instruments are not available to a small country, it will operate a second-best policy as described above. The global allocation result is then no longer optimal since international relative prices of goods and factors do not reflect their actual global scarcities. It nevertheless remains rational for other small countries to adhere to first-best optimal policies, provided they are not confronted with additional restrictions. If strategic behaviour of some countries is also a fact, a globally efficient allocation result again cannot be achieved, especially since it has to be expected that affected countries will respond with retaliation.

From this section it has become clear that international economic integration significantly influences the possibilities of an autonomous environmental policy, even with respect to purely national environmental externalities. The following section will expand consideration to the specific restrictions for national policy actions that result from transborder environmental problems.

3.4   INTERNATIONAL EXTERNALITIES

In the treatment of market failures resulting from external effects we have so far ignored the problems of assigning the competence which is needed for an elimination of these unwanted effects. It was always implicitly assumed in the previous section that there exists an authority with the political power to enforce the desired internalization measures. However, the failure explicitly to specify this authority means that an essential facet of the externality problem is excluded. The previous analysis was further based on the assumption that the effects of an externality coincide with the sphere of influence of a government authority. If a regulatory authority has full information and, in addition, differentiated tax rates are at its disposal, the internalization of a local externality would also be possible for a government institution whose jurisdiction by far exceeds the sphere of effect of the externality or where it is generated. In the case of Meade's additive atmosphere externality, which deserves a uniform Pigou tax for internalization purposes, a government whose jurisdiction reaches further than the sphere of activity of the externality needs to be able to intervene selectively in the market system, which is spatially differentiated. However, if it is not possible to design a spatially differentiated tax system that takes care of different types of additive atmosphere externalities, an internalization would best be carried out in accordance with the subsidiarity principle: the internalization must be reserved for the regional authority whose jurisdiction currently coincides with the area of influence and generation of the externality.

International externalities constitute an important extension of the analysis. Especially in the field of environmental economics, this kind of externality plays an important role: air or water pollution very often do not remain within the country of origin but harm other countries. Examples such as CO_2 emissions or acid rain have already been mentioned. Furthermore, it is mostly a group of countries that simultaneously act as polluters. Since these countries are themselves affected by the externality, this phenomenon corresponds to an aggregate externality in the form of congestion.

It can be expected that sovereign states care only for marginal environmental damage arising to their home country; marginal environmental damage to other countries remains neglected. As a most drastic case, one may assume that an externality does not harm the country of origin but one or several neighbour countries. An internalization by the generating country is hardly conceivable in these circumstances. Since an important characteristic of international environmental externalities is that their areas of influence are larger than the jurisdictions of national governments, the number of countries involved is a crucial feature of these problems. The direction of influence of an externality – with reference to p. 23 – can be categorized as follows (see Mäler 1990):[32] (i) unidirectional externalities which are only exported but not imported by a polluting country – the pollution of a river which runs into another country and acid rain can serve as examples; (ii) reciprocal externalities that have an effect in two directions – e.g. water pollution by the states adjoining a lake. The states involved in such an externality will have a

---

[32]Every environmental problem (including purely national ones) can be described through a pollutant-transport matrix in which transportation coefficients indicate both direction and quantity of pollutants. For an application to the example of acid rain in Europe see Mäler (1989).

greater interest in coordinating their actions than in the first case, since each of them is affected by the pollution. When cross-border environmental problems are covered in the following sections, the analysis is restricted to reciprocal, non-exhaustible and aggregate externalities that affect a group of countries and which have the characteristic of a pure international public good: a reduction in their level benefits all countries (non-rivalry) and no country can be excluded from the resulting welfare effects (non-excludability). This again is Meade's additive atmosphere externality. At the international level this is optimally internalized by means of a uniform tax rate across all individuals in all countries. The most serious global environmental problems such as the anthropogenic greenhouse effect and the destruction of the ozone layer, have such characteristics. Other important features, as for instance the time dimension and the degree of uncertainty concerning causes and consequences of the respective environmental problem, remain unconsidered.[33]

Since national internalization efforts can be interpreted as a voluntary provision of an international public (environmental) good, conditions can be derived by analogy to the case of national public goods which ensure that its provision is efficient from the global point of view. If international externalities represent the only distortion, global efficiency is achieved if each country involved internalizes global and not only domestic marginal environmental damage. With numerous countries involved in the provision problem, efficiency requires the fulfilment of a modified Samuelson condition:[34] the provision of an international environmental public good is globally efficient if the sum of marginal rates of substitution of all economic agents involved in the home country as well as in foreign countries corresponds to the marginal rates of transformation in each country.[35] Accordingly, not only must the provision of the public good achieve an efficient level (efficiency in pro-

---

[33] A theoretical introduction to the problem of international stock externalities can be found in van der Ploeg and de Zeeuw (1992). For the role of uncertainty in the context of climate policy design see Larson and Tobey (1994).

[34] This condition, however, implicitly assumes the possibility of transfer payments between countries.

[35] An application of the Samuelson condition to international environmental problems can be found in Arnold (1984) for a model with two countries and two goods (a private consumption good and the international public environmental good).

vision), but additionally the good must be produced with globally the least opportunity cost (cost-efficiency). The first is tantamount to the complete global internalization of external environmental damages; the latter implies that the marginal cost of providing the environmental good (which is the marginal cost of abatement) is equalized across countries. Both efficiency aspects can only be realized if all countries involved in the pollution problem are included. The group of countries that have to coordinate their national environmental policies is hence normatively determined by the spatial dimension of the externality.[36]

Globally efficient provision of international environmental goods is impeded since environmental policies are pursued by national governments which aim at maximizing their own population's welfare.[37] They behave strategically in interaction with other governments, which leads to incentive problems with respect to environmental decision-making. In principle, it would be possible for governments to cooperate in order to internalize transborder environmental externalities. This, however, conflicts with the public-good characteristic of national environmental policy measures. Every country has an incentive to act as a free rider, i.e. to stay ecopolitically passive but still to profit from other states' efforts. If the countries involved behave in such a way, they will not cooperate even if, by doing so, every country would reach a higher welfare level. The fundamental incentive problem of this decision situation is the well-known 'prisoner's dilemma'. Here, the dominant strategy for each player is non-cooperation (see, for example, Althammer and Buchholz 1993; Sandler 1996). Certainly, cooperation would benefit each individual country provided that the other players also cooperate; but the individual advantage is even greater if a country does not cooperate unilaterally. In Figure 3.5 a situation of isolated actions is depicted for the case of two identical countries A and B. National marginal environmental damages are represented by curves $MED_{A,B}$. Summing vertically (due to the public-good characteristic of the externality) produces the

---

[36]This principle, however, is called into question since there are also reasons for international cooperation in the case of purely national externalities (see e.g. Hoel 1997*a,b*; Kox and van der Tak 1996).

[37]Here, we ignore distributional conflicts within a country and therefore political-economy aspects.

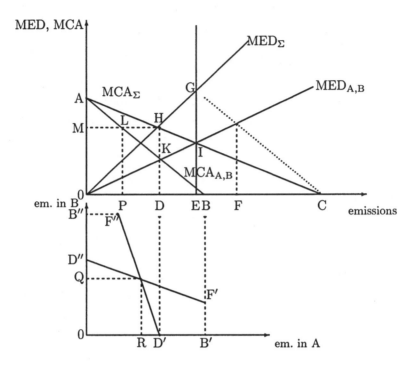

Source: Own presentation, partly based on Endres (1993), p. 54.

Figure 3.5: Isolated actions in the presence of international externalities

global marginal environmental damages line MED_Σ. The marginal cost of abatement represented by line AB is likewise assumed to be identical for both countries. Due to its private-good character it must be aggregated horizontally to get the global marginal cost of abatement (line AC). The Pareto-optimal emission level is D, where the global marginal environmental damage curve and the global marginal cost of abatement curve intersect; national emission contributions amount to P. Isolated behaviour of both countries however leads to an emission level E, which is higher since each country ignores the damage imposed on the other. In order to show this, the behaviour of country A for a given emission level of country B is considered first.

- If country B decides to have a national emission level equal to zero, the world emission level without an internalization policy undertaken by country A lies at point B. If country A autonomously internalizes domestic environmental damages, it will reduce its emission level to point D since there its national marginal cost of abatement corresponds to national marginal environmental damage. Although the global externality level incidentally corresponds to the efficient level D in the example,[38] global allocation is still not efficient because the marginal cost of abatement in both countries differs. In this case the provision level of the public good 'environmental quality' is globally efficient whereas cost-effectiveness is not realized. This inefficiency is represented by the sum of the areas of welfare triangles KHL and LAM. It results from the additional costs for country A if it were to reduce emissions from D to P (area DKLP) and the diminuition of abatement costs for country B if it were to extend emissions from zero to level P (area PLA0).
- If country B does not internalize at all, the emission level realized if country A also refrains from internalizing is C. Moving the national marginal cost of abatement curve of country A to point C (see the dotted line), a reduction of its externality level to point F would be optimal.

If both countries behave in this manner and moreover assume that the behaviour of the other country will not change in reaction to its own measures, the Nash equilibrium will be realized at point E. This has been derived in the lower part of Figure 3.5 according to the above discussion: if country B does not pollute, country A chooses emission level 0D', which corresponds to level 0D in the upper part of the figure. If country B realizes emission level 0B" (which is equivalent to level 0B), country A pollutes at level B"F", which corresponds to the distance BF. The reaction curve for country A is represented by line F"D'. The derivation of country B's reaction curve is analogous and shown by line D"F' (since distance 0D" corresponds to distance 0D). The point of intersection of

---

[38]This results from the fact that at point D not only the global marginal environmental damage, but by chance also the global marginal cost of abatement is twice as high as the national marginal environmental damage and the marginal cost of abatement, respectively, of country A.

both lines is the Nash equilibrium, with the corresponding emission levels 0R for country A and 0Q for country B – which are identical. These national pollution levels sum to the global emission level E which will be realized in the Nash equilibrium. Compared to the Pareto-optimal situation, a global welfare loss remains of the size of the triangle GHI. As long as governments are not able to commit themselves credibly to cooperative behaviour, cooperation between countries represents no equilibrium. This result, however, has to be qualified in a context of repeated decisions. The 'shadow of the future' then implies that gains from non-cooperative behaviour are weighed against expected utility losses (for instance through credible penalization strategies) in future periods. Provided that future benefits are not discounted too strongly, even the social optimum is a possible cooperative solution. This applies to an infinite time horizon game (Folk theorem) as well as in a limited sense also to a finitely repeated prisoner's dilemma game (see, for example, Kreps et al. 1982).[39] If more than two countries are involved, free-rider incentives can alternatively lead to a coordination problem which in game theory is known as the 'chicken game' (Lipnowski and Maital 1983): in contrast to the prisoner's dilemma, cooperative behaviour is rational for some countries despite non-cooperation of other countries. The result of the chicken game is always a partial cooperation. However, it is most advantageous for each country not to belong to the cooperating countries in the Nash equilibrium. Each government therefore has an incentive to indicate that it will abstain from the environmental agreement. The coordination problem occurs since *ex ante* it remains open which states will be involved in the cooperation and which will not. In order to avoid multiple Nash equilibria, it has to be assumed that countries involved in the negotiations differ sufficiently from each other, for example with respect to their utility gains from an environmental agreement or with respect to their bargaining power (see, for example, Schmidt 2000, ch. 5).

The classical way to overcome the falling-apart of individual and collective rationality is to equip a supranational institution with in-

---

[39] However, Dockner and Long (1993) show within a dynamic two-country model with a stock externality that under the assumption of non-linear Markov strategies the global first-best optimum can be a subgame-perfect equilibrium; punishment mechanisms are not required.

ternational environmental competence. In the ideal case this leads to an international first-best solution. This possibility corresponds to the branch 'complete cooperation' in Figure 3.1. However, such an institution is – at least at the global level – not a realistic policy option in the foreseeable future because of the aforementioned incentive problems. Therefore, since the usual welfare-theoretic advice of environmental economics actually presupposes a sufficient sovereignty power for complete internalization, it is of only minor applicability to international environmental problems. The sovereignty of national governments implies that the internalization of cross-border externalities has to be supported at the national level. Therefore, all solution approaches, if evaluated from the international perspective, take place in a second-best framework. This holds even if the environmental externality represents the only distortion and if national Pigou taxes are available; the internalization remains incomplete. National governments can pursue two different decentralized strategies in order to cope with transborder environmental problems: either they take part in incomplete cooperations or they initiate unilateral actions that above all include aspects of an indirect internalization. Intergovernmental cooperations that are depicted in the middle and on the left of the right branch of Figure 3.1 will be investigated in the following subsection. In subsection 3.4.2, unilateral actions (on the right of the right branch of Figure 3.1) will be discussed.

3.4.1   Coordinated Actions

In the case of a decentralized internalization of cross-border environmental externalities, it seems reasonable first to investigate the possibilities of a negotiation solution between the involved states according to Coase. As already explained, his efficiency thesis says that under certain conditions the social optimum will be realized by means of negotiations (Figure 3.1, on the left of the right branch). The relevance of the Coase negotiation solution presented in section 3.2 can be illustrated for a unidirectional externality in the two-country case. It is assumed that pollution generated by country A is harmful exclusively to country B. This scenario is represented by Figure 3.6. The straight line MCA_A reflects the marginal cost of abatement accruing to country A if it reduces its

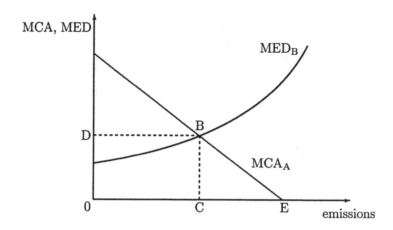

Source: Baumol and Oates (1988), p. 280.

Figure 3.6: Unidirectional externality

pollution level. The MED_B curve corresponds to the social marginal environmental damage of country B from pollution. Accordingly, point B would be the internationally efficient activity level. In order to achieve this level and at the same time to avoid country A being worse off compared to starting point E, a compensation payment from country B to country A is needed, at least of the size of triangle BCE.[40] World welfare gains (the area between the MCA and MED curves to the right of C) would have to be split up between both countries in order to strengthen the compliance of country A with the cooperation agreement. This aim may be achieved by a compensatory payment from country B to country A at level 0D per unit of reduced emissions. The present example corresponds to the situation of a voluntary negotiation solution according to Coase, since country A, because of its sovereignty, cannot be deterred from polluting and therefore *de facto* has the property right connected with the economic good damaged by emissions (e.g. a river). If the countries involved into a transborder externality can agree upon a

---

[40]However, this result contradicts the 'polluter pays principle' demanded by the OECD (see OECD 1976).

cooperation, this corresponds to an internalization without state intervention as proposed by Coase. The (internationally efficient) outcome of these negotiations must then be implemented nationally in an equally efficient manner by means of, e.g., Pigou taxes.

However, these conditions are hardly met, particularly for international environmental externalities with a (great) number of countries involved. First, property rights are rarely assigned to international environmental goods.[41] Even if property rights were assigned in national contracts, compliance with these contracts cannot be enforced at the international level. This, however, is a crucial condition of the Coase theorem. A third premise that is in strong contrast to reality is the non-existence of transaction costs. There is evidence that the costs of negotiation, implementation and monitoring are likely to be very high.[42] The great number of potentially cooperating countries, in particular, will impede a Coase solution. Finally the approach neglects additional distortions in the economies involved, which for instance are caused by strategic trade policies.

However, it may be possible to implement an incomplete cooperation. As outlined, the central premise of the Coase approach reflects the real decision situation in the course of international environmental negotiations just as little as the already mentioned (static) prisoner's dilemma. The states involved can communicate and negotiate with each other; they can conclude an environmental agreement and monitor the other countries' compliance up to a certain degree. Moreover, they normally decide repeatedly on whether to cooperate and can therefore renegotiate an agreement once it has failed. Finally, different economic as well as political arrangements are available to the countries, which help to stabilize cooperative solutions so that at least partial improvements compared to the *status quo* may be attainable (Figure 3.1, in the middle of the right branch).

---

[41] In international law this is reflected by calling such goods *res nulli* or *res communis*.

[42] The newer negotiation theory explains this cost by the fact that not all conceivable events (often lying in the far future) can be explicitly included in the contract (theory of incomplete contracts) and that the negotiation partners suffer from incomplete information.

The core of every environmental convention is the agreed level of environmental care as well as the assignment of the required measures to the individual signatory states. When a convention is designed, it must be clarified within the contract which instruments should be applied to obtain the negotiated targets. In this context, not only must the described incentive problems of cooperative solutions at the international level be considered, but also the specifics of the respective environmental problems and the countries involved. The issue of instrument selection therefore contains two further aspects: (i) the internalization of cross-border environmental externalities and (ii) the incentive compatibility of the agreed measures.

Internalization

The problem of internalization needs to be solved both at the international and the national level. From an economic point of view – as discussed in section 3.2 – the policy advice for both levels would be to implement market-consistent instruments like Pigou taxes or tradable emission permits. Only such instruments satisfy the minimal cost principle and are dynamically efficient, since they offer incentives for investments in environmentally sound technologies. This also applies when an environmental standard is first agreed and it is decided afterwards which instrument to use so as to comply nationally with the standard at least cost.[43] This procedure appears reasonable when it is almost impossible to carry out an explicit cost–benefit analysis, as in the case of the anthropogenic greenhouse effect due to its intertemporal and global character. As indicated, the DIW report is based on exactly this procedure.

When costs and benefits are known with certainty by both the government and the individual agents and when markets are perfectly competitive, the effects of tradable emission permits and emission taxes only differ with respect to the distribution of income. This result is analogous to the findings derived for the national level. The distribution of income resulting from licences is dependent upon the method of distribution of licences across and within countries. Apart from these differences, the

---

[43]This corresponds to the standard-price approach already addressed in connection with the DIW report (see Baumol and Oates 1971).

choice between the two internalization systems under certainty primarily depends on administrative convenience. If competition is imperfect, however, it is possible that with both instruments large countries try strategically to exploit their market power in international markets (Misiolek and Elder 1989). When costs and benefits are uncertain, the equivalence argument does not apply (Weitzman 1974). If, for instance, the global marginal cost of abatement increases more rapidly than the associated marginal utility diminishes, the social cost of incorrect determination of a pollution-tax level is lower than that resulting from a suboptimal determination of an emission standard; the tax is superior to the standard. When the opposite holds, quantity restrictions are to be preferred. Nevertheless, suspected threshold effects or the danger that developments lead to a catastrophe call, rather, for a standard (see Myles 1995, ch. 10, sec. 7).

The required institutional superstructure and the extent of national sovereignty which has to be given up are further central selection criteria for the internalization instrument because they essentially influence the respective national political acceptance. For both licences and taxation an international authority needs to (i) determine the current tax rate or the number of certificates in circulation, (ii) monitor the national implementation of measures, and (iii) redistribute resulting proceeds to the individual countries. The redistribution of tax proceeds is equivalent to the initial allocation of emission-permit endowments across countries (including possible later allotments) and determines how the gains from cooperation are distributed among the countries involved. Because of differences concerning the implementation, the equivalence between taxes and permits cannot be extended to the international level without any problem:[44] in the case of the greenhouse effect, for example, substantial differences between national energy prices resulting from diverse distortions on energy markets have to be considered when corrective taxes are implemented. For tradable permits, transaction costs would have to be kept as low as possible in order to realize sufficiently high turnovers on the international market for emission permits.

---

[44]See e.g. Hoel (1997*b*) for the issue of instrument selection in the context of internationally coordinated reductions of CO_2 emissions; for implementation aspects of the certificate solution see Tietenberg (1994).

International environmental negotiations mostly lead to agreements on quotas, for example in the form of proportional emission reductions. If the quota corresponds to the globally optimal emission level, only the trading of these pollution rights on an international, competitive market would be needed to achieve an efficient internalization of transboundary pollution damages. If, however, market-consistent internalization instruments cannot be agreed upon at the international level, arrangements will stick to the internationally determined quotas. Remaining on this first step to an international certificate solution has the serious disadvantage that cost-efficiency is not achieved at the international level if the countries involved differ with respect to their marginal cost of abatement in the initial equilibrium. In the case of identical marginal cost of abatement, a proportional reduction is also only efficient if cost curves are linear (see, for example, Endres 1993).[45] In the Framework Convention on Climate Change, it was attempted to take these circumstances into account by designing a concept called 'activities implemented jointly'. According to this, signatory states with high marginal cost of abatement are allowed to meet their reduction obligations in countries with low marginal cost of abatement, since foreign emission reductions can at least partly be attributed to own obligations.[46] In the case of full attribution to the obligations of the donor country that bears the cost of abatement activities abroad, the joint implementation concept entails a complete equalization of national marginal cost of abatement, and therefore cost-efficiency. Since the contractual reduction obligations of the receiving countries are not affected by such joint implementation projects, the arrangement comes close to trading of pollution permits. It can therefore serve as a preliminary stage to a later certificate solution.

---

[45] Schmidt examines the influence of different country sizes on cost-efficiency in non-cooperative Nash as well as Stackelberg equilibria (see Schmidt 2000, ch. 3, sec. 2).

[46] In this case, the ratio in which emission reductions are attributed to the obligations of both countries implicitly determines the amount of a transfer to the receiving country. The amount of the transfer is equal to zero in the case of full attribution, and the entire gains from increased cost-efficiency go to the donor country – a cause of massive criticism by the developing countries on the joint implementation concept.

Incentive compatibility

For international cooperations to be viable they must be designed in an incentive-compatible manner. Two facets of incentive-compatibility can be distinguished: participation incentives which are relevant for *ex ante* considerations and compliance incentives which become crucial *ex post*. Participation incentives need to exist before the initial agreement on a convention (Black et al. 1993), but also after it has taken effect in order to attract non-signatories to an accession to the treaty. Basically, the participation should include all countries involved in the environmental problem – in the case of truly global environmental problems, all states on the globe. In addition, incentives have to be given which avoid the default risk, so that compliance is guaranteed by the cooperating parties throughout the contract period.[47] Both aspects of incentive compatibility can at least partially be realized by means of a suitable distribution of the rights and duties arising from an environmental convention – i.e. the welfare gains from ecopolitical cooperation.[48]

There is a close interdependence between incentive compatibility of environmental agreements, the choice of the internalization instrument, and the agreed abatement level. This is particularly true if countries are heterogeneous (Barrett 1992).[49] Under the assumption that signatory states agree upon proportional emission reductions in accordance with the preferences of the median country and that compliance is guaranteed, cooperation will not be complete. The coalition of countries will be smaller the more ambitious the chosen abatement target (Hoel 1992). The outcome of only partial cooperation does not hereby depend on the quota solution, which is exogenous to Hoel's model. Finus and Rundshagen (1998) show within an extended model framework (i) where the

---

[47] However, conflicts between these two aspects of incentive compatibility can result if – for example through a minimum ratification clause (analysed by Black et al. 1993) – incentives are created for ratifying the convention by as many states as possible which subsequently, however, do not comply.

[48] Apart from direct effects on the distribution of welfare gains across countries arising from an environmental agreement, indirect effects such as changes in the terms of trade or in factor rewards must also be considered within a general equilibrium analysis (see e.g. McGuire 1982, p. 350).

[49] See e.g. Cline (1992) and Pearce (1990) for aspects of incentive compatibility with respect to internationally tradable CO_2 emission certificates.

internalization instrument is endogenously determined, (ii) where apart from participation incentives also compliance incentives are considered, and (iii) where the preferences of the marginal signatory country (and not the median country) are relevant so that, again, there will only be a subcoalition of cooperating countries. Furthermore, a uniform quota will generally be preferred to the more efficient emission tax.

The additional economic instruments that can be integrated into a treaty in order to secure cooperative behaviour can be subdivided into so-called (i) internal stabilization instruments, (ii) external stabilization instruments, and (iii) flexible adaptation mechanisms of an environmental convention (Heister et al. 1995, p. 16). Internal instruments concern the agreed ecopolitical measures themselves (e.g. emission reductions), when cooperating countries punish a breach of contract, for instance by a reduction of their own future internalization efforts. External stabilization instruments exceed the internalization commitments and exclusively serve the objective of incentive compatibility (e.g. transfers, sanctions). Flexible adjustments of the contract finally allow countries to adapt an environmental agreement to new conditions or to scientific progress before these factors cause a breakdown of the cooperation.[50]

The possibility of internal stabilization is given by the periodically repeated decisions that have to be made among the countries. As a result, a national government must weigh present utility gains from noncooperative behaviour against future losses due to penalization. It applies to all internal stabilization instruments that penalization must be technically feasible by changing countries' own emission levels. If for example new emission-reducing technologies have been implemented because of international environmental cooperation which cannot easily be reversed, penalization is impossible or at least involves high cost.

External stabilization instruments for example are transfers and sanctions which must be agreed upon in a convention and which are used contingent on a specific behaviour. Sanctions (like internal penalization strategies) modify the national benefit from a breach of contract, but their success does not depend on a repeated decision process. Transfers,

---

[50]See Schmidt (2000) for a comprehensive analysis of instruments aiming at providing incentive compatibility.

however, provide positive incentives for cooperative behaviour by redistributing the welfare gains from ecopolitical cooperation in a predetermined manner. A defecting country has to weigh lost transfers – which can be interpreted as sanctions – against the gains resulting from the breach of the contract. Within an incentive-compatible environmental agreement, transfers will always and sanctions will never become effective. Either instrument may induce both participation and compliance incentives. A further instrument for external stabilization is the deposit of securities with a neutral third party. This can underline the willingness to commit oneself convincingly to the fulfilment of the agreed obligations.[51] The institutional set-up for the deposit could be an international fund which manages the deposited financial resources according to the regulations of the environmental agreement. The withheld resources of defecting states could for example be used for compensating complying countries for the incurred cost of imposing additional sanctions, thus making such sanctions more credible (see Heister et al. 1995, p. 38). The practicability of such a fund solution depends on the independence of the international organization from national governments.

The third category of instruments contributing to incentive compatibility are provisions for a flexible adaptation of an agreement to new general conditions, thereby avoiding the substance of the ecopolitical cooperation to be undermined. A change of, for example, important general economic data, which could not be anticipated when the agreement was signed and which may lead to unexpectedly high costs for some contracting parties, can endanger cooperation. In order to make an existing contract more flexible (i) obligations can be connected to central economic features like economic or population growth or (ii) escape clauses can be admitted.

In addition to the three categories of instruments presented general measures supporting cooperation should also be mentioned. A key factor for negotiations is the amount and quality of available information. This becomes obvious if one thinks of the uncertainty connected with physical-biological relationships and the economic effects of (eco)political

---

[51]The deposit of securities can be implemented alternatively through the exchange of so-called 'hostages' or 'pledges' (Williamson 1983).

measures in the face of international environmental externalities. Improving the information level and making it accessible to all countries is often assigned to international organizations and research institutions.

A last instrument which has been proposed in political discussions is forerunner behaviour of individual governments in international environmental care. A national government for example could decide to exceed the agreed internalization obligations of an environmental agreement by reducing own emissions by more than stipulated in the contract. The motivation is to give an example which other potentially cooperating countries think is worth following, thus encouraging imitation. Alternatively, individual countries may decide to start an environmental programme even before an environmental agreement is actually concluded, in order to raise the information level for negotiations by means of pilot projects or to support new technologies. However, forerunner behaviour can be counterproductive since it may lead to lower global emission reductions (see Hoel 1991; Endres and Finus 1998).[52]

The coordinated action of a subgroup of states can be interpreted as unilateral action, since such a coalition is outwardly confronted with the same factors as separately acting countries. The close relationship to unilateral actions becomes particularly evident if some countries behave as forerunners. Consequently, there is no clearcut dividing line between cooperative and unilateral internalization efforts. Summing up, it can be stated that the instruments available for cooperative internalization approaches are mostly not sufficient to guarantee complete and stable cooperation. As a rule, only partial internalization will be achieved through a subgroup of countries.

---

[52]Hoel (1991) shows this in the context of a Nash negotiation solution. However, the result depends on the assumption that the marginal cost of abatement of the forerunner country rises sufficiently more than that of the reacting country and is only valid in the case of elastic reaction curves. As soon as many countries are involved, the effect via the adaptation of the marginal cost of abatement fades into the background compared to price effects and possibly imitation effects. In the paper by Endres and Finus (1998), unilateral actions are modelled as a result of optimizing behaviour; moreover, the authors analyse an environmental agreement on proportional emission reductions.

3.4.2   Unilateral Actions

Alternative to coordinated actions, every government can decide single-handedly to carry out measures which protect the international environment. In Figure 3.1 this is on the right of the right branch. A country that wishes to carry out certain unilateral environmental policy measures has to weigh the advantages against the disadvantages. One advantage is that unilateral actions require neither laborious negotiation nor agreement processes. Due to sovereignty, every state is free to carry out environmental policies at its own discretion. The idea of giving a good example (as addressed above) is a possible motive, too. Finally there can exist non-ecological reasons, e.g. competitive advantages on future markets to be realized by the early development of ecopolitically induced non-polluting technologies (see Porter and van der Linde 1995). However, the diverse interactions of unilateral environmental policies with other national objectives have to be considered. Therefore a basic and comprehensive analysis of the welfare effects within a general equilibrium framework is needed. Even if strategic aspects or the impact of national policies on foreign transborder externality generation are not in the foreground of a country's considerations, these interactions are of considerable importance for national welfare. If they remain neglected when national policies are designed, unilateral ecopolitical actions may well produce counterproductive effects on a country's income and environmental situation. Obviously, aspects like international or global efficiency are irrelevant if international cooperation does not exist.

Faced with international externalities, the internalization instrument of the Pigou tax loses its first-best character in two respects. Foreign transborder pollution cannot be regulated by means of national tax legislation. Consequently, internalization of external costs suffered at home is impossible due to lack of competence. In section 3.3, when the internalization of national externalities was discussed against the background of further distortions, the result was that a national Pigou tax did not bring forth a first-best result. The parallel is due to the fact that in the case of international externalities, too, there is a lack of instruments. Furthermore, the increasing international mobility of goods and factors implies that Pigou conditions can no longer ensure efficiency, even where no further distortions except externalities exist. The expected substitution effect resulting from a national, marginal rise in the pollution tax will induce an international reallocation of mobile factors or a delocation of industries. The increase in foreign production may partially or completely ruin domestic endeavours to improve the environmental situation: in the context of CO_2 this is the so-called 'carbon leakage' effect.[53] Merrifield (1988) analyses the change in the global pollution level in a model with two countries and internationally mobile goods and factors (capital). Other, immobile production factors are labour, which is assumed to be fixed in quantity, and pollution abatement equipment, which is a pure intermediate good and by itself a non-productive factor. Both countries each produce one composite good. The part of production not consumed in the country itself is left for exports. In the course of production, emissions are released which contribute to a transnational pollution level. This transborder pollution is modelled as a pure public good and has an influence on the scarcity of capital. A reduced pollution level brings in its wake more available capital and in this way improved (global) production possibilities. An influence of the externality on the representative individuals' utility in both countries is not modelled; these depend exclusively on consumption levels. The model endogenously determines factor prices, terms of trade, production levels in both countries, as well as their shares in the entire world's capital stock and the global pollution level. Merrifield derives the result that the global pollution level could actually rise in reaction to a unilaterally imposed tax on the output of the polluting industry. If this is the case, the change in the transnational pollution level due to a reduction in one country's emissions is more than offset, on account of capital movements that increase the other country's output and emissions. The mode of action is as follows: the tax on the output of the polluting industry raises the consumer price for this good whereas the price received by producers falls. Factor rewards fall, too, prompting some capital to migrate abroad. Producers in the other country demand additional capital because its price has fallen relative to wages and because the higher consumer price for the

---

[53]Pezzey (1992) estimates that a unilateral CO_2 reduction policy undertaken by the EU would be countervailed by 80 per cent through an increase in emissions of third states.

import good increases the demand for the own good. For the result of an increased global emission level to be revealed, the unilaterally acting country in the initial equilibrium needs to produce pollution-extensively in the sense that its share in global emissions is less than the share of employed capital in the total, internationally mobile capital stock (see Merrifield 1988, p. 271). Alternatively to such an indirect effect via price changes, an increase in environmentally harmful emissions in ecopolitically passive countries, following unilateral environmental policy measures of one or several other countries, can be induced directly. This happens if increased abatement levels in the internalizing home country lead to reduced marginal environmental damage abroad, and adaptation of the marginal cost of abatement causes an increase of foreign emissions.[54] However, the leakage effect refers primarily to adaptations that result indirectly from changes of relative (international) prices (see e.g. Felder and Rutherford 1993).

In a small country, the internalization of externalities caused at home leads to a rise in the factor price of environment and therefore to a weakened competitive position of the country provided the other countries do not likewise commit themselves to environmental care. A unilateral environmental policy is only worthwhile if an improved environmental situation can be achieved in the own country. If, however, the externality, for instance the anthropogenic greenhouse effect, has a global effect and, moreover, shows the characteristics of a pure public good (as assumed in this section), the national environmental situation will not change and the costs of the intensified environmental policy will reduce national welfare in the country. In such a case, unilateral actions of a small country are not rational. This result can be confirmed by slightly modifying a model of Markusen (1975) that analyses the case of two countries with two consumer goods which are traded internationally. Domestic and foreign production of one of both goods is associated with a transborder externality. As policy instruments, an environmental tax in the form of a production tax, a consumption tax, as well as a tariff

---

[54]This effect is the stronger, the more elastically the countries respond mutually to changes in the abatement levels, that is the steeper the slope of the reaction curve of the respective country (see e.g. Carraro and Siniscalco 1993; Hoel 1991). For an illustration of this aspect see Figure 3.5 on p. 50.

imposed on the polluting good are available. Provided that a country has no influence on international prices, neither a unilateral environmental policy nor a national tariff policy is profitable (Markusen 1975, p. 19, for $E_1 = S_1 = 0$). There is an analogy with the zero tax result of the environmental tax which was stated in section 3.3, p. 42, in the context of an ecological tax reform. There, utility gains from an improved environmental situation remain unconsidered if the tax system is optimized from the fiscal point of view. Instead, in the case outlined here, they are negligible. Alternatively, it is possible that a country has actually no monopoly power but contributes considerably to global – and hence also national – pollution through its domestic production. Reinterpreting Markusen's model in this way, the following features result for the analysed policy instruments:[55] if in the two-good case with one dirty good only one national policy instrument is available, an optimal consumption tax is equal to zero; an optimal production tax or a tariff however is different from zero. Since the latter taxes affect the domestic production structure, their optimal levels reflect the influence of domestic pollution on the global emission level. The tariff on the polluting good will always be negative; the production tax directly assessing the externality is positive. In contrast to the discussion of national externalities in section 3.3, interactions between the tax instruments are at first ignored here. However, the argumentation is analogous. If two instruments are available to the government – the tariff and the production tax – the optimal production tax internalizes the national contribution to the domestically suffered pollution level, while the optimal tariff rate is equal to zero. The reason for this result is that the production tax assesses domestic externality generation directly and therefore represents the more effective internalization instrument.

Let it be assumed next that the countries have sufficient market power to influence prices on world markets. They then have the possibility to affect the foreign production structure and therefore to indirectly internalize transborder pollution caused abroad. Moreover, ecopolitical efforts of acting countries can be shielded against undesired adjustments

---

[55]The following remarks in this paragraph can be derived by inserting $E_1 = 0$ and $S_1 > 0$ into the results of Markusen (1975, pp. 19–25).

in environmentally passive countries, which result from a change in relative prices.[56] However, this influence via the price vector – unlike a direct internalization – occurs only indirectly since the externality-generating activity itself cannot be assessed. In addition to this indirect internalization, it is possible to exert an influence on world market prices in order strategically to raise own welfare (e.g. via terms of trade). A rational national policy has to consider the targets of direct and indirect internalization of transborder externalities as well as the exploitation of a dominant market position on international markets simultaneously.[57] Consequently, a global first-best result is not only not attainable but, additionally, national governments do not strive for it at all.

In order to illustrate the aspects of an indirect internalization, the discussion is first limited to models with international trade and transborder externalities. Factors are internationally immobile. As already said, the possibilities of a direct internalization by means of Pigou taxes are restricted if goods markets are internationally integrated. In addition to the behavioural change induced directly in domestic economic agents, higher costs because of a rise in pollution taxes entail an intersectoral reallocation of factors across industries. International trade flows and therefore the country's terms of trade consequently change. If the set of instruments in the Markusen model outlined above is limited to an environmental tax, the analysis of a unilateral, marginal pollution tax increase must – in addition to changes in the domestic pollution level – also account for the induced impact on foreign emissions as well as for the influence on the country's terms of trade. The first-order conditions of an optimal emission tax require that these counteracting marginal effects exactly balance. The Pigou criteria have to be modified (Markusen 1975, p. 25).

Tariff policy of a large country in this model likewise has an effect on all three listed national objectives. The imposition of a tariff on an import good whose production causes transborder pollution induces

---

[56] Corresponding possibilities are also open to subcoalitions of countries that have agreed on tighter environmental standards. Such a subcoalition can externally be regarded as a single unilaterally acting country. See e.g. Bohm (1993) or Hoel (1994) in the context of global warming.

[57] Aspects of retaliation are not being dealt with here.

an excess supply of this good on international markets. Consequently, its price goes down. Foreign production of this good declines, which is perceived as a cleaner environment in both countries. In the case described here, the improvement in its terms of trade hence offers a country the possibility also to internalize such externalities which cannot be assessed directly because of a lack of political competence. In addition to the improvement of the country's income situation (theory of optimal tariffs), the chance of an indirect internalization hence becomes a further target of national tariff policy. However, an increase in the national import tariff simultaneously leads to an increase in domestic pollution which has to be weighed against the positive effects previously described (Markusen 1975, p. 23).[58]

The optimal design of national environmental policies depends on which set of instruments is available to the government. If the set is restricted to only one policy instrument, the optimization takes place within a national second-best setting and considers all three national targets simultaneously. The national first-best result depicted on the right of the right branch of Figure 3.1 can be achieved in the Markusen example if, apart from the production tax directly counteracting the environmentally harmful activity, a tariff is also available to the government. The production tax retrieves its efficiency characteristics in the Pigou sense, since it corresponds to national marginal environmental damage in the optimum. However, it only accounts for marginal environmental damage suffered at home, not for global marginal environmental damage. The optimal tariff rate is defined with respect to the other two targets (foreign pollution generation, improvement of the terms of trade). Its sign is clearly positive with regard to both objectives provided that the dirty good is the import good. Otherwise, its sign is uncertain (Markusen 1975, p. 19).

Another important issue is the influence of international mobility of factors on the design of national environmental policies, an issue which will be thoroughly analysed in Chapter 5.

Ludema and Wooton (1994) analyse Nash equilibria of strategic trade

---

[58]The argumentation for an export good whose production is associated with trans-border pollution is similar and is not pursued here.

policy within a simple model that additionally accounts for ecopolitical objectives. Their model includes two countries, of which the foreign country only produces but does not consume the sole traded consumption good. The home country produces, imports and consumes the consumption good and is harmed by pollution arising from foreign production. The foreign country, for its part, is not affected by its pollution. Domestic production causes no pollution. The instruments available are a production tax in the foreign country and an import tariff in the home country. The tariff pursues not only trade, but also ecopolitical objectives. Compared to the situation without pollution, the domestic reaction curve shifts outward in the tax rate diagram, while the foreign reaction curve remains unchanged. In the Nash equilibrium, the level of the globally aggregated tax burden on the polluting good is higher than in the global optimum, when it just corresponds to global marginal environmental damage (Ludema and Wooton 1994, p. 955). If the countries are members of a customs union, the above-mentioned instruments must no longer be used. Instead, it is assumed that the foreign country may use an environmental tax. A foreign firm can lower its tax burden by reducing emissions per unit of output. In this case, a partial 'internalization' of the externality through the foreign government is rational although individuals abroad are not affected. The foreign country's activity is, however, not driven by the suffering in the domestic country resulting from foreign pollution but rather by the strategic improvement in its terms of trade. The environmental tax serves as a substitute for the unavailable export tax and likewise causes a strategic shortage of foreign goods supply. The analysis illustrates once again the interdependence of national trade policy and environmental policy.

If the government for the purpose of welfare maximization not only has to consider the effects mentioned but is, moreover, dependent on tax revenues, international externalities increase by an additional facet the economic analysis of an ecological tax reform previously carried out. The fiscal objective can be pursued if the system of government proceeds and expenditures is embedded into models with international externalities. Such an analysis will likewise be carried out for the case of international capital mobility in Chapter 5. Again, if an environmental tax, apart from correcting for environmental distortions, has the additional benefit of reducing the excess burden of a distorting tax system, it achieves a double dividend in Goulder's strong form (which was introduced in section 3.3). Even if a country has influence neither on prices on the international markets nor on the national environmental situation, pursuing a unilateral ecological tax reform can be welfare-enhancing, provided the cost of internalization can be overcompensated by means of a decreased excess burden of the domestic tax system (Goulder's fiscal dividend). The precondition, however, is a tax system that is imperfect or fiscally inefficient in the initial equilibrium. The environmental dividend in this scenario is equal to zero since environmental quality remains unchanged. The relocation of industries as well as the migration of capital following unilateral environmental policy measures, however, may also cause a rise in the excess burden of the national tax system because of the erosion of domestic tax bases. For a large country, the strategic component of national tax policies must also be considered: the influence of a pollution tax increase and the induced adaptation of other, distorting taxes on its terms of trade as well as on the return on imported or exported capital are to be included in the analysis. Furthermore, these aspects determine the possiblities of a double dividend from a unilateral environmental tax reform. A double dividend may be reaped if the initial tax system is not second-best optimal from a fiscal point of view, so that for example strategic potentials are left unexploited. The cause, *inter alia*, can be agreements within international law. In accordance with the sign of its interactions, the optimal environmental tax deviates from the Pigou tax criteria. If, on the other hand, a non-distorting lump-sum tax were available to the state for financing its budget, the analysis would again take place in the national first-best framework.

3.5   CONCLUSIONS

This chapter has surveyed the influence of international aspects on the design of national environmental policies. Fields of interest to be analysed in greater detail in the following chapters have been embedded in a more general context in order to illustrate their relevance and to give an idea of the relative importance of each specific issue.

The chapter started with a general discussion of the normative basics of an internalization of external effects. The survey then turned to the more specific aspects of national environmental policies which are subject to a fundamental and growing economic integration into the world economy. It was demonstrated that, in the case of national externalities, considerable repercussions on national welfare result because of international economic integration, provided that other distortions exist within the economy apart from the environmental ones. In this context, the possibility of reaping a double dividend with the help of an ecological tax reform was also briefly discussed. This issue will be subject to a thorough analysis in Chapter 4 which deals with different concepts and their plausibility. The analysis received a further international component by extending it to transborder externalities. The political decision-maker is – just as before in the case of national externalities – confronted with an additional restriction even if pollution represents the only distortion and a national Pigou tax is available. An internalization can be carried out only through cooperation between governments or unilateral policy measures of individual countries. Both approaches are impaired by serious weaknesses. Unilateral measures, which will also be dealt with in Chapter 5, are mainly reserved for large countries with sufficient power in international markets. Additionally, they are confronted with the risk of retaliation. Cooperative approaches to environmental policy also do not normally succeed in reducing environmental damage to a globally efficient level. Particularly when a large number of states is involved, there is a latent incentive to free-ride on the ecopolitical measures of other countries. Therefore, environmental agreements must be designed in an incentive-compatible way. But still, in most cases, cooperation is restricted to a subgroup of states. If, on the other hand, almost complete cooperation can be observed and the number of signatory states is very high, agreements will either not be complied with, due to incentive problems, or they are of low substance, so that no country is confronted with too high costs that would lead to defection.

The scenarios discussed in the various subsections must not be seen as isolated, but rather as complementary:

    i. if the states involved in a transborder but not global externality agree upon complete cooperation and possibly even the installation of a supranational institution, environmental policy should be designed in accordance with the aspects valid for national environmental problems (section 3.3);

    ii. if cooperation is incomplete, the coalition outwardly has to consider the same factors as a country acting unilaterally (subsection 3.4.2);

    iii. in any cooperation strategic behaviour cannot be excluded if national governments are allowed to choose independently the set of instruments with which they want to realize their agreed-upon abatement targets. In this respect subsection 3.4.2 complements the discussion of the choice of instruments in subsection 3.4.1;

    iv. incentive compatibility of an international environmental agreement may also need to take into consideration the remarks in section 3.3 for national environmental problems. This applies if further distortions exist apart from the environmental one (for example on account of a governmental budget restriction) which influence the distribution of the gains from cooperation.

From a global point of view, it is not clear whether environmental cooperation with few participating countries but ambitious environmental targets is more efficient than cooperation with many participants and low obligations. Furthermore, nationally differing levels of public goods in the global optimum imply differing marginal costs of public funds across countries. Even in the case of an international externality which has the characteristic of a pure public good (like the anthropogenic greenhouse effect), the implementation of a uniform tax rate for all countries would no longer be globally efficient. Therefore it is uncertain whether (incomplete) international cooperations – which as a political compromise are likely to include a uniform regulation for all countries – produce better efficiency results than unilateral environmental policies.

In this chapter it has been pointed out that one of the central features of the DIW report as well as one of the dominating issues in the political and theoretical discussion is the double-dividend characteristic of ecological tax reforms. The evaluation criteria have so far been exogenous to the discussion, since a concept formulated by Goulder was applied throughout. What follows is an analysis that goes deeper by inquiring into the aptitude and applicability of this concept and by comparing it with an alternative concept.

Chapter 4

The double dividend of ecological tax reforms

4.1 INTRODUCTION

As discussed in detail in the preceding chapter, the internalization of negative external effects such as environmental depletion leads to social welfare gains due to the reduction of the externality level, but also induces costs arising from the necessity to meet the tighter environmental standard. In a first-best framework when there is solely an environmental distortion, the first-order condition of an efficient externality level demands that the cost of reducing the externality-generating activity and the social utility gain resulting from an improvement in environmental quality be equal at the margin. If the internalization is pursued by means of an environmental tax, this tax must be implemented at the level that equals the aggregate marginal environmental damage that each individual imposes on others in the optimum.[1] In this setting, it is efficient to redistribute tax proceeds to the individuals in a lump-sum fashion. It has already been mentioned that compensation of those who suffer from the externality would induce a change in their behaviour

---

[1]In the following the analysis is again restricted to Meade's additive atmosphere externality. The optimal Pigou tax is hence a uniform tax across all individuals that equals marginal environmental damage in the optimum.

in order to get higher compensatory payments, and hence is inefficient (Baumol and Oates 1988, pp. 23–24).

In a second-best framework with additional distortions, if for instance a government budget has to be financed from distortionary taxes, in contrast to the above-described scenario a partial equilibrium analysis is no longer sufficient for deriving an optimal internalization strategy. Changes in one market generate first-order spill-over effects in other markets. This is the starting point of the reflection that an environmental tax reform must allow the reaping of a double dividend. The underlying idea is simple and convincing: apart from the amelioration of the environment, the excess burden of the distortionary tax system can be lowered if the additional funds from the environmental tax are recycled by reducing the rates of the other taxes. The catch-phrase *double dividend* has not only been very popular in the political discussion but has also gained huge attention in the theoretical literature. But since it was interpreted in different ways, Goulder (1995) categorized three different interpretations and distinguished a weak, medium and strong form of a double dividend. Nevertheless, some papers that deal with the double-dividend issue still refer to additional concepts (e.g. Böhringer et al. 1997, Bovenberg and de Mooij 1994c, Goulder et al. 1997). And sometimes the respective concept that underlies an analysis is not made explicit at all (e.g. Böhringer et al. 1994). Common to all double-dividend concepts is that they decompose the overall welfare effect of an ecological tax reform in order to identify the different mechanisms at work. It is apparent therefore that in the second-best optimum where, subject to the existing constraints, no further welfare gain is attainable, either both dividends are equal to zero or one is positive and the other negative, together summing to zero. Yielding a double dividend is hence no rational policy goal since this reveals that possibly even considerable welfare gains have been left unexploited. The primary use of the concepts is to facilitate the understanding of environmental taxation analysis when it changes from a first-best to a second-best framework with additional distortion. Apart from this rather theoretical aspect, the decomposition of the overall welfare may be of interest to policy-makers who are lacking the information they need in order exactly to determine the welfare changes of a certain policy reform. Goulder raises this more applied issue in connection with his stronger concepts and claims that it would help politicians to overcome information hurdles.

The aim of this chapter is to discuss the two most popular double-dividend concepts found in the literature and to formalize them within the same consistent theoretical framework.[2] Schöb (1996) introduced a method that allows for a very proper and convenient decomposition of the overall welfare effect resulting from a marginal ecological tax reform which he applies to Goulder's concept in the strong form. In this chapter, Schöb's decomposition method is transferred to a model framework that seems more appropriate for the purpose here. The following analysis uses a simple trade model and concentrates on the welfare effects arising in a small open economy that unilaterally carries out an ecological tax reform. Externalities are assumed to be only national, and the additional distortions within the economy stem from the imposition of a tariff in order to generate public funds. Then Schöb's decomposition is applied to the other frequently employed concept apart from Goulder's concept in the strong form in order to provide it with the analytical formalization it is lacking so far. It will be called the 'Pearce concept' since Pearce – although implicitly – based his reasoning with respect to a double dividend of environmental taxes on exactly this concept (see Pearce 1991).

Because of the hidden nature of the underlying concepts, the double-dividend debate suffers from a certain diffuseness.[3] Applying Goulder's concept in the strong form[4] and Pearce's concept to one and the same theoretical framework allows us to work out their differences as well as to discuss the (very often only implicitly made) assumptions connected

---

[2]This chapter is based on Killinger (1997).

[3]In the meantime, this point of view earlier raised by Killinger (1997) has also been adopted by Bovenberg and van Hagen (1999), who identify four ambiguities with respect to the double-dividend concept and by Fullerton and Gravelle (1999), who discuss several problems with the double-dividend literature, one of which is that the double-dividend hypothesis 'is not well defined, or at least not commonly stated' (p. 75). They conclude that 'there is no such thing as "the" double-dividend hypothesis' (p. 76).

[4]Henceforth, this concept will, for simplification purposes, simply be denoted as the 'Goulder concept'.

to them. The issues that will be raised are information requirements, the likelihood that a double dividend can indeed be realized, and the aptitude of both concepts. In this context we shall analyse whether Goulder's concept indeed serves the stated purpose of being a guide to effectively circumventing governmental lack of information, for instance with respect to the social damage function. Different from most other contributions to the double-dividend issue, this chapter does not consider endogenous labour supply but incorporates foreign trade and hence external distortions. It allows for interdependencies between environmental quality and private-good consumption which are (for instance in the case of tourism) probably more realistic than the – generally ignored – influence of changes in the environment on labour supply. The analysis is restricted to welfare considerations of a marginal ecological tax reform; i.e. the signs of the dividends reflect the net impact on welfare of the effects they include. The analysis does not cover comparative statics of optimal policies in reaction to an exogenous change in individuals' environmental preferences (see, for example, Bovenberg and van der Ploeg 1994*a,b* and 1996 or Nielsen et al. 1995). In any case, the latter analyses are confronted with the difficulty that the new optimum following an exogenous shift in individual preferences is evaluated with the preferences in the initial equilibrium. Alternative concepts with higher employment of the production factor labour in models with voluntary (for example Bovenberg and de Mooij 1994*b*) or involuntary unemployment (for example Schneider 1997) or rises in optimal public sector sizes (for example Bovenberg and de Mooij 1994*b* or Bovenberg and van der Ploeg 1996) as dividends are not considered in this chapter.[5] The analysis is further restricted to a marginal introduction or increase of exclusively an environmental tax, the proceeds of which are then used to reduce other distortionary taxes. The tax reform is hence not seen as part of a more general restructuring of a distortionary tax system that allows for additional instruments, as in Ruocco and Wiegard (1997).

In the following section 4.2 the two concepts will be introduced. Section 4.3 contains a simple trade model which allows formally to embed

---

[5] In Schneider's model a decrease in involuntary unemployment is always connected to a rise in welfare, however.

and discuss the concepts in section 4.4. Section 4.5 includes a discussion of the second-best optimal environmental tax level compared to the Pigou level. The results are summarized in the final section, 4.6.

4.2   THE TWO MAIN CONCEPTS

4.2.1   Goulder Concept

The decomposition of the global welfare effect resulting from an ecological tax reform in a second-best setting in this first concept is related to Goulder's (1995) double dividend in the strong form. It can be interpreted as a distinction between ecological and fiscal effects. The first dividend comprises the change in the environmental situation resulting not only from the rise in the pollution tax rate, but also from adapting the other tax rates. The cost of internalization reflected by the erosion of the pollution tax base due to the intended substitution away from environmentally harmful activities[6] as well as the general equilibrium changes in the other tax bases are assigned to the second dividend, i.e. the cost side of the tax reform. This second or fiscal dividend reflects the change in the excess burden of the existing tax system from a public finance point of view, where environmental considerations are excluded. The excess burden increases by the marginal cost of funds caused by the rise in the pollution tax rate and – if the recycling effect is positive, i.e. if the environmental tax is on the increasing branch of its Laffer curve – diminishes by that of the adapting tax rates.

The aim of Goulder's double-dividend definition in the strong form is to implement a criterion which concentrates on the effects united within the fiscal dividend and thereby involves relatively low information hurdles: 'The revenue-neutral substitution of the environmental tax for typical or representative distortionary taxes involves a zero or negative gross cost' (Goulder 1995, p. 159). With the expression *gross cost* he

---

[6] As indicated in Chapter 3, p. 33, this is only true for an aggregate externality where the contribution of every single polluter is negligible. If it is not, the marginal cost of abatement in equilibrium is equal to the foregone marginal pollution tax revenue due to tax base erosion plus the marginal private welfare loss that results from own pollution generation.

indicates that his evaluation 'abstracts from welfare effects associated with policy-related changes in environmental quality' (ibid., p. 161), i.e. from the environmental dividend. He claims that by using his definition, 'policymakers would not need to establish magnitudes of environmental benefits to justify the tax swap on overall benefit–cost grounds' (ibid., p. 162). Goulder hence takes the view that in the political discussion the force of arguments significantly increases if an ecological tax reform can be identified to be beneficial, although the evaluation is restricted to the cost side. His intention, therefore, is to draw a dividing line between measurable effects and those which cannot be measured. The concept is widespread in the literature and is used for instance by Bovenberg and de Mooij (1994*b* and 1996), Schöb (1996), Ruocco and Wiegard (1997), and Böhringer et al. (1997).

4.2.2   Pearce Concept

An alternative concept for a double-dividend evaluation which was mainly initiated by Pearce (1991), refers to the historical development of the discussion concerning ecological tax reforms in a second-best setting. The first dividend contains the general equilibrium effects on the environment resulting from a rise in the pollution tax and the induced adaptation of the other tax rates. The environmental effect is weighted with the difference between the marginal social utility of environmental quality, i.e. the shadow price of environmental quality, and the pollution tax rate, or equivalently the marginal product of the environment in the production process (in case the tax is levied on the production side). These are the criteria known from the first-best framework. The second dividend incorporates the remaining effects of an ecological tax reform in a second-best world that stem from the prevailing distortions in the tax system. This tax interaction effect can alternatively be interpreted as the change in tax proceeds from the other tax sources due to general equilibrium spillover effects of the pollution tax change on the other tax bases. If both dividends are positive, there is a double dividend. The concept has been repeatedly applied in the literature (Parry 1995, Goulder et al. 1997) without having been formalized so far. The balancing of cost and utility directly connected with a reduction in environmental depletion within one dividend is hence the main difference to the Goulder concept, which unites all cost components, i.e. direct and indirect ones, arising in the course of an ecological tax reform within the non-environmental or fiscal dividend.

In order to formalize both concepts, a simple model will now be introduced. In section 4.4 it will be possible to analyse and compare the concepts within this framework.

4.3   THE MODEL

The model refers to a small open economy.[7] To keep things as simple as possible the analysis is restricted to the two-goods case. There are n factors of production, represented by vector v, which are fixed in supply, and therefore they are not made explicit.[8] The only factor that is perfectly elastic in supply is an environmental resource ε. The resource input is defined as the share of the resource which is used up during the production process. It can alternatively be interpreted as emissions resulting from the production process as a side product which is negatively perceived by the individuals.[9]

4.3.1   Consumer Behaviour

There is only one representative consumer, so that distributional aspects are disregarded. The utility function of the representative individual is $u(c_1, c_2, \varepsilon)$, where c_i, $i = 1, 2$, is the consumption of both goods. Pollution ε, in contrast, takes the form of a public bad, and hence the level of its consumption is beyond the consumer's control.[10] Preferences are then represented by the expenditure function, which is defined as

$$e\left((p_1 + t), p_2, u_0, \varepsilon\right) = \min_c \left\{ (p_1 + t) c_1 + p_2 c_2 : u \geq u_0 \right\}$$

---

[7]Dixit and Norman (1980) provide an exposition of the standard model which is here altered so as to include a national environmental externality.

[8]Bold-face letters are used for vector notation.

[9]Henceforth the expressions *environmental resource* and *pollution* will be used synonymously.

[10]For the modelling of a public bad as a quantity constraint see Cornes (1992).

$e(\cdot)$ is increasing in u and ε and is defined as the minimum cost of attaining utility level u_0 given the vector of prices of the consumption goods p, the level of tariff t on good 1, and the pollution level ε. An increase in the level of pollution harms the representative consumer and therefore raises the minimum cost of attaining a given utility level. The partial derivative of the expenditure function with respect to the level of pollution $(\partial e/\partial \varepsilon)$ is the marginal willingness to pay for reductions in pollution and equals the marginal environmental damage.

4.3.2   Firm Behaviour

The production side of the economy is condensed in the aggregate revenue function.[11] Given prices p_i, $i = 1, 2$, of the consumer goods and the level of both pollution taxes and tariffs, firms maximize their individual profits. In doing so, they collectively maximize GNP at domestic prices. The private sector of the economy thus acts as if it solves the problem

$$r(p_1 + t, p_2, v, \varepsilon) = \max_{x} \left\{ (p_1 + t)\, x_1 + p_2 x_2 : x \in T(v, \varepsilon) \right\}$$

where x_i, $i = 1, 2$, is production of both goods, and T is the technology set. The production function underlying the GNP function is linearly homogeneous, concave, and non-decreasing, and $\partial^2 r/\partial \varepsilon^2 < 0$. The environmental resource is a free public good, and it is used up to the point where its marginal product $\partial r/\partial \varepsilon$ is zero if there is no environmental regulation. Otherwise it is adjusted to the pollution tax level. The externality is assumed to be of an eyesore type, i.e. it only affects individual utility but it does not generate detrimental effects on the countries' production possibilities.

4.3.3   Government Behaviour

The government maximizes the representative consumer's utility and is assumed to be confronted with an exogenous budget constraint. Tax revenue is used to finance an exogenously determined level B of public

---

[11] This revenue function is known as the GNP function. It has the properties of a restricted profit function.

goods, the production of which is not modelled

$$B = \tau \cdot \varepsilon + t \cdot m \qquad (4.1)$$

The two tax instruments, an environmental tax τ and a tariff t levied on imports m of good 1, hence jointly finance the governmental budgetary needs. Therefore, the decision problem of the government concerns the level at which both tax instruments are employed.

4.3.4 Equilibrium

Equilibrium in the economy is then described by the following equations

$$e(p_1 + t, p_2, u, \varepsilon) = r(p_1 + t, p_2, \varepsilon) - \tau \cdot \varepsilon \qquad (4.2\text{a})$$

$$\frac{\partial r(p_1 + t, p_2, \varepsilon)}{\partial \varepsilon} = \tau \qquad (4.2\text{b})$$

$$t \cdot m(p_1 + t, p_2, \varepsilon, u) + \tau \cdot \varepsilon = B \qquad (4.2\text{c})$$

$$m = c_1(p_1 + t, p_2, u, \varepsilon)$$
$$\qquad - x_1(p_1 + t, p_2, \varepsilon) \qquad (4.2\text{d})$$

where expression $t \cdot m(\cdot) - B$ in income identity (4.2a) has already been replaced by $(-\tau \cdot \varepsilon)$ according to condition (4.2c).

Apart from (4.2d), which defines excess demand for good 1, the following definitions are used

$$c_1(p_1 + t, p_2, u, \varepsilon) \stackrel{\text{def}}{=} \frac{\partial e(p_1 + t, p_2, u, \varepsilon)}{\partial(p_1 + t)} \qquad (4.3\text{a})$$

$$x_1(p_1 + t, p_2, \varepsilon) \stackrel{\text{def}}{=} \frac{\partial r(p_1 + t, p_2, \varepsilon)}{\partial(p_1 + t)} \qquad (4.3\text{b})$$

in which c_1 is the Hicksian demand function and x_1 the supply function for good 1. It is assumed that good 1 is imported ($m > 0$). The Marshallian demand function for good 1 is denoted by $d_1(p_1 + t, p_2, \varepsilon, y)$.

From duality theory, the following relations are known

$$d_1(p_1 + t, p_2, \varepsilon, e(p_1 + t, p_2, u, \varepsilon)) \equiv c_1(p_1 + t, p_2, u, \varepsilon) \tag{4.4a}$$

$$\left.\frac{\partial d_1}{\partial y}\right|_{y=e(p_1+t,p_2,u,\varepsilon)} \equiv \frac{\partial c_1}{\partial u}\bigg/\frac{\partial e}{\partial u} \tag{4.4b}$$

$$\left.\frac{\partial d_1}{\partial(p_1 + t)}\right|_{y=e(p_1+t,p_2,u,\varepsilon)} = \frac{\partial c_1}{\partial(p_1 + t)}$$

$$- d_1 \left.\frac{\partial d_1}{\partial y}\right|_{y=e(p_1+t,p_2,u,\varepsilon)} \tag{4.4c}$$

since in equilibrium $d_1 = c_1$. Relations (4.4c) is the Slutsky decomposition. In order to find an analogous decomposition for import demand m, the following system is considered

$$e(p_1 + t, p_2, u, \varepsilon) = r(p_1 + t, p_2, \varepsilon) \tag{4.5a}$$

$$m = c_1(p_1 + t, p_2, u, \varepsilon) - x_1(p_1 + t, p_2, \varepsilon) \tag{4.5b}$$

Total differentiation with respect to prices and the environment results in

$$\begin{bmatrix} 1 & 0 \\ -\dfrac{\partial d_1}{\partial y} & 1 \end{bmatrix} \begin{bmatrix} \dfrac{\partial e}{\partial u}\, du \\ dm \end{bmatrix} = \begin{bmatrix} -m & -\left(\dfrac{\partial e}{\partial \varepsilon} - \dfrac{\partial r}{\partial \varepsilon}\right) \\ S & \dfrac{\partial m}{\partial \varepsilon} \end{bmatrix} \begin{bmatrix} d(p_1 + t) \\ d\varepsilon \end{bmatrix} \tag{4.6}$$

Here, (4.4b) was used, and the definitions

$$S \stackrel{\text{def}}{=} \frac{\partial m}{\partial(p_1 + t)} \quad \text{and} \quad \frac{\partial m}{\partial \varepsilon} \stackrel{\text{def}}{=} \frac{\partial c_1}{\partial \varepsilon} - \frac{\partial x_1}{\partial \varepsilon} \tag{4.7}$$

As the Slutsky decomposition of Marshallian import demand with respect to prices we then obtain

$$dm = D(dp_1 + dt), \text{ by using definition} \tag{4.8a}$$

$$D \stackrel{\text{def}}{=} S - m\frac{\partial d_1}{\partial y} \tag{4.8b}$$

For the Slutsky decomposition of Marshallian import demand with respect to the environment the result is

$$dm = E \cdot d\varepsilon, \text{ where } E \text{ is defined as} \tag{4.9a}$$

$$E \stackrel{\text{def}}{=} \frac{\partial m}{\partial \varepsilon} - \left(\frac{\partial e}{\partial \varepsilon} - \frac{\partial r}{\partial \varepsilon} \right) \frac{\partial d_1}{\partial y} \tag{4.9b}$$

Condition $D < 0$ characterizes a normal reaction of import demand.

4.3.5 Stability Condition with Respect to Tariff

The stability condition of system (4.2) for the tariff can be found by total differentiation. In the following, this condition will allow us to determine the sign of the determinant of its Jacobian. Furthermore, it will alleviate the interpretation of the multipliers to be derived from comparative static analysis of the equilibrium conditions (4.2).

$$H \begin{bmatrix} \dfrac{\partial e}{\partial u} \dfrac{du}{dp_1} \\[2mm] \dfrac{d\varepsilon}{dp_1} \\[2mm] \dfrac{dt}{dp_1} \\[2mm] \dfrac{dm}{dp_1} \end{bmatrix} = - \begin{bmatrix} m \\[2mm] \dfrac{\partial^2 r}{\partial \varepsilon \, \partial(p_1 + t)} \\[2mm] 0 \\[2mm] -S \end{bmatrix} \tag{4.10}$$

The matrix H is

$$H \stackrel{\text{def}}{=} \begin{bmatrix} 1 & \dfrac{\partial e}{\partial \varepsilon} & m & 0 \\[3mm] 0 & \dfrac{\partial^2 r}{\partial \varepsilon^2} & \dfrac{\partial^2 r}{\partial \varepsilon \, \partial(p_1 + t)} & 0 \\[3mm] 0 & \tau & m & t \\[3mm] -\dfrac{\partial d_1}{\partial y} & -\dfrac{\partial m}{\partial \varepsilon} & -S & 1 \end{bmatrix} \tag{4.11}$$

with determinant

$$|H| = (m + tD) \frac{\partial^2 r}{\partial \varepsilon^2} - Et \frac{\partial^2 r}{\partial \varepsilon \, \partial(p_1 + t)} - \tau \left(1 - t \frac{\partial d_1}{\partial y} \right) \frac{\partial^2 r}{\partial \varepsilon \, \partial(p_1 + t)} \tag{4.12}$$

$$= \left(\frac{\partial e}{\partial \varepsilon} t \frac{\partial d_1}{\partial y} - \tau - t \frac{\partial m}{\partial \varepsilon} \right) \frac{\partial^2 r}{\partial \varepsilon \, \partial(p_1 + t)} + (m + tD) \frac{\partial^2 r}{\partial \varepsilon^2} \tag{4.13}$$

Stability requires that import demand decrease as a reaction to an increase in p_1. From (4.10) we obtain

$$\frac{dm}{dp_1} = \frac{m\frac{\partial^2 r}{\partial\varepsilon^2}}{|H|}\left(D + \frac{\left(\frac{\partial x_1}{\partial\varepsilon}\right)^2}{\frac{\partial^2 r}{\partial\varepsilon^2}} - \frac{\frac{\partial d_1}{\partial\varepsilon}\frac{\partial x_1}{\partial\varepsilon}}{\frac{\partial^2 r}{\partial\varepsilon^2}}\right) \overset{!}{<} 0 \qquad (4.14)$$

In order to interpret the stability condition, the same analysis is used, but now for the case where t changes, p_1 is fixed, and B is free to adapt. This leads to

$$\begin{bmatrix} 1 & \frac{\partial e}{\partial\varepsilon} & 0 & 0 \\ 0 & \frac{\partial^2 r}{\partial\varepsilon^2} & 0 & 0 \\ 0 & \tau & -1 & t \\ -\frac{\partial d_1}{\partial y} & -\frac{\partial m}{\partial\varepsilon} & 0 & 1 \end{bmatrix} \begin{bmatrix} \frac{\partial e}{\partial u}\frac{du}{dt} \\ \frac{d\varepsilon}{dt} \\ \frac{dB}{dt} \\ \frac{dm}{dt} \end{bmatrix} = - \begin{bmatrix} m \\ \frac{\partial^2 r}{\partial\varepsilon\,\partial(p_1+t)} \\ m \\ -S \end{bmatrix} \qquad (4.15)$$

The general equilibrium effect of a tariff increase on tax proceeds is

$$\frac{dB}{dt} = \frac{1}{\frac{\partial^2 r}{\partial\varepsilon^2}}\left((m+tD)\frac{\partial^2 r}{\partial\varepsilon^2} - tE\frac{\partial^2 r}{\partial\varepsilon\,\partial(p_1+t)}\right.$$

$$\left. -\tau\left(1 - t\frac{\partial d_1}{\partial y}\right)\frac{\partial^2 r}{\partial\varepsilon\,\partial(p_1+t)}\right)$$

$$= \frac{|H|}{\frac{\partial^2 r}{\partial\varepsilon^2}} \qquad (4.16)$$

Assuming a decreasing marginal product of the environmental resource or tantamount environmental depletion (i.e. $\partial^2 r/\partial\varepsilon^2 < 0$), multiplier (4.16) shows that the sign of $|H|$ indicates on which side of the Laffer curve of the tariff the economy is operating. If $|H| > 0$, then $dB/dt < 0$, and an increase in the tariff reduces revenue (to be called the Reagan regime). If $|H| < 0$, an increase in the tariff increases revenue since $dB/dt > 0$ (Carter regime).

If the assumptions are

- a normal reaction of import demand $(D < 0)$ and
- that supply and demand for good 1 react in opposite directions if environmental quality changes so that

$$\frac{\partial d_1}{\partial \varepsilon} \frac{\partial x_1}{\partial \varepsilon} < 0$$

it can be seen from (4.14) that a Carter regime is necessary and sufficient for stability. Furthermore, the sign of determinant $|H|$ is determined to be negative due to stability requirements.

4.3.6 Stability Condition with Respect to Environmental Tax

The stability condition for system (4.2) with respect to the environmental tax τ can again be found by totally differentiating the system. But in contrast to subsection 4.3.5, the environmental tax is now endogenous and permanently adapting so as to meet the budget constraint

$$H^* \begin{bmatrix} \dfrac{\partial e}{\partial u} \dfrac{du}{dp_1} \\[2mm] \dfrac{d\varepsilon}{dp_1} \\[2mm] \dfrac{d\tau}{dp_1} \\[2mm] \dfrac{dm}{dp_1} \end{bmatrix} = - \begin{bmatrix} m \\[2mm] \dfrac{\partial^2 r}{\partial \varepsilon \, \partial(p_1 + t)} \\[2mm] 0 \\[2mm] -S \end{bmatrix} \qquad (4.17)$$

The matrix H^* is

$$H^* \stackrel{\text{def}}{=} \begin{bmatrix} 1 & \dfrac{\partial e}{\partial \varepsilon} & \varepsilon & 0 \\[2mm] 0 & \dfrac{\partial^2 r}{\partial \varepsilon^2} & -1 & 0 \\[2mm] 0 & \tau & \varepsilon & t \\[2mm] -\dfrac{\partial d_1}{\partial y} & -\dfrac{\partial m}{\partial \varepsilon} & 0 & 1 \end{bmatrix} \qquad (4.18)$$

with determinant

$$|H^*| = Et + \left(\tau + \varepsilon \frac{\partial^2 r}{\partial \varepsilon^2} \right) \left(1 - t \frac{\partial d_1}{\partial y} \right)$$

$$= - \left(\frac{\partial e}{\partial \varepsilon} - \tau - t \frac{\partial m}{\partial \varepsilon} \right) + \left(\frac{\partial e}{\partial \varepsilon} + \varepsilon \frac{\partial^2 r}{\partial \varepsilon^2} \right) \left(1 - t \frac{\partial d_1}{\partial y} \right) \qquad (4.19)$$

Stability requires that import demand decreases as a reaction to an increase in p_1. From (4.17) we obtain

$$\frac{dm}{dp_1} = \frac{1}{|H^*|} \left(\tau D + \varepsilon \left(D \frac{\partial^2 r}{\partial \varepsilon^2} - E \frac{\partial^2 r}{\partial \varepsilon \, \partial (p_1 + t)} \right) \right) \overset{!}{<} 0 \qquad (4.20)$$

In order to interpret the stability condition, the same analysis is followed, this time for the case where τ changes, p_1 is fixed, and B is free to adapt. The finding is

$$
\begin{bmatrix}
1 & \dfrac{\partial e}{\partial \varepsilon} & 0 & 0 \\[2mm]
0 & \dfrac{\partial^2 r}{\partial \varepsilon^2} & 0 & 0 \\[2mm]
0 & \tau & -1 & t \\[2mm]
-\dfrac{\partial d_1}{\partial y} & -\dfrac{\partial m}{\partial \varepsilon} & 0 & 1
\end{bmatrix}
\begin{bmatrix}
\dfrac{\partial e}{\partial u} \dfrac{du}{d\tau} \\[2mm]
\dfrac{d\varepsilon}{d\tau} \\[2mm]
\dfrac{dB}{d\tau} \\[2mm]
\dfrac{dm}{d\tau}
\end{bmatrix}
= -
\begin{bmatrix}
\varepsilon \\[2mm]
-1 \\[2mm]
\varepsilon \\[2mm]
0
\end{bmatrix}
\qquad (4.21)
$$

This yields

$$\frac{dB}{d\tau} = \frac{1}{\dfrac{\partial^2 r}{\partial \varepsilon^2}} \left(tE + \left(\tau + \varepsilon \frac{\partial^2 r}{\partial \varepsilon^2} \right) \left(1 - t \frac{\partial d_1}{\partial y} \right) \right) = \frac{|H^*|}{\dfrac{\partial^2 r}{\partial \varepsilon^2}} \qquad (4.22)$$

A Carter regime ($|H^*| < 0$) is hence neither necessary nor sufficient for stability with respect to the environmental tax. This means that a scenario where additional tax revenues from a marginal increase in the pollution tax rate are negative is compatible with stability. In this case the revenue-recycling effect would of course be negative, too, since the distortionary tariff would have to be raised in the course of an ecological tax reform in order to meet the government budget restriction. It becomes apparent that this would tear down the main column in the double-dividend calculation.

4.3.7   General Equilibrium Analysis

It is now necessary to go very quickly through some comparative statics and to derive all the multipliers needed in the remainder of this chapter in order to analyse the two concepts concerning the double-dividend characteristic of an environmental tax reform.

Effects on utility

The effect of an ecological tax reform on the utility of the representative individual is determined by implicitly differentiating system (4.2) with respect to the environmental tax τ. The change in the environmental tax rate has an effect on the endogenous variables; these are utility u, the pollution level ε, and imports m. The tariff level t is likewise endogenous to the system as its revenue has to close the gap between the tax proceeds stemming from the pollution tax and the governmental budgetary needs

$$
H
\begin{bmatrix}
\dfrac{\partial e}{\partial u}\dfrac{du}{d\tau} \\[2ex]
\dfrac{d\varepsilon}{d\tau} \\[2ex]
\dfrac{dt}{d\tau} \\[2ex]
\dfrac{dm}{d\tau}
\end{bmatrix}
= -
\begin{bmatrix}
\varepsilon \\[1ex]
-1 \\[1ex]
\varepsilon \\[1ex]
0
\end{bmatrix}
\tag{4.23}
$$

Matrix H and its determinant are the same as in (4.11) and (4.12), respectively. From (4.23) results the desired multiplier for changes in utility

$$
\frac{\partial e}{\partial u}\frac{du}{d\tau} = \frac{-1}{|H|}\left[\left(\frac{\partial e}{\partial \varepsilon} - \tau - t\frac{\partial m}{\partial \varepsilon}\right)\left(m + \varepsilon\frac{\partial^2 r}{\partial \varepsilon\,\partial(p_1 + t)}\right) \right.
$$

$$
\left. + \left(\frac{\partial e}{\partial \varepsilon} + \varepsilon\frac{\partial^2 r}{\partial \varepsilon^2}\right) tS\right]
\tag{4.24}
$$

The assumptions are still

- a decreasing marginal product of the environmental resource or tantamount environmental depletion (i.e. that $\partial^2 r/\partial\varepsilon^2 < 0$),
- stability of the system so that

$$
\frac{\partial d_1}{\partial \varepsilon}\frac{\partial x_1}{\partial \varepsilon} < 0 \Longrightarrow \frac{dB}{dt} > 0 \Longrightarrow |H| < 0 \text{ , and}
$$

- a normal reaction of import demand ($D < 0$).

It can then be seen from welfare multiplier (4.24) that sufficient conditions for welfare to increase in the course of the tax reform are the following:

- Supply of good 1 has to rise with the externality level (i.e. that[12]

$$\frac{\partial^2 r}{\partial \varepsilon \, \partial(p_1 + t)} > 0 \quad \text{(good 1 is pollution-intensive)} \qquad (4.25)$$

$$\implies \frac{\partial m}{\partial \varepsilon} < 0 \text{ which follows from stability and definition (4.7)),}$$

- the pollution tax rate in the initial equilibrium has to be below marginal environmental damage (i.e. $\partial e / \partial \varepsilon > \tau$), and
- condition

$$\left(\frac{\partial e}{\partial \varepsilon} + \varepsilon \frac{\partial^2 r}{\partial \varepsilon^2} \right) < 0 \quad \text{must apply} \qquad (4.26)$$

$$\iff \frac{\frac{\partial e}{\partial \varepsilon}}{\tau} < - \eta_{(\partial r / \partial \varepsilon, \varepsilon)} \qquad (4.27)$$

if written in elasticity notation.[13]

Concentrating on condition (4.27), it follows from the above assumption $\partial e / \partial \varepsilon > \tau$ that $\eta_{(\partial r / \partial \varepsilon, \varepsilon)} < -1$. The condition hence demands the marginal product of the environmental resource to be rather elastic with respect to its use in production, which means that the erosive effect on the pollution tax base is not very serious. Interpreting the condition in non-elasticity notation, i.e. considering condition (4.26), it follows that the welfare effect

$$\frac{-1}{|H|} \left(\frac{\partial e}{\partial \varepsilon} + \varepsilon \frac{\partial^2 r}{\partial \varepsilon^2} \right) tS$$

---

[12] The following interpretation refers to the Rybczynski effect $(\partial^2 r / (\partial (p_1 + t) \, \partial \varepsilon))$. $(\partial^2 r / (\partial \varepsilon \, \partial(p_1 + t))) = (\partial^2 r / (\partial(p_1 + t) \, \partial \varepsilon))$ always holds if the Young theorem applies, as assumed from now on.

[13] Elasticities throughout the book are defined as

$$\eta_{(x,y)} \overset{\text{def}}{=} \frac{\partial x}{\partial y} \cdot \frac{y}{x}$$

from increased tariff revenue due to a change in the price of good 1, as it can be isolated from welfare multiplier (4.24), must be positive. The second term in brackets reflects the positive partial effect of the tax reform on tariff revenue since revenue-recycling induces a lower tariff and consequently a *ceteris paribus* higher import demand for good 1. The rise in tariff revenue via income effects however leads to a negatively perceived increase in national pollution which is reflected by the first term in brackets.

Effects on tariff

The effects of a marginal increase in the environmental tax on the tariff that can be determined from the system of total differentials in (4.23) are

$$\frac{dt}{d\tau} = \frac{1}{|H|} \left(\left(\frac{\partial e}{\partial \varepsilon} - \tau - t\frac{\partial m}{\partial \varepsilon} \right) - \left(\frac{\partial e}{\partial \varepsilon} + \varepsilon \frac{\partial^2 r}{\partial \varepsilon^2} \right) \left(1 - t\frac{\partial d_1}{\partial y} \right) \right) \quad (4.28)$$

$$= -\frac{|H^*|}{|H|} \quad (4.29)$$

with determinant $|H^*|$ as derived in (4.19). If, in addition, the assumption

$$\left(1 - t\frac{\partial d_1}{\partial y} \right) > 0 \quad (4.30)$$

is made which can be supposed to be the normal case, condition (4.26) holding is sufficient for a decreasing tariff following a rise in the environmental tax rate, i.e. for a positive revenue-recycling effect. Furthermore, multiplier (4.22) shows that a necessary and sufficient condition for a decreasing tariff in reaction to a rise in the environmental tax rate (i.e. multiplier (4.28) is negative) is that the environmental tax is on the increasing branch of its Laffer curve (i.e. that $dB/d\tau > 0$).

Effects on environment

The effects of a marginal increase in the environmental tax on environmental quality can also be found from (4.23)

$$\frac{d\varepsilon}{d\tau} = \frac{1}{|H|} \left(\left(m + \varepsilon \frac{\partial^2 r}{\partial \varepsilon\, \partial(p_1 + t)} \right) \left(1 - t\frac{\partial d_1}{\partial y} \right) + tS \right) \quad (4.31)$$

One recognizes that if conditions (4.25) and (4.30) hold, a positive effect on the environment, i.e. that $d\varepsilon/d\tau < 0$, depends on the income effect $tS/|H|$ resulting from changes in tariff income. These changes result from adaptations of uncompensated excess demand for good 1 to price changes of good 1. The environmental effect becomes positive if the positive income effect is rather small.

Effects on imports

The effects of a marginal increase in the environmental tax on imports are

$$\frac{dm}{d\tau} = \frac{1}{|H|} \left(E \left(m + \varepsilon \frac{\partial^2 r}{\partial \varepsilon \, \partial(p_1 + t)} \right) - S \left(\tau + \varepsilon \frac{\partial^2 r}{\partial \varepsilon^2} \right) \right) \qquad (4.32)$$

The sign of the multiplier is positive if conditions (4.25), (4.26) and $\partial e/\partial \varepsilon > \tau$ hold. It can be seen from definition (4.9b) that $E < 0$ then follows from stability. The conditions to be fulfilled mean that both the income effect (second term in brackets in (4.32)) and the environmental effect (first term in brackets in (4.32)) of a pollution tax rise point in the same direction and lead to an increase in excess demand for good 1.

Marginal social cost of tariff funds

The analysis will rely on the concept of marginal cost of funds used by Schöb (1996) and Ruocco and Wiegard (1997). The notion 'marginal social cost of funds' (MSCF) for the tariff is defined so as to reflect the total welfare effect, i.e. including environmental effects, if the budgetary needs of the government are marginally extended in a setting where the tariff is endogenously determined so that its revenues fill the gap between pollution tax proceeds and the budget constraint. Differentiating system (4.2) with respect to B leads to

$$H \begin{bmatrix} \dfrac{\partial e}{\partial u} \dfrac{du}{dB} \\[2ex] \dfrac{d\varepsilon}{dB} \\[2ex] \dfrac{dt}{dB} \\[2ex] \dfrac{dm}{dB} \end{bmatrix} = \begin{bmatrix} 0 \\[2ex] 0 \\[2ex] 1 \\[2ex] 0 \end{bmatrix} \qquad (4.33)$$

where matrix H and its determinant are given in (4.11) and (4.12), respectively. Then follows

$$\frac{\partial e}{\partial u}\frac{du}{dB} = \frac{1}{|H|}\left[\frac{\partial e}{\partial \varepsilon}\frac{\partial^2 r}{\partial \varepsilon\, \partial(p_1 + t)} - m\frac{\partial^2 r}{\partial \varepsilon^2}\right] \tag{4.34}$$

which allows us to define

$$\text{MSCF}_t \stackrel{\text{def}}{=} -\frac{\partial e}{\partial u}\frac{du}{dB}\bigg|_{t\,\text{endog.}} \tag{4.35}$$

If condition (4.25) holds, the marginal social cost of the tariff is positive, which means that the total welfare effect from marginally increasing the budgetary needs of the government in the above-described setting is negative.

Marginal social cost of pollution tax funds

Analogously to the MSCF connected with the tariff, those of the pollution tax have to be determined in a setting where this tax is endogenous. From total differentials of system (4.2) therefore we obtain

$$H^* \begin{bmatrix} \dfrac{\partial e}{\partial u}\dfrac{du}{dB} \\[2mm] \dfrac{d\varepsilon}{dB} \\[2mm] \dfrac{d\tau}{dB} \\[2mm] \dfrac{dm}{dB} \end{bmatrix} = \begin{bmatrix} 0 \\ 0 \\ 1 \\ 0 \end{bmatrix} \tag{4.36}$$

where matrix H^* and its determinant are given in (4.18) and (4.19), respectively. Multiplier

$$\frac{\partial e}{\partial u}\frac{du}{dB} = \frac{1}{|H^*|}\left(-\frac{\partial e}{\partial \varepsilon} - \varepsilon\frac{\partial^2 r}{\partial \varepsilon^2}\right) \tag{4.37}$$

is needed for definition

$$\text{MSCF}_\tau \stackrel{\text{def}}{=} -\frac{\partial e}{\partial u}\frac{du}{dB}\bigg|_{\tau\,\text{endog.}} \tag{4.38}$$

The marginal social cost of the environmental tax is positive if the tax is on the increasing branch of its Laffer curve, i.e. $|H^*| < 0$, and condition (4.26) holds.

4.3.8   The Benchmark Case

Since both concepts concerning the double dividend in a second-best setting presented in section 4.2 in one way or another refer to the Pigou analysis, a first-best framework is now introduced as a benchmark for further discussion. This will help to gain a better understanding of the differences between both concepts. Therefore, the model needs to be adapted to the case where a lump-sum tax is available to the government, which means that the budget can be financed without any distortion of the system. This also means that the government no longer levies a tariff $(t = 0)$. The set of equilibrium conditions (4.2) therefore changes to

$$e(p_1, p_2, u, \varepsilon) = r(p_1, p_2, \varepsilon) - \tau \cdot \varepsilon - h \qquad (4.39a)$$

$$\frac{\partial r(p_1, p_2, \varepsilon)}{\partial \varepsilon} = \tau \qquad (4.39b)$$

$$\tau \cdot \varepsilon + h = B \qquad (4.39c)$$

$$m = c_1(p_1, p_2, u, \varepsilon) - x_1(p_1, p_2, \varepsilon) \qquad (4.39d)$$

where condition (4.39c) has already been inserted into income identity (4.39a) and where h reflects the non-distorting head tax. The environmental tax is exogenous to the system, whereas the head tax level is varied in order to meet the governmental budget constraint. Totally differentiating the above system (4.39) leads to

$$H_{fb} \begin{bmatrix} \dfrac{\partial e}{\partial u} \dfrac{du}{d\tau} \\[2mm] \dfrac{d\varepsilon}{d\tau} \\[2mm] \dfrac{dh}{d\tau} \\[2mm] \dfrac{dm}{d\tau} \end{bmatrix} = - \begin{bmatrix} \varepsilon \\[2mm] -1 \\[2mm] \varepsilon \\[2mm] 0 \end{bmatrix} \qquad (4.40)$$

The matrix H_{fb} is given by[14]

$$H_{\text{fb}} \stackrel{\text{def}}{=} \begin{bmatrix} 1 & \dfrac{\partial e}{\partial \varepsilon} & 1 & 0 \\[2ex] 0 & \dfrac{\partial^2 r}{\partial \varepsilon^2} & 0 & 0 \\[2ex] 0 & \tau & 1 & 0 \\[2ex] -\dfrac{\partial d_1}{\partial y} & -\dfrac{\partial m}{\partial \varepsilon} & 0 & 1 \end{bmatrix} \qquad (4.41)$$

and its determinant by

$$|H_{\text{fb}}| = \frac{\partial^2 r}{\partial \varepsilon^2} \qquad (4.42)$$

The welfare multiplier for a marginal variation of the environmental tax where pollution tax proceeds partly replace the head tax is

$$\frac{\partial e}{\partial u}\frac{du}{d\tau} = -\frac{\dfrac{\partial e}{\partial \varepsilon} - \tau}{\dfrac{\partial^2 r}{\partial \varepsilon^2}} \qquad (4.43)$$

This multiplier is positive as long as the pollution tax rate τ is below marginal environmental damage, or equivalently, below the shadow price of the environment $\partial e/\partial \varepsilon$. It can be seen that a pollution tax rate at the Pigou level ($\tau = \partial e/\partial \varepsilon$) is a first-order condition for a welfare optimum, i.e. that multiplier (4.43) equals zero.

For the decomposition of the total welfare effect, use is now made of the concept of MSCF which was introduced in subsection 4.3.7, p. 92. The MSCF of the head tax reflects the effects on utility if governmental budgetary needs are marginally extended. Considerations refer to the case where the head tax is endogenous so that its revenues fill the gap between pollution tax proceeds and the budget constraint. From total

---

[14]Subscript 'fb' stands for 'first-best'.

differentials of system (4.39) we obtain

$$
H_{fb}
\begin{bmatrix}
\dfrac{\partial e}{\partial u}\dfrac{du}{dB} \\[2ex]
\dfrac{d\varepsilon}{dB} \\[2ex]
\dfrac{dh}{dB} \\[2ex]
\dfrac{dm}{dB}
\end{bmatrix}
=
\begin{bmatrix}
0 \\
0 \\
1 \\
0
\end{bmatrix}
\tag{4.44}
$$

where matrix H_{fb} and its determinant are the same as in (4.41) and (4.42), respectively. This entails

$$
\frac{\partial e}{\partial u}\frac{du}{dB} = \frac{1}{|H_{fb}|}\left(-\frac{\partial^2 r}{\partial \varepsilon^2}\right) = -1
\tag{4.45}
$$

and the definition

$$
\text{MSCF}_h \stackrel{\text{def}}{=} -\left.\frac{\partial e}{\partial u}\frac{du}{dB}\right|_{h\,\text{endog.}} = 1
\tag{4.46}
$$

Analogously, the MSCF of the pollution tax must be determined in a setting where this tax is endogenous. From total differentials of system (4.39) we therefore obtain

$$
H_{fb}^{*}
\begin{bmatrix}
\dfrac{\partial e}{\partial u}\dfrac{du}{dB} \\[2ex]
\dfrac{d\varepsilon}{dB} \\[2ex]
\dfrac{d\tau}{dB} \\[2ex]
\dfrac{dm}{dB}
\end{bmatrix}
=
\begin{bmatrix}
0 \\
0 \\
1 \\
0
\end{bmatrix}
\tag{4.47}
$$

where matrix H_{fb}^{*} is

$$
H_{fb}^{*} \stackrel{\text{def}}{=}
\begin{bmatrix}
1 & \dfrac{\partial e}{\partial \varepsilon} & \varepsilon & 0 \\[2ex]
0 & \dfrac{\partial^2 r}{\partial \varepsilon^2} & -1 & 0 \\[2ex]
0 & \tau & \varepsilon & 0 \\[2ex]
-\dfrac{\partial d_1}{\partial y} & -\dfrac{\partial m}{\partial \varepsilon} & 0 & 1
\end{bmatrix}
\tag{4.48}
$$

with determinant

$$|H^*_{\text{fb}}| = \tau + \varepsilon \frac{\partial^2 r}{\partial \varepsilon^2} \tag{4.49}$$

The result is

$$\frac{\partial e}{\partial u}\frac{du}{dB} = \frac{1}{|H^*_{\text{fb}}|}\left(-\frac{\partial e}{\partial \varepsilon} - \varepsilon \frac{\partial^2 r}{\partial \varepsilon^2}\right) = -\frac{\frac{\partial e}{\partial \varepsilon} + \varepsilon \frac{\partial^2 r}{\partial \varepsilon^2}}{\tau + \varepsilon \frac{\partial^2 r}{\partial \varepsilon^2}} \tag{4.50}$$

and the definition

$$\text{MSCF}_\tau \overset{\text{def}}{=} -\left.\frac{\partial e}{\partial u}\frac{du}{dB}\right|_{\tau\text{ endog.}} \tag{4.51}$$

Following Schöb (1996), the MSCF is decomposed into two components: first, a direct (welfare) cost component caused by the increase in a particular tax rate, with environmental quality assumed to be constant; second, an indirect effect reflecting the isolated welfare effect due to a change in environmental quality. The direct cost, divided by actual marginal tax revenues, is named marginal cost of public funds (MCF). The indirect effect, likewise related to actual marginal tax revenues, is called marginal environmental impact (MEI) of the respective tax. As will be seen, this way of decomposing the overall welfare effect portrays Goulder's double-dividend concept.

Head tax

To derive the MCF for the head tax, the externality level ε and the pollution tax τ must be kept constant. A marginal variation of the head tax in the course of an incremental tax reform alters the public budget level B endogenously

$$\begin{bmatrix} 1 & 0 & 0 \\ 0 & -1 & t \\ -\frac{\partial d_1}{\partial y} & 0 & 1 \end{bmatrix}\begin{bmatrix} \frac{\partial e}{\partial u}\frac{du}{dh} \\ \frac{dB}{dh} \\ \frac{dm}{dh} \end{bmatrix} = -\begin{bmatrix} 1 \\ 1 \\ 0 \end{bmatrix} \tag{4.52}$$

Solving (4.52) yields

$$\frac{\partial e}{\partial u}\frac{du}{dh}\bigg|_{\bar{\varepsilon}} = -1 \tag{4.53}$$

and the definition

$$\text{MCF}_h \overset{\text{def}}{=} -\frac{\partial e}{\partial u}\frac{du}{dh}\bigg|_{\bar{\varepsilon}} \cdot \frac{1}{\dfrac{dB}{dh}} = 1 \tag{4.54}$$

dB/dh can be determined from the complete system (4.39), i.e. the set of equilibrium conditions that also accounts for environmental effects, where h changes, p_1 and τ are fixed, and B is free to adapt. Then follows

$$\begin{bmatrix} 1 & \dfrac{\partial e}{\partial \varepsilon} & 0 & 0 \\[2mm] 0 & \dfrac{\partial^2 r}{\partial \varepsilon^2} & 0 & 0 \\[2mm] 0 & \tau & -1 & 0 \\[2mm] -\dfrac{\partial d_1}{\partial y} & -\dfrac{\partial m}{\partial \varepsilon} & 0 & 1 \end{bmatrix} \begin{bmatrix} \dfrac{\partial e}{\partial u}\dfrac{du}{dh} \\[2mm] \dfrac{d\varepsilon}{dh} \\[2mm] \dfrac{dB}{dh} \\[2mm] \dfrac{dm}{dh} \end{bmatrix} = - \begin{bmatrix} 1 \\[2mm] 0 \\[2mm] 1 \\[2mm] 0 \end{bmatrix} \tag{4.55}$$

From this results

$$\frac{dB}{dh} = -\frac{1}{\dfrac{\partial^2 r}{\partial \varepsilon^2}}\left(-\frac{\partial^2 r}{\partial \varepsilon^2}\right) = 1 \tag{4.56}$$

For the MEI_h multiplier $d\varepsilon/dh$ is derived in the case where the pollution tax is constant and the public budget is free to adapt according to system (4.55)

$$\frac{d\varepsilon}{dh}\bigg|_{\bar{\tau}} = 0 \tag{4.57}$$

Multiplier (4.57) weighted with the negative of the marginal willingness to pay for the environment then defines the MEI of the head tax as

$$\text{MEI}_h \overset{\text{def}}{=} -\frac{\partial e}{\partial \varepsilon} \cdot \frac{d\varepsilon}{dh}\bigg|_{\bar{\tau}} \cdot \frac{1}{\dfrac{dB}{dh}} = 0 \tag{4.58}$$

Environmental tax

To define the MCF of the environmental tax, system (4.39) is considered for the case of an incremental green tax reform (i.e. B is endogenous) where environmental degradation ε and the head tax h are constant, and the pollution tax τ is exogenously altered. The finding

$$
\begin{bmatrix}
1 & 0 & 0 \\
0 & -1 & 0 \\
-\dfrac{\partial d_1}{\partial y} & 0 & 1
\end{bmatrix}
\begin{bmatrix}
\dfrac{\partial e}{\partial u}\dfrac{du}{d\tau} \\[2mm]
\dfrac{dB}{d\tau} \\[2mm]
\dfrac{dm}{d\tau}
\end{bmatrix}
= -
\begin{bmatrix}
\varepsilon \\
\varepsilon \\
0
\end{bmatrix}
\tag{4.59}
$$

leads to

$$
\left.\frac{\partial e}{\partial u}\frac{du}{d\tau}\right|_{\bar\varepsilon} = -\varepsilon
\tag{4.60}
$$

and to the definition

$$
\mathrm{MCF}_\tau \stackrel{\text{def}}{=} -\left.\frac{\partial e}{\partial u}\frac{du}{d\tau}\right|_{\bar\varepsilon} \cdot \frac{1}{\dfrac{dB}{d\tau}} = \varepsilon \cdot \frac{1}{\dfrac{dB}{d\tau}}
\tag{4.61}
$$

where $dB/d\tau$ can be determined in setting (4.39) when τ changes, p_1 and h are fixed, and B is free to adapt so that

$$
\begin{bmatrix}
1 & \dfrac{\partial e}{\partial \varepsilon} & 0 & 0 \\[2mm]
0 & \dfrac{\partial^2 r}{\partial \varepsilon^2} & 0 & 0 \\[2mm]
0 & \tau & -1 & 0 \\[2mm]
-\dfrac{\partial d_1}{\partial y} & -\dfrac{\partial m}{\partial \varepsilon} & 0 & 1
\end{bmatrix}
\begin{bmatrix}
\dfrac{\partial e}{\partial u}\dfrac{du}{d\tau} \\[2mm]
\dfrac{d\varepsilon}{d\tau} \\[2mm]
\dfrac{dB}{d\tau} \\[2mm]
\dfrac{dm}{d\tau}
\end{bmatrix}
= -
\begin{bmatrix}
\varepsilon \\
-1 \\
\varepsilon \\
0
\end{bmatrix}
\tag{4.62}
$$

From this follows

$$
\frac{dB}{d\tau} = \frac{\varepsilon \cdot \dfrac{\partial^2 r}{\partial \varepsilon^2} + \tau}{\dfrac{\partial^2 r}{\partial \varepsilon^2}} = \frac{|H_{\text{fb}}^*|}{\dfrac{\partial^2 r}{\partial \varepsilon^2}} = \varepsilon + \frac{\tau}{\dfrac{\partial^2 r}{\partial \varepsilon^2}}
\tag{4.63}
$$

$dB/d\tau = \varepsilon$ from (4.59) cannot be used since in the general equilibrium every variation in τ leads to a change in ε which must also be taken into consideration.

For the indirect effect of the pollution tax, multiplier $d\varepsilon/d\tau$ is derived for the case where the head tax is constant and the public budget is free to adapt according to (4.62)

$$\frac{d\varepsilon}{d\tau}\bigg|_{\overline{h}} = \frac{1}{\frac{\partial^2 r}{\partial \varepsilon^2}} \tag{4.64}$$

Weighting also multiplier (4.64) with the negative of the marginal willingness to pay for the environment now defines the MEI of the pollution tax

$$\text{MEI}_\tau \stackrel{\text{def}}{=} -\frac{\partial e}{\partial \varepsilon} \cdot \frac{d\varepsilon}{d\tau}\bigg|_{\overline{h}} \cdot \frac{1}{\frac{dB}{d\tau}} = -\frac{\partial e}{\partial \varepsilon} \cdot \frac{1}{\frac{\partial^2 r}{\partial \varepsilon^2}} \cdot \frac{1}{\frac{dB}{d\tau}} \tag{4.65}$$

It can be seen that definitions (4.54), (4.58), (4.61) and (4.65) are indeed appropriate for a decomposition of the MSCF since

$$\text{MSCF}_h \equiv -\frac{\partial e}{\partial u}\frac{du}{dB}\bigg|_{h\,\text{endog.}} = \text{MCF}_h - \text{MEI}_h \tag{4.66}$$

$$\text{MSCF}_\tau \equiv -\frac{\partial e}{\partial u}\frac{du}{dB}\bigg|_{\tau\,\text{endog.}} = \text{MCF}_\tau - \text{MEI}_\tau \tag{4.67}$$

As is known, a green tax reform generally consists of an increase in the pollution tax and a fall in the other tax instruments which offsets the additional tax revenue from the pollution tax. Consequently, with the MSCF defined positively

$$\text{MSCF}_h - \text{MSCF}_\tau = (\text{MEI}_\tau - \text{MEI}_h) + (\text{MCF}_h - \text{MCF}_\tau)$$

where

$$(\text{MEI}_\tau - \text{MEI}_h) = \frac{1}{\frac{dB}{d\tau}} \cdot \left(-\frac{\frac{\partial e}{\partial \varepsilon}}{\frac{\partial^2 r}{\partial \varepsilon^2}} \right) \tag{4.68}$$

and

$$(\text{MCF}_h - \text{MCF}_\tau) = \frac{1}{\frac{dB}{d\tau}} \cdot \left(\varepsilon + \frac{\tau}{\frac{\partial^2 r}{\partial \varepsilon^2}} - \varepsilon \right) = \frac{1}{\frac{dB}{d\tau}} \cdot \frac{\tau}{\frac{\partial^2 r}{\partial \varepsilon^2}} \tag{4.69}$$

so that

$$\text{MSCF}_h - \text{MSCF}_\tau = \frac{\partial e}{\partial u}\frac{du}{d\tau} \cdot \frac{1}{\dfrac{dB}{d\tau}} \tag{4.70}$$

As long as the environmental tax is on the increasing branch of the Laffer curve (i.e. $dB/d\tau > 0$), equation (4.70) shows that

$$\frac{\partial e}{\partial u}\frac{du}{d\tau}\left\{\begin{array}{c}>\\=\\<\end{array}\right\}0 \iff \text{MSCF}_h\left\{\begin{array}{c}>\\=\\<\end{array}\right\}\text{MSCF}_\tau$$

$$\iff (\text{MEI}_\tau - \text{MEI}_h) + (\text{MCF}_h - \text{MCF}_\tau)\left\{\begin{array}{c}>\\=\\<\end{array}\right\}0 \tag{4.71}$$

This means that if the MSCF of the tax to be substituted for the environmental tax – in this case the head tax – is higher than that of the environmental tax itself, the ecological tax reform is welfare-enhancing.

In (4.71) the effects are rearranged according to Goulder's decomposition of the dividends. The first term in brackets is proportional to the environmental dividend. It consists of the marginal welfare gains from environmental improvement following the increase in pollution tax τ and the induced change in head tax h, respectively. The second bracketed term is proportional to the fiscal dividend. It results from a change in the MCF arising from changes in both taxes. The proportionality factor for both dividends is the inverse of multiplier $dB/d\tau$. The strong form of Goulder's double-dividend hypothesis holds if both bracketed terms in presentation (4.71) are positive.

The next step is to modify Schöb's method of using the MSCF in order to decompose the overall utility effect in a different manner, which is compatible with the Pearce concept. For this, direct cost of internalization (DCI) is defined as that part of the MCF which is *directly* attributable to the abatement efforts and which is reflected by the foregone pollution tax revenues due to the erosion of the tax base. Since both tax instruments involved in an ecological tax reform have a potential impact on the environmental situation and hence on the pollution tax base, DCI is defined with respect to either instrument. Again, the erosion effect is normalized with the actual marginal tax revenues from the corresponding tax instrument.

Head tax

To derive the erosion effect on the pollution tax base resulting from a marginal change in the head tax – in analogy to the MEI – system (4.39) is considered for the case of an incremental tax reform (i.e. B is endogenous) where the pollution tax τ is constant. Using multiplier (4.57), the definition is

$$\text{DCI}_h \overset{\text{def}}{=} -\tau \cdot \left. \frac{d\varepsilon}{dh} \right|_\tau \cdot \frac{1}{\dfrac{dB}{dh}} = 0 \tag{4.72}$$

where the environmental effect is weighted with the pollution tax rate τ, or equivalently, with the marginal product of environment in production. dB/dh is equal to multiplier (4.56).

Environmental tax

For the DCI of the environmental tax, system (4.39) is considered for the case where the head tax h is constant and the public budget B is endogenous. Referring to multiplier (4.64), we can define that

$$\text{DCI}_\tau \overset{\text{def}}{=} -\tau \cdot \left. \frac{d\varepsilon}{d\tau} \right|_h \cdot \frac{1}{\dfrac{dB}{d\tau}} = -\tau \cdot \frac{1}{\dfrac{\partial^2 r}{\partial \varepsilon^2}} \cdot \frac{1}{\dfrac{dB}{d\tau}} \tag{4.73}$$

where $dB/d\tau$ is known from multiplier (4.63). In the figures in section 3.2 which represent partial equilibrium analyses in first-best settings, the marginal cost of abatement is identical to the DCI of the pollution tax introduced here. This is because the adaptation of the head tax – which is implicitly also included in the above-mentioned figures – causes no spill-over effects on the pollution tax base so that its DCI is equal to zero.

The definition used for the net marginal cost of funds (NMCF) connected with the corresponding tax instrument is the difference between its MCF and DCI

$$\text{NMCF}_h \overset{\text{def}}{=} \text{MCF}_h - \text{DCI}_h = 1 \cdot \frac{1}{\dfrac{dB}{dh}} \tag{4.74}$$

$$\text{NMCF}_\tau \stackrel{\text{def}}{=} \text{MCF}_\tau - \text{DCI}_\tau = \frac{\tau + \varepsilon \dfrac{\partial^2 r}{\partial \varepsilon^2}}{\dfrac{\partial^2 r}{\partial \varepsilon^2}} \cdot \frac{1}{\dfrac{dB}{d\tau}} \qquad (4.75)$$

By opposing MEI to DCI, we define the net marginal environmental impact (NMEI) of either tax instrument as

$$\text{NMEI}_h \stackrel{\text{def}}{=} \text{MEI}_h - \text{DCI}_h = 0 \qquad (4.76)$$

$$\text{NMEI}_\tau \stackrel{\text{def}}{=} \text{MEI}_\tau - \text{DCI}_\tau = -\left(\frac{\partial e}{\partial \varepsilon} - \tau\right) \cdot \frac{1}{\dfrac{\partial^2 r}{\partial \varepsilon^2}} \cdot \frac{1}{\dfrac{dB}{d\tau}} \qquad (4.77)$$

In analogy to the Schöb decomposition, the change in MSCF results

$$\text{MSCF}_h - \text{MSCF}_\tau = (\text{NMEI}_\tau - \text{NMEI}_h) + (\text{NMCF}_h - \text{NMCF}_\tau)$$

$$= \frac{1}{\dfrac{dB}{d\tau}} \left(-\frac{\dfrac{\partial e}{\partial \varepsilon} - \tau}{\dfrac{\partial^2 r}{\partial \varepsilon^2}}\right)$$

$$= \frac{\partial e}{\partial u}\frac{du}{d\tau} \cdot \frac{1}{\dfrac{dB}{d\tau}} \qquad (4.78)$$

As long as the environmental tax is on the increasing branch of the Laffer curve (i.e. $dB/d\tau > 0$), equation (4.78) shows that

$$\frac{\partial e}{\partial u}\frac{du}{d\tau} \begin{Bmatrix} > \\ = \\ < \end{Bmatrix} 0$$

$$\Longleftrightarrow \quad (\text{NMEI}_\tau - \text{NMEI}_h) + \underbrace{(\text{NMCF}_h - \text{NMCF}_\tau)}_{=0} \begin{Bmatrix} > \\ = \\ < \end{Bmatrix} 0 \qquad (4.79)$$

$$\Longleftrightarrow \quad (\text{MEI}_\tau - \text{MEI}_h) + (\text{DCI}_h - \text{DCI}_\tau) \begin{Bmatrix} > \\ = \\ < \end{Bmatrix} 0 \qquad (4.80)$$

The interesting point is that the first bracketed term in (4.79) is equal to the LHS of (4.71) and (4.80), and therefore equal to the global welfare effect; the second bracketed term is equal to zero. This means that expressions $(\mathrm{MCF}_h - \mathrm{MCF}_\tau)$ and $(\mathrm{DCI}_h - \mathrm{DCI}_\tau)$ are equivalent within this framework. These findings reveal that the two most common concepts for double-dividend evaluation, namely the Goulder concept and the Pearce concept, rely on different conceptual platforms and can be traced back to a differing interpretation of the first-best scenario: Goulder's concept interprets the first-order condition for an optimal pollution tax in a first-best setting as an opposition of the changes in the marginal cost of funds – representing the fiscal effect of an environmental tax reform (equation (4.69)) – to the net impact on the environmental situation (equation (4.68)). The Pearce concept, however, interprets the same first-order condition as a comparison of the shadow price of the environment with the direct cost of internalization (i.e. the pollution tax rate), the difference of both weighted with the change in pollution $d\varepsilon/d\tau$. This comparison represents the first dividend of the Pearce concept. The second dividend is defined as a residual that reflects additional effects. It becomes apparent that according to Goulder's concept there are two dividends,[15] even if the analysis takes place in a first-best setting. According to the Pearce concept, however, just one 'dividend' can be observed in a first-best setting. The second only arises if additional effects show up due to additional distortions, i.e. in a second-best setting. The first dividend of the Pearce concept can therefore be interpreted as a reflection of the conditions in a first-best analysis.

4.4   APPLICATION OF THE CONCEPTS

Returning to the second-best framework, where the environmental tax partly replaces the distorting tariff, the two double-dividend concepts will be applied to the model represented by equation system (4.2) that contains trade distortions. Statements which are explicitly or implicitly connected to the concepts will be discussed in order to evaluate how justified or appropriate the respective concepts are.

---

[15] Either of which can be equal to zero, positive or negative.

4.4.1 The Goulder Concept

To begin with, Goulder's strong double-dividend definition will be applied to the framework. From (4.23) it follows that

$$\frac{\partial e}{\partial u}\frac{du}{d\tau} = \underbrace{-\frac{\partial e}{\partial \varepsilon}\frac{d\varepsilon}{d\tau}}_{\text{1st dividend}} \underbrace{- m\frac{dt}{d\tau} - \varepsilon}_{\text{2nd dividend}} \qquad (4.81)$$

where $d\varepsilon/d\tau$ and $dt/d\tau$ are the multipliers (4.31) and (4.28), respectively. The first dividend is the marginal general equilibrium welfare gain due to the environmental improvement following the green tax reform. This effect not only incorporates the environmental effects resulting from an increase in the pollution tax, but also all repercussions on the environment emerging from an adaptation of the tariff due to revenue-recycling and spill-over effects. The second dividend incorporates the fiscal effects and therefore reflects the gross cost according to Goulder's definition. Its first term is the revenue-recycling effect, whereas the second one, namely $(-\varepsilon)$, is the negative tax rate effect or tax-withdrawing effect connected with a rise in the environmental tax rate. Bovenberg and de Mooij (1996) ascribe these two effects in the fiscal dividend to the notion *tax burden effect*. Both other effects known from the literature, namely the tax base erosion effect and the tax interaction effect, do not explicitly show up in this decomposition.

Applying Schöb's decomposition of the total welfare effect, analogously to the analysis in the benchmark scenario, the MSCF is decomposed into MCF and MEI caused by the change in either tax instrument.

Tariff

To derive the MCF of the tariff, the following consideration refers to the set of equilibrium conditions (4.2) in the case of an incremental tax reform (i.e. B is endogenous) where the externality level ε and the pollution tax τ are constant, and tariff t is exogenously altered. Starting from

$$
\begin{bmatrix}
1 & 0 & 0 \\
0 & -1 & t \\
-\dfrac{\partial d_1}{\partial y} & 0 & 1
\end{bmatrix}
\begin{bmatrix}
\dfrac{\partial e}{\partial u}\dfrac{du}{dt} \\[2mm]
\dfrac{dB}{dt} \\[2mm]
\dfrac{dm}{dt}
\end{bmatrix}
= -
\begin{bmatrix}
m \\
m \\
-S
\end{bmatrix}
\tag{4.82}
$$

and deriving

$$
\left. \frac{\partial e}{\partial u}\frac{du}{dt}\right|_{\bar{\varepsilon}} = -m
\tag{4.83}
$$

the following definition is used

$$
\mathrm{MCF}_t \stackrel{\text{def}}{=} - \left.\frac{\partial e}{\partial u}\frac{du}{dt}\right|_{\bar{\varepsilon}} \cdot \frac{1}{\dfrac{dB}{dt}} = m \cdot \frac{1}{\dfrac{dB}{dt}}
\tag{4.84}
$$

where dB/dt is known from multiplier (4.16). For the MEI_t multiplier $d\varepsilon/dt$ is derived for the case where the pollution tax is constant and the public budget is free to adapt according to (4.15)

$$
\left.\frac{d\varepsilon}{dt}\right|_{\bar{\tau}} = - \frac{\dfrac{\partial^2 r}{\partial\varepsilon\,\partial(p_1 + t)}}{\dfrac{\partial^2 r}{\partial\varepsilon^2}}
\tag{4.85}
$$

Multiplier (4.85) weighted with the negative of the marginal willingness to pay for the environment then defines the MEI of the tariff as

$$
\mathrm{MEI}_t \stackrel{\text{def}}{=} -\frac{\partial e}{\partial\varepsilon}\cdot\left.\frac{d\varepsilon}{dt}\right|_{\bar{\tau}}\cdot\frac{1}{\dfrac{dB}{dt}} = \frac{\partial e}{\partial\varepsilon}\cdot\left[\frac{\dfrac{\partial^2 r}{\partial\varepsilon\,\partial(p_1 + t)}}{\dfrac{\partial^2 r}{\partial\varepsilon^2}}\right]\cdot\frac{1}{\dfrac{dB}{dt}}
\tag{4.86}
$$

Environmental tax

For the MCF of the environmental tax, equation system (4.2) is considered in the case of an incremental green tax reform (i.e. B is endogenous) where environmental degradation ε and tariff t are constant. Since this scenario is identical with the benchmark case, a fall-back upon definition (4.60) results

$$\text{MCF}_\tau \overset{\text{def}}{=} -\left.\frac{\partial e}{\partial u}\frac{du}{d\tau}\right|_{\bar{\varepsilon}} \cdot \frac{1}{\dfrac{dB}{d\tau}} = \varepsilon \cdot \frac{1}{\dfrac{dB}{d\tau}} \tag{4.87}$$

where $dB/d\tau$ is known from multiplier (4.22). For the indirect effect of the pollution tax, definition (4.65) is referred to

$$\text{MEI}_\tau \overset{\text{def}}{=} -\left.\frac{\partial e}{\partial \varepsilon} \cdot \frac{d\varepsilon}{d\tau}\right|_{\bar{t}} \cdot \frac{1}{\dfrac{dB}{d\tau}} = -\frac{\partial e}{\partial \varepsilon} \cdot \frac{1}{\dfrac{\partial^2 r}{\partial \varepsilon^2}} \cdot \frac{1}{\dfrac{dB}{d\tau}} \tag{4.65}$$

Now again

$$\text{MSCF}_t \equiv -\left.\frac{\partial e}{\partial u}\frac{du}{dB}\right|_{t \, \text{endog.}} = \text{MCF}_t - \text{MEI}_t \tag{4.88}$$

$$\text{MSCF}_\tau \equiv -\left.\frac{\partial e}{\partial u}\frac{du}{dB}\right|_{\tau \, \text{endog.}} = \text{MCF}_\tau - \text{MEI}_\tau \tag{4.89}$$

Applying the definitions to a revenue-neutral green tax reform where the pollution tax increases and the tariff adapts corresponding to the additional tax revenues, it becomes evident that

$$\text{MSCF}_t - \text{MSCF}_\tau = (\text{MEI}_\tau - \text{MEI}_t) + (\text{MCF}_t - \text{MCF}_\tau)$$

where

$$(\text{MEI}_\tau - \text{MEI}_t) = \frac{-1}{\dfrac{dB}{d\tau}} \cdot \left(\frac{\partial e}{\partial \varepsilon} \cdot \frac{\dfrac{\partial^2 r}{\partial \varepsilon \, \partial(p_1 + t)} \dfrac{dB}{d\tau} + \dfrac{dB}{dt}}{\dfrac{\partial^2 r}{\partial \varepsilon^2} \cdot \dfrac{dB}{dt}} \right)$$

$$= \frac{-1}{\dfrac{dB}{d\tau}} \cdot \frac{\partial e}{\partial \varepsilon} \frac{d\varepsilon}{d\tau} \tag{4.90}$$

and

$$(\text{MCF}_t - \text{MCF}_\tau) = \frac{-1}{\dfrac{dB}{d\tau}} \cdot \left(m\frac{dt}{d\tau} + \varepsilon \right) \quad \text{since} \quad \frac{\dfrac{dB}{d\tau}}{\dfrac{dB}{dt}} = \frac{|H^*|}{|H|} = -\frac{dt}{d\tau}$$

$$\tag{4.91}$$

so that

$$\text{MSCF}_t - \text{MSCF}_\tau = \frac{\partial e}{\partial u}\frac{du}{d\tau} \cdot \frac{1}{\dfrac{dB}{d\tau}} \tag{4.92}$$

As long as not only the tariff but also the environmental tax is on the increasing branch of the Laffer curve (i.e. $dB/d\tau > 0$), equation (4.92) shows that

$$\frac{\partial e}{\partial u}\frac{du}{d\tau} \left\{ \begin{matrix} > \\ = \\ < \end{matrix} \right\} 0 \iff \text{MSCF}_t \left\{ \begin{matrix} > \\ = \\ < \end{matrix} \right\} \text{MSCF}_\tau$$

$$\iff (\text{MEI}_\tau - \text{MEI}_t) + (\text{MCF}_t - \text{MCF}_\tau) \left\{ \begin{matrix} > \\ = \\ < \end{matrix} \right\} 0 \tag{4.93}$$

In (4.93) the effects are again arranged according to Goulder's decomposition of the dividends, which also corresponds to the presentation in equation (4.81). The first term in brackets consists of the marginal impact on welfare due to a change in environmental quality following the increase in pollution tax τ and the induced change in tariff t, respectively. It is proportional to the environmental dividend. The second bracketed term is proportional to the fiscal dividend. It results from a change in the MCF of both taxes. From definition (4.84) in conjunction with the RHS of presentation (4.91) it can be seen that the MCF_t corresponds to the revenue-recycling effect $(-m \cdot dt/d\tau)$ and the MCF_τ to the tax rate effect $(-\varepsilon)$ in equation (4.81). The proportionality factor for both dividends is the inverse of multiplier $dB/d\tau$. A double dividend again requires that both bracketed terms in (4.93) be positive.

Measurability

Goulder's intention for his concept was the separation of measurable effects from those which cannot be measured. Regarding multiplier (4.81), it can be noticed that from estimating the system of demand functions one gets insight into the level of both multipliers $dt/d\tau$ and $d\varepsilon/d\tau$. The level of externality ε as well as the level of imports m in the initial equilibrium, the latter being the weight for multiplier $dt/d\tau$, are also observable. However, the impact of a change in environmental quality on utility, which is reflected by the marginal willingness to pay for the environment $\partial e/\partial \varepsilon$, cannot be easily determined. Therefore, the quantitive amount of the first dividend is indeed uncertain. Derivative $\partial e/\partial \varepsilon$ is also a component of multiplier $dt/d\tau$, which has been derived in (4.28). There it belongs to an effect that reflects changes in private demand due to a change in the environmental situation – effects generally not considered in the literature. But multiplier $dt/d\tau$ can nevertheless be determined from the system of demand functions, and therefore the level of the second dividend can be determined much more easily than that of the environmental one. Goulder proposes to rely exclusively on the fiscal dividend since information requirements would be significantly lower. Furthermore, a positive sign of the second dividend indicates that the green tax reform is a 'no-regret policy', i.e. a free lunch. It would hence be interesting to show that it is possible for the environmental dividend in the course of a green tax reform to be negative while the fiscal one is positive. For the environmental effect of a marginal increase in the environmental tax to be negative or multiplier (4.31) to be positive is hence a necessary and sufficient condition for the first of Goulder's dividends to be negative.[16] In this case it would no longer be a rational guidance to evaluate only the second dividend and to take the positive sign of the first one for granted.

Condition for positive fiscal dividend

From multiplier (4.81) it is obvious that for the second of Goulder's dividends to be positive demands that

$$\left(-m\frac{dt}{d\tau} - \varepsilon\right) \overset{!}{>} 0 \qquad (4.94)$$

Inserting

$$\frac{\dfrac{dB}{d\tau}}{\dfrac{dB}{dt}} = \frac{|H^*|}{|H|} = -\frac{dt}{d\tau}$$

---

[16] Bovenberg and de Mooij (1996) and Schöb (1996) indeed show that the environmental dividend of an ecological tax reform may become negative.

into (4.94) results in

$$\left(m\frac{\frac{dB}{d\tau}}{\frac{dB}{dt}} - \varepsilon\right) = \frac{m\frac{dB}{d\tau} - \varepsilon\frac{dB}{dt}}{\frac{dB}{dt}} \overset{!}{>} 0$$

Since stability requires dB/dt to be positive, this condition is fulfilled if

$$m\frac{dB}{d\tau} - \varepsilon\frac{dB}{dt} > 0$$

Written in elasticity notation, the condition for the second dividend to be positive is

$$\frac{\eta_{(B,\tau)}}{\eta_{(B,t)}} > \frac{\tau\cdot\varepsilon}{t\cdot m} = \frac{\beta}{\alpha} \tag{4.95}$$

where

$$\alpha \overset{\text{def}}{=} \frac{t\cdot m}{B} \qquad \text{and} \qquad \beta \overset{\text{def}}{=} \frac{\tau\cdot\varepsilon}{B} = 1 - \alpha$$

denote the revenue shares of the respective taxes in total tax proceeds. The necessary and sufficient condition for the second dividend to be positive is hence that the ratio of revenue elasticities of both taxes must be greater than the respective ratios of revenue shares. That the environmental tax is on the increasing branch of its Laffer curve ($dB/d\tau > 0 \iff \eta_{(B,\tau)} > 0$) is a necessary condition for a positive second dividend.

Condition for negative environmental dividend

From multiplier (4.81) in combination with (4.90) it can be seen that for the first of Goulder's dividends to be negative demands that

$$-\frac{\partial e}{\partial\varepsilon}\frac{d\varepsilon}{d\tau} = (\text{MEI}_\tau - \text{MEI}_t)\cdot\frac{dB}{d\tau} \overset{!}{<} 0 \tag{4.96}$$

From definitions (4.86) and (4.65) it is known that

$$(\text{MEI}_\tau - \text{MEI}_t) = -\frac{\frac{\partial e}{\partial\varepsilon}}{\frac{\partial^2 r}{\partial\varepsilon^2}}\left(\frac{\frac{\partial^2 r}{\partial\varepsilon\,\partial(p_1 + t)}}{\frac{dB}{dt}} + \frac{1}{\frac{dB}{d\tau}}\right) \tag{4.97}$$

Inserted into condition (4.96) and taking care of the stability requirement $dB/dt > 0$, the result is

$$\frac{dB}{d\tau} \frac{\partial^2 r}{\partial\varepsilon\, \partial(p_1 + t)} + \frac{dB}{dt} \overset{!}{<} 0 \qquad (4.98)$$

Again using elasticity notation, the condition for the first dividend to be negative is derived as

$$\frac{\eta_{(B,\tau)}}{\eta_{(B,t)}} \gtrless -\frac{\beta}{\alpha} \cdot \frac{m}{x_1} \cdot \frac{1}{\eta_{(x_1,\varepsilon)}} \quad \text{for} \quad \frac{\partial^2 r}{\partial\varepsilon\, \partial(p_1 + t)} \lessgtr 0 \qquad (4.99)$$

from which it follows that

$$\eta_{(B,\tau)} \gtrless 0$$

respectively. $\eta_{(x_1,\varepsilon)}$ is the supply elasticity of good 1 with respect to a change in resource input. Its sign corresponds to that of derivative $\partial^2 r/(\partial\varepsilon\, \partial(p_1 + t))$, which reflects the marginal change in domestic supply of good 1 in reaction to a change in the pollution level and is hence a kind of Rybczynski effect.[17] Condition (4.99) again is necessary and sufficient.

For conditions for a positive fiscal and a negative environmental dividend to be met simultaneously hence requires

$$\frac{\eta_{(B,\tau)}}{\eta_{(B,t)}} > \frac{\beta}{\alpha} \quad \wedge \quad \frac{\eta_{(B,\tau)}}{\eta_{(B,t)}} \lessgtr -\frac{\beta}{\alpha} \cdot \frac{m}{x_1} \cdot \frac{1}{\eta_{(x_1,\varepsilon)}} \quad \text{for} \quad \frac{\partial^2 r}{\partial\varepsilon\, \partial(p_1 + t)} \lessgtr 0$$

$$(4.100)$$

respectively. As the lower line in condition (4.100) contains a contradiction, the only possible condition for the dividends to have the requested opposite signs is

$$\frac{\eta_{(B,\tau)}}{\eta_{(B,t)}} > \max\left[\frac{\beta}{\alpha}; -\frac{\beta}{\alpha} \cdot \frac{m}{x_1} \cdot \frac{1}{\eta_{(x_1,\varepsilon)}}\right] \quad \text{for} \quad \frac{\partial^2 r}{\partial\varepsilon\, \partial(p_1 + t)} < 0 \quad (4.101)$$

From this it follows that the pollution tax must be on the increasing side of its Laffer curve ($\eta_{(B,\tau)} > 0$). The condition for a negative sign of the

---

[17] If $\partial^2 r/(\partial\varepsilon\, \partial(p_1 + t)) = \partial x_1/\partial\varepsilon < 0$, stability requires that $\partial d_1/\partial\varepsilon > 0$. This means that $\partial m/\partial\varepsilon > 0$ according to definition (4.7).

first dividend to become binding is[18]

$$\left(m + \varepsilon \frac{\partial^2 r}{\partial \varepsilon \, \partial(p_1 + t)}\right) \overset{!}{>} 0 \iff -\frac{m}{x_1} \frac{1}{\eta_{(x_1,\varepsilon)}} > 1$$

The intuition behind the result in (4.101) is that if the rise in the pollution tax leads to a relatively high amount of additional tax revenue, this in turn allows the government to reduce the tariff rate substantially (LHS of condition (4.101)). Domestic production of the protected sector which uses the environment relative extensively $(\partial^2 r/(\partial \varepsilon \, \partial(p_1 + t)) < 0)$ therefore goes down, and that of the other, relatively dirty, good rises. Consequently, an environmental tax reform may lead to a reduction in the excess burden of the tax system, but simultaneously to a deterioration of the environmental situation. In this case it would not be sufficient to evaluate the fiscal dividend only and to take the positive sign of the environmental one for granted. It may even happen that a green tax reform is actually welfare-decreasing despite a positive second dividend; this result occurs if the fiscal dividend is not big enough to overcompensate the negative environmental dividend.

Goulder's concept as an answer to a situation where information is not complete is associated with two possible errors:

1. It may happen that an ecological tax reform is supported due to a positive second dividend although the negative environmental dividend more than offsets the positive effects of the fiscal dividend and the overall welfare effect becomes negative. But estimating the system of demand functions in order to determine the sign of the fiscal dividend also gives insight into the sign of the first one. A consequent interpretation of Goulder's concept would then lead to the conclusion that in the case of a negative environmental dividend an environmental tax reform is inopportune even if the second dividend is positive and absolutely larger.
2. Alternatively – and certainly more probably – the government will be advised to refrain from the tax reform due to a negative second

---

[18]The bracketed term is a component of multiplier (4.31) $d\varepsilon/d\tau$. For $1 - t \cdot \partial d_1/\partial y > 0$ the above bracketed term being negative is a sufficient condition for a positive environmental dividend, i.e. $d\varepsilon/d\tau < 0$.

dividend although the first one is positive and absolutely larger. Not pursuing a green tax reform due to the negative sign of the second dividend may then be a very costly policy.

The necessary and sufficient conditions for the different possible outcomes with respect to the sign of the dividends are summarized in Table 4.1. From the conditions for a negative fiscal dividend and a pos-

Table 4.1: Necessary and sufficient conditions for the Goulder concept

No.	Condition	D_1[a]	D_2	$r_{\varepsilon p}$[b]	$\frac{d\varepsilon}{d\tau}$	$\frac{dB}{d\tau}$
(i)	$\dfrac{\eta_{(B,\tau)}}{\eta_{(B,t)}} > \max\left[\dfrac{\beta}{\alpha}\,;\, -\dfrac{\beta}{\alpha}\cdot\dfrac{m}{x_1}\cdot\dfrac{1}{\eta_{(x_1,\varepsilon)}}\right]$	$-$	$+$	$-$	$+$	$+$
(ii)		$+$	$+$	$+$	$-$	$+$
(iii)	$\dfrac{\eta_{(B,\tau)}}{\eta_{(B,t)}} < \min\left[\dfrac{\beta}{\alpha}\,;\, -\dfrac{\beta}{\alpha}\cdot\dfrac{m}{x_1}\cdot\dfrac{1}{\eta_{(x_1,\varepsilon)}}\right]$	$-$	$-$	$+$	$+$	$-$
(iv)		$+$	$-$	$-$	$-$	$-$
(v)	$\dfrac{\beta}{\alpha} < \dfrac{\eta_{(B,\tau)}}{\eta_{(B,t)}} < -\dfrac{\beta}{\alpha}\cdot\dfrac{m}{x_1}\cdot\dfrac{1}{\eta_{(x_1,\varepsilon)}}$	$+$	$+$	$-$	$-$	$+$
(vi)	$-\dfrac{\beta}{\alpha}\cdot\dfrac{m}{x_1}\cdot\dfrac{1}{\eta_{(x_1,\varepsilon)}} < \dfrac{\eta_{(B,\tau)}}{\eta_{(B,t)}} < \dfrac{\beta}{\alpha}$	$-$	$-$	$-$	$+$	$+$
(vii)		$+$	$-$	$+$	$-$	$-$

[a]D_i, $i = 1, 2$, stands for the first and second dividend, respectively.
[b]$r_{\varepsilon p}$ stands for $\partial^2 r/(\partial\varepsilon\,\partial(p_1 + t))$.

itive environmental one at the same time in lines (iv) and (vii) it is obvious that $\eta_{(B,\tau)}$ (i.e. column $dB/d\tau$ in the table) is not restricted in sign. The necessary and sufficient conditions for a double dividend according to Goulder's concept are outlined in lines (ii) and (v). As can be seen, derivative $\partial^2 r/(\partial\varepsilon\,\partial(p_1 + t))$ is not committed to a certain sign, which means that good 1 can be pollution-intensive or pollution-extensive. Lines (i), (ii) and (v) show that $\eta_{(B,\tau)} > 0$ is necessary for a double dividend to occur since, if negative, it is incompatible with a positive second dividend. Only if conditions (ii) or (v) are met will an environmental tax reform be regarded as a sensible policy option. In all other cases the Goulder concept is not appropriate to give policy advice. In cases (iii) and (vi) an ecological tax reform definitely leads to a deterioration of welfare. In all cases it is not clear whether the environmental tax is already above its Pigou level, i.e. higher than marginal environmental damage reflected by the shadow price of the environment $\partial e/\partial \varepsilon$.

The important question is whether the Goulder concept is more than a theoretically viable decomposition of the overall welfare effect of an ecological tax reform. Goulder claims that his concept is of practical use since it would support the decision process of policy-makers. A double dividend backs an environmental tax reform even if no information is available on the marginal willingness to pay for the environment. This statement is true where individuals within an economy are identical. It hence applies to the analytical framework used in this chapter. But Goulder does not restrict his proposition to certain model assumptions. Therefore, the relevance of his statement has to be validated in a more general context. As long as the economy under consideration is more or less populous, a tax reform that from a social point of view gives rise to a double dividend according to the Goulder concept will produce losers and winners even though the gross cost of the tax reform is negative. This result emerges because the change in the price vector induced by the tax changes affects individuals in a different manner. Whether somebody loses or wins depends on items such as, for example, preferences or factor income. A marginal pollution tax reform in this case can only be justified in the Kaldor–Hicks–Scitovsky sense that winners can potentially compensate those who are put at a disadvantage. This of course is not sufficient in the face of democratic political decision-making since there decisions in the political process depend on votes. A policy measure that would lead to a Pareto improvement in the Kaldor–Hicks–Scitovsky interpretation will not necessarily be supported by the majority. But, if it is strictly Pareto improving, it will be carried unanimously, as in the case of identical individuals.

The conclusion is that the Goulder concept is of only limited practical relevance for policy advice in the sense that it helps to overcome information hurdles, and this despite being very restrictive in the sense that a double dividend is not very likely to occur.

Fiscally optimized tax system

In a setting which is not first-best from a fiscal point of view, the analysis is always restricted to a subset of policy instruments. To begin with an abstraction from environmental concerns: the notion 'second-best' describes an optimal situation where only the first-best instrument with respect to revenue-raising is not available. In this setting, a rise in the environmental tax cannot contribute to the efficiency of the tax system from a fiscal point of view (i.e. environmental quality is assumed to be constant). Starting the analysis of a marginal green tax reform from an optimized tax system is analogous to analysing the effects of a marginal increase in the environmental tax with respect to just one other distortionary tax. Furthermore, if the environmental tax is available and already in place in the initial equilibrium, a fiscally optimized tax system implies that the MCF are equalized across all tax sources – also that of the environmental tax. Referring back to Schöb's decomposition of the overall welfare effect in direct and indirect effects according to presentation (4.93) shows that in this case no welfare gains with respect to fiscal efficiency can be realized from pollution taxes substituting for other taxes. Now a tax system will be called third-best which is optimized subject to the limited set of instruments but which is not appropriate to achieve a second-best or a first-best allocation. The possibility of fiscal efficiency gains emerging from an environmental tax reform arises if in the initial tax system the environmental tax rate is exogenously fixed at a fiscally suboptimal level.[19] In this case tax sources differ with respect to their MCF. Therefore, Bovenberg and de Mooij's claim that pollution taxes raise the overall tax burden (i.e. the reduction in after-tax private incomes associated with a given level of public revenues) if the existing tax structure is aimed at revenue-raising rather than at environmental protection (i.e. the tax system is optimal from a fiscal point of view) has to be modified: it is only true for the case that the pollution tax is above its fiscally optimal level in the initial equilibrium (i.e. $\mathrm{MCF}_\tau > \mathrm{MCF}_t$ in (4.93)).

---

[19]See also Schöb (1997, p. 175). Bovenberg and de Mooij (1996, p. 5), likewise call this scenario 'third-best'.

If the total differential of subequation (4.2c) is considered

$$dB = m \cdot dt + \varepsilon \cdot d\tau + \tau \cdot d\varepsilon \overset{!}{=} 0 \quad \text{with} \quad dm = 0$$

$$\Longleftrightarrow \qquad -\frac{m \cdot dt + \varepsilon \cdot d\tau}{d\tau} = \frac{\tau \cdot d\varepsilon}{d\tau} \tag{4.102}$$

it can be seen that even in the case when the tariff is a first-best instrument, since $dm = 0$ and spill-over effects are hence absent, the fiscal dividend in Goulder's definition – reflected by the LHS of equation (4.102) as can be seen from equation (4.81) – may become positive. This peculiar case occurs if the green tax reform leads to a further deterioration of the environment, i.e. $d\varepsilon/d\tau > 0$. This is confirmed by Table 4.1 where it is shown that $d\varepsilon/d\tau > 0$ is not compatible with a double dividend, but is so with a positive second dividend. This means that in this case the initial tax system is not optimized from a public finance point of view because of too low a level of the environmental tax rate – even though it substitutes for a lump-sum tax.

After this discussion it can finally be stated that a necessary (but not sufficient) condition for a double dividend according to the Goulder concept to occur is that the initial tax system is suboptimal from the environmental as well as from the fiscal point of view. Fiscal suboptimality can also exist in a fiscally optimized tax system if tax bases have been left unexploited in the initial equilibrium due to a lack of instruments. A trivial scenario would be a situation where the initial tax system is optimized not only with respect to fund-raising but also concerning the internalization of environmental externality generation but where no environmental tax is available to the government. This would mean that the other optimal tax rates would incorporate their general equilibrium impact on the environmental situation in order indirectly to internalize the externality – an issue that will be dealt with in greater depth in Chapter 5. In this case a double dividend in Goulder's strong form can be expected since the environmental situation would probably improve if the most appropriate tax instrument could be applied.[20] The government would get an additional tax instrument to use which is equivalent to one restriction less. The efficiency of the tax system could also be increased from a fiscal point of view.

---

[20] According to the targeting principle.

4.4.2   The Pearce Concept

The next step will be to draw attention to the other double-dividend concept which – as already mentioned in the introduction to this chapter – is being frequently applied but which has not been formalized so far. In order to apply the Pearce concept to the model (in analogy to the Goulder concept above), (4.81) is slightly reformulated to

$$
\frac{\partial e}{\partial u}\frac{du}{d\tau} = -\left(\frac{\partial e}{\partial \varepsilon} - \tau\right)\frac{d\varepsilon}{d\tau} - \left(\tau\frac{d\varepsilon}{d\tau} + m\frac{dt}{d\tau} + \varepsilon\right)
$$

$$
= -\underbrace{\left(\frac{\partial e}{\partial \varepsilon} - \tau\right)\frac{d\varepsilon}{d\tau}}_{\text{1st dividend}} + \underbrace{t\frac{dm}{d\tau}}_{\text{2nd dividend}} \tag{4.103}
$$

which renders a criterion for a double dividend that concentrates on the differences emerging from the transition of the analysis from a first-best framework to a second-best setting. The concept does justice to the development of the discussion concerning the double-dividend characteristic of an ecological tax reform. The first dividend confronts marginal changes in utility with the marginal direct cost of abatement connected with the change in environmental quality $d\varepsilon/d\tau$. The latter is adapted to the second-best setting by incorporating all general equilibrium effects. Effect $(\tau \cdot d\varepsilon/d\tau)$ as stated before can alternatively be interpreted as the general equilibrium effect of an ecological tax reform on pollution tax income because of changes in its tax base; in accordance with the literature this is called the tax base erosion effect. As already shown, the erosion effect of the pollution tax on its own tax base is also present in the first-best setting. The effect of the tariff change on the pollution tax base is, strictly speaking, a tax interaction effect rather than a tax base erosion effect. This interpretation, however, would complicate the terminology significantly. The second dividend exists if the last term in (4.103) is positive. It consists of the general equilibrium effects of the environmental tax reform on the tariff base. This tax interaction effect, according to the first line in presentation (4.103), consists of the revenue-recycling effect $(-m \cdot dt/d\tau)$, the tax rate effect or tax-withdrawing effect of the pollution tax $(-\varepsilon)$, and the negative of the tax base erosion effect $(-\tau \cdot d\varepsilon/d\tau)$. The decomposition of the overall welfare effect of an ecological tax reform into these two dividends allows a clearcut application of the terms 'tax base erosion effect' and 'tax interaction effect'. The first dividend consists of the environmental effect and the tax base erosion effect, both referring to general equilibrium adaptations of the pollution tax base; the second reflects the tax interaction effect. The revenue-recycling effect is given implicitly as a component of the tax interaction effect.[21]

Different from the Goulder concept, the Pearce concept relies on the understanding that in the first-best setting analysed in subsection 4.3.8 the marginal utility gain from an improved environment is compared to the direct cost of internalization (DCI) and not to the change in the marginal cost of funds (MCF) – which, as already seen, are identical in a first-best setting. According to the analysis in the first-best setting, therefore, DCI is defined as that part of the MCF which is directly attributable to the internalization and which is reflected by the foregone pollution tax revenues due to the erosion of its tax base. The erosion effect again is related to actual marginal tax revenues from the respective tax instruments.

Tariff

To derive the DCI for the tariff, the system of equilibrium conditions (4.2) will be considered for the case of an incremental tax reform (i.e. the public budget B is endogenous) where the pollution tax τ is constant. Using multiplier (4.85), the definition used is

$$\text{DCI}_t \stackrel{\text{def}}{=} -\tau \cdot \frac{d\varepsilon}{dt}\bigg|_{\tau} \cdot \frac{1}{\dfrac{dB}{dt}} = \tau \cdot \frac{\dfrac{\partial^2 r}{\partial \varepsilon\, \partial(p_1 + t)}}{\dfrac{\partial^2 r}{\partial \varepsilon^2}} \cdot \frac{1}{\dfrac{dB}{dt}} \qquad (4.104)$$

---

[21]Parry (1995) uses a somewhat different terminology. The counterpart to the above revenue-recycling effect is his *revenue effect (RE)* which is defined in a slightly different manner since 'it refers to the welfare gain from using environmental tax revenues to cut distortionary taxes, relative to the case where revenues are returned lump-sum' (Parry 1995, p. S-64). This definition is identical to Goulder's definition of the double dividend in the weak form. Parry's tax interaction effect is named *interdependency effect (IE)*.

where the environmental effect is weighted with the negative of the marginal product of pollution in production or equivalently the pollution tax rate τ. dB/dt is multiplier (4.16).

Environmental tax

For the DCI of the environmental tax, system (4.2) is considered for the case of an incremental green tax reform (i.e. B is endogenous) where now tariff t is constant. With the help of multiplier (4.64) it is defined as

$$\text{DCI}_\tau \overset{\text{def}}{=} -\tau \cdot \left.\frac{d\varepsilon}{d\tau}\right|_{\bar{t}} \cdot \frac{1}{\dfrac{dB}{d\tau}} = -\tau \cdot \frac{1}{\dfrac{\partial^2 r}{\partial \varepsilon^2}} \cdot \frac{1}{\dfrac{dB}{d\tau}} \tag{4.105}$$

where $dB/d\tau$ is known from multiplier (4.22).

The net marginal cost of funds (NMCF) of the respective tax instruments, then, is the difference between their MCF already derived in (4.84) and (4.87) and their DCI

$$\text{NMCF}_t \overset{\text{def}}{=} \text{MCF}_t - \text{DCI}_t = \frac{m \dfrac{\partial^2 r}{\partial \varepsilon^2} - \tau \dfrac{\partial^2 r}{\partial \varepsilon \, \partial (p_1 + t)}}{\dfrac{\partial^2 r}{\partial \varepsilon^2}} \cdot \frac{1}{\dfrac{dB}{dt}}$$

$$= \left.\frac{dB}{dt}\right|_{\overline{m}} \cdot \frac{1}{\dfrac{dB}{dt}} \tag{4.106}$$

$$\text{NMCF}_\tau \overset{\text{def}}{=} \text{MCF}_\tau - \text{DCI}_\tau = \frac{\tau + \varepsilon \dfrac{\partial^2 r}{\partial \varepsilon^2}}{\dfrac{\partial^2 r}{\partial \varepsilon^2}} \cdot \frac{1}{\dfrac{dB}{d\tau}} = \left.\frac{dB}{d\tau}\right|_{\overline{m}} \cdot \frac{1}{\dfrac{dB}{d\tau}} \tag{4.107}$$

On the RHS of (4.106) and (4.107) we made use of two multipliers $dB/dt|_{\overline{m}}$ and $dB/d\tau|_{\overline{m}}$ that can be determined from a system where imports m are constant, the public budget B is free to adapt, and the tariff t and the pollution tax τ, respectively, are exogenously altered

$$
\begin{bmatrix}
1 & \dfrac{\partial e}{\partial \varepsilon} & 0 \\[2mm]
0 & \dfrac{\partial^2 r}{\partial \varepsilon^2} & 0 \\[2mm]
0 & \tau & -1
\end{bmatrix}
\begin{bmatrix}
\dfrac{\partial e}{\partial u} \cdot du \\[2mm]
d\varepsilon \\[2mm]
dB
\end{bmatrix}
= -
\begin{bmatrix}
m \cdot dt + \varepsilon \cdot d\tau \\[2mm]
\dfrac{\partial^2 r}{\partial \varepsilon \, \partial (p_1 + t)} \cdot dt - d\tau \\[2mm]
m \cdot dt + \varepsilon \cdot d\tau
\end{bmatrix}
$$

$$(4.108)$$

Both multipliers will be needed for the discussion in the remainder of this section.

According to the first-best case, where the shadow price of the environment, weighted with the improvement in environmental quality, is opposed to DCI, with the help of definitions (4.86) and (4.65) the net marginal environmental impact (NMEI) of either tax instrument is defined as

$$
\text{NMEI}_t \overset{\text{def}}{=} \text{MEI}_t - \text{DCI}_t = \left(\frac{\partial e}{\partial \varepsilon} - \tau \right) \cdot \frac{\dfrac{\partial^2 r}{\partial \varepsilon \, \partial (p_1 + t)}}{\dfrac{\partial^2 r}{\partial \varepsilon^2}} \cdot \frac{1}{\dfrac{dB}{dt}} \qquad (4.109)
$$

$$
\text{NMEI}_\tau \overset{\text{def}}{=} \text{MEI}_\tau - \text{DCI}_\tau = - \left(\frac{\partial e}{\partial \varepsilon} - \tau \right) \cdot \frac{1}{\dfrac{\partial^2 r}{\partial \varepsilon^2}} \cdot \frac{1}{\dfrac{dB}{d\tau}} \qquad (4.110)
$$

In analogy with Schöb's decomposition, the result for the change in the marginal social cost of funds is

$$
\text{MSCF}_t - \text{MSCF}_\tau = (\text{NMEI}_\tau - \text{NMEI}_t) + (\text{NMCF}_t - \text{NMCF}_\tau)
$$

where

$$
(\text{NMEI}_\tau - \text{NMEI}_t) = \frac{-1}{\dfrac{dB}{d\tau}} \left(\left(\frac{\partial e}{\partial \varepsilon} - \tau \right) \left(- \frac{\dfrac{\partial^2 r}{\partial \varepsilon \, \partial (p_1 + t)}}{\dfrac{\partial^2 r}{\partial \varepsilon^2}} \cdot \frac{dt}{d\tau} + \frac{1}{\dfrac{\partial^2 r}{\partial \varepsilon^2}} \right) \right)
$$

$$
= \frac{-1}{\dfrac{dB}{d\tau}} \left(\frac{\partial e}{\partial \varepsilon} - \tau \right) \frac{d\varepsilon}{d\tau} \qquad (4.111)
$$

with $d\varepsilon/d\tau$ as multiplier (4.31), and

$$(\text{NMCF}_t - \text{NMCF}_\tau) = \frac{-1}{\dfrac{dB}{d\tau}} \left(\frac{\tau + \varepsilon \dfrac{\partial^2 r}{\partial \varepsilon^2}}{\dfrac{\partial^2 r}{\partial \varepsilon^2}} + \frac{m \dfrac{\partial^2 r}{\partial \varepsilon^2} - \tau \dfrac{\partial^2 r}{\partial \varepsilon \, \partial (p_1 + t)} \dfrac{dt}{d\tau}}{\dfrac{\partial^2 r}{\partial \varepsilon^2}} \right)$$

$$= \frac{1}{\dfrac{dB}{d\tau}} \cdot t \cdot \frac{dm}{d\tau} \qquad\qquad (4.112)$$

with $dm/d\tau$ as multiplier (4.32). This leads to

$$\text{MSCF}_t - \text{MSCF}_\tau = \frac{\partial e}{\partial u} \frac{du}{d\tau} \cdot \frac{1}{\dfrac{dB}{d\tau}} \qquad\qquad (4.113)$$

As long as the environmental tax is on the increasing branch of the Laffer curve (i.e. $dB/d\tau > 0$), equation (4.113) shows that

$$\frac{\partial e}{\partial u} \frac{du}{d\tau} \left\{ \begin{matrix} > \\ = \\ < \end{matrix} \right\} 0$$

$$\Longleftrightarrow \quad (\text{NMEI}_\tau - \text{NMEI}_t) + (\text{NMCF}_t - \text{NMCF}_\tau) \left\{ \begin{matrix} > \\ = \\ < \end{matrix} \right\} 0$$

$$\Longleftrightarrow \quad \Big[(\text{MEI}_\tau - \text{MEI}_t) - (\text{DCI}_\tau - \text{DCI}_t) \Big]$$

$$+ \Big[(\text{MCF}_t - \text{MCF}_\tau) - (\text{DCI}_t - \text{DCI}_\tau) \Big] \left\{ \begin{matrix} > \\ = \\ < \end{matrix} \right\} 0 \qquad (4.114)$$

where the effects are rearranged according to the decomposition of the dividends in equation (4.103): the first term in square brackets is proportional to the first dividend and consists of the difference in *net* marginal impacts on the environment of the increase in the green tax τ and the induced change in the tariff t, respectively, and net DCI. The second square bracketed term is proportional to the second dividend and reflects the change in the marginal cost of funds arising from changes in both taxes *net* of the DCI of either tax instrument. Equation (4.112) in conjunction with equation (4.103) shows that this term is proportional to the tax interaction effect $(t \cdot dm/d\tau)$. As can be seen from equation (4.113), the proportionality factor for both bracketed terms again is the inverse of multiplier $dB/d\tau$. A double dividend in this definition accrues if both square bracketed terms in (4.114) are positive.

Condition for negative first dividend

The condition for a negative environmental dividend as defined in this concept is mainly the same as for condition (4.99), which was derived for the Goulder concept. But since now the DCI is incorporated in the dividend, there are four necessary and sufficient conditions for its negative sign

$$\frac{\eta_{(B,\tau)}}{\eta_{(B,t)}} > -\frac{\beta}{\alpha} \cdot \frac{m}{x_1} \cdot \frac{1}{\eta_{(x_1,\varepsilon)}} \quad \text{for} \quad \frac{\partial^2 r}{\partial \varepsilon \, \partial(p_1+t)} \lessgtr 0 \quad \text{and} \quad \frac{\partial e}{\partial \varepsilon} \gtrless \tau$$

or

$$\frac{\eta_{(B,\tau)}}{\eta_{(B,t)}} < -\frac{\beta}{\alpha} \cdot \frac{m}{x_1} \cdot \frac{1}{\eta_{(x_1,\varepsilon)}} \quad \text{for} \quad \frac{\partial^2 r}{\partial \varepsilon \, \partial(p_1+t)} \gtrless 0 \quad \text{and} \quad \frac{\partial e}{\partial \varepsilon} \gtrless \tau$$

respectively, from which follows that $dB/d\tau$ is not restricted in sign. The difference from condition (4.99) is that now it matters whether the environmental tax in the initial equilibrium is below or above the marginal environmental damage. As long as the tax rate lies below marginal environmental damage, the above conditions do not deviate from those in (4.99).

Condition for positive second dividend

Inserting expressions (4.106) and (4.107) into the second bracketed term in presentation (4.114) leads to

$$(\text{NMCF}_t - \text{NMCF}_\tau) \cdot \frac{dB}{d\tau} \overset{!}{>} 0 \iff \frac{\frac{dB}{d\tau}}{\frac{dB}{dt}} \overset{!}{>} \frac{\frac{dB}{d\tau}\big|_{\overline{m}}}{\frac{dB}{dt}\big|_{\overline{m}}} \tag{4.115}$$

and since it is the effect on the tariff base that makes the difference between the LHS and the RHS, the condition can be translated into

$$\implies \quad t\frac{dm}{d\tau}\Big|_{\bar{t}} \overset{!}{>} t\frac{dm}{dt}\Big|_{\bar{\tau}} \tag{4.116}$$

A necessary and sufficient condition for a positive second dividend is that the marginal impact of the pollution tax on the tariff base has to be larger than that of the tariff itself. Since the effect of a tariff reduction on its own base is *ceteris paribus* positive, the condition demands that the effect of the rise in the pollution tax on the tariff base be positive or at least smaller in absolute terms than that of the tariff itself. This makes clear that in the model of, for example, Bovenberg and de Mooij (1994a) – already discussed in Chapter 3, p. 40 – there exists no positive second dividend even if the relatively weak Pearce concept was applied.[22] Due to the weak separability between environment and consumption of the private and the public good in the utility function, the explicit tax on labour (in their model identical with a uniform tax on consumption goods) charges the factor labour more efficiently – from a public finance point of view – than the discriminating pollution tax. This means that the erosion of the labour tax base in reaction to a tax increase is larger for the environmental tax than for the labour tax. This result changes if the separability assumption were given up so that it is not a uniform labour tax that charges labour most efficiently but a discriminating consumption tax that takes account of the substitution elasticity between private consumption and leisure.

Using an alternative approach to deriving necessary and sufficient conditions for a positive second dividend, according to the presentation of the concept in multiplier (4.103) the result is

$$-\left(\tau\frac{d\varepsilon}{d\tau} + m\frac{dt}{d\tau} + \varepsilon\right) \overset{!}{>} 0$$

Substituting $dt/d\tau$ by expression (4.91) and writing in elasticity notation, the final outcome is

$$\frac{\eta_{(B,\tau)}}{\eta_{(B,t)}} \overset{!}{>} \frac{\beta}{\alpha} \cdot \left(1 + \eta_{(\varepsilon,\tau)}\right) \tag{4.117}$$

This condition facilitates a comparison with the one derived in (4.95) for the Goulder concept. It is evident that condition (4.117) is less strict in

---

[22]Goulder et al. (1997), who use this concept in a model very similar to that of Bovenberg and de Mooij, indeed derive the result that the second dividend is negative (p. 7).

the case where the effect on the environment is positive (i.e. $\eta_{(\varepsilon,\tau)} < 0$). The negative correlation of condition (4.117) with the environmental impact of the tax reform increases the possibility of a positive second and a negative first dividend.

The necessary and sufficient conditions for the possible constellations with respect to the sign of both dividends are summarized in Table 4.2. Lines (iii) and (ix) show the conditions for those cases where the envi-

Table 4.2: Necessary and sufficient conditions for the Pearce concept

No.	Condition	D_1^a	D_2	$r_{\varepsilon p}^b$	$\frac{d\varepsilon}{d\tau}$	$\frac{dB}{d\tau}$	$\frac{\partial e}{\partial \varepsilon} - \tau$
(i)		−	+	−	+	+	+
(ii)	$\frac{\eta_{(B,\tau)}}{\eta_{(B,t)}} > \max\left[\Xi^c; \Upsilon^d\right]$	+	+	−	+	+	−
(iii)		+	+	+	−		+
(iv)		−	+	+	−		−
(v)		+	−	−	−		+
(vi)	$\frac{\eta_{(B,\tau)}}{\eta_{(B,t)}} < \min\left[\Xi; \Upsilon\right]$	−	−	−	−		−
(vii)		−	−	+	+	−	+
(viii)		+	−	+	+	−	−
(ix)	$\Xi < \frac{\eta_{(B,\tau)}}{\eta_{(B,t)}} < \Upsilon$	+	+	−	−		+
(x)		−	+	−	−		−
(xi)		−	−	−	+	+	+
(xii)	$\Upsilon < \frac{\eta_{(B,\tau)}}{\eta_{(B,t)}} < \Xi$	+	−	−	+	+	−
(xiii)		+	−	+	−		+
(xiv)		−	−	+	−		−

[a]D_i, $i = 1, 2$, stands for the first and second dividend, respectively.
[b]$r_{\varepsilon p}$ stands for $\partial^2 r / (\partial \varepsilon \, \partial(p_1 + t))$.
[c]With $\Xi \equiv (\beta/\alpha)\left(1 + \eta_{(\varepsilon,\tau)}\right)$.
[d]With $\Upsilon \equiv -(\beta/\alpha) \cdot (m/x_1) \cdot (1/\eta_{(x_1,\varepsilon)})$.

ronmental tax reform leads to a double dividend in the definition of the Pearce concept and where additionally the pollution tax rate in the initial equilibrium is below the shadow price of the environment, i.e. marginal environmental damage. The case in line (ii) is in a way obscure since in this scenario an environmental tax reform would yield a double dividend, although environmental quality is worsened. This of course can only happen if the pollution tax rate in the initial equilibrium lies above marginal environmental damage. Furthermore, it can be realized that $dB/d\tau < 0$ is also compatible with a positive sign of the second dividend – a difference from the Goulder concept. The first dividend can likewise become positive and negative for $dB/d\tau < 0$. If conditions in lines (vi), (vii), (xi) and (xiv) in conjunction with all other equilibrium conditions hold, the environmental tax reform is undoubtedly welfare-decreasing. Since a green tax reform is usually justified on ecological grounds, the cases where the pollution tax rate lies above marginal environmental damage in the initial equilibrium (i.e. $(\partial e/\partial\varepsilon - \tau) < 0$) can be regarded as less relevant.

Measurability

In analogy to the analysis of the Goulder concept we shall now evaluate whether the Pearce concept is of more than only theoretical interest. Distinct from Goulder's concept, it interprets the welfare multiplier for a green tax reform in a first-best setting, which was analysed as a benchmark in subsection 4.3.8, as a balance of marginal environmental damage and DCI, the latter being reflected by the loss in pollution tax proceeds due to the erosion of its tax base. Therefore, in Goulder's definition, the DCI is part of the MCF in the fiscal dividend. It may be recalled that Goulder's motivation for his concept was that policy-makers should rely exclusively on the cost side of the environmental tax reform and an evaluation of the changes in utility from the improvement in the environmental situation would no longer be necessary. It has been shown that this is not true if one abstracts from the rather special model assumptions underlying the analysis within this chapter, and assumes that individuals are not identical. This difficulty of course exists for any cost–benefit analysis. The point, however, is that the potential of the Goulder concept to alleviate policy decision-making – a characteristic which Goulder stresses very intensively – is considerably restricted. Furthermore, if individuals are identical, the difficulty exists that the environmental, first dividend may become negative in a second-best framework.[23]

---

[23] It has of course also been stated that this problem is of limited relevance since the evaluation of the cost side is also based on information on the change in the

But how does the Pearce concept perform if there is no full information available to the government? Equivalent to the Goulder concept, the second dividend consisting of the tax interaction effect $(t \cdot dm/d\tau)$ can be determined by estimating the system of demand functions. This also applies to the DCI, i.e. expression $(\tau \cdot d\varepsilon/d\tau)$ being part of the first dividend in equation (4.103). But since this DCI is opposed to marginal environmental damage which is uncertain, more information is needed in order to determine the sign of the first dividend. Suppose the benevolent government guarantees a positive second dividend according to the Pearce concept as well as a positive effect of the tax reform on the environmental situation (i.e. $d\varepsilon/d\tau < 0$), and suppose furthermore a setting with many individuals who are completely identical. If, as in the model, pollution tax payments are levied on the production side, individuals perceive a loss in production due to the higher price of the environmental resource as a loss in pollution tax income. The individual marginal willingness to pay for the environment is therefore compared to the loss in tax income attributable to each individual, which is equivalent to the case of a pollution tax on the consumer side. Putting the question to a vote as to whether the first dividend is positive will be answered in the affirmative if marginal environmental damage is greater than DCI, i.e. if $(\partial e/\partial \varepsilon > \tau)$. This means that the decision of the individual is based on the same marginal calculation as that of a benevolent central planner. A voting mechanism according to the majority rule would therefore be sufficient for approaching the Pareto-optimal allocation, i.e. it leads to a unanimously supported decision which directs reforms to the second-best optimum and is appropriate for informing the government about the sign of the first dividend. The prisoner's dilemma characteristic of a situation with externalities where negotiations, according to Coase, are not possible can hence be overcome by regulative intervention by the state by means of a voting mechanism. In the case of incomplete information and identical individuals, the government can also determine the sign of both dividends if it relies on the Pearce concept, which is by far less re-

---

environmental situation which is tantamount to an alteration of the pollution tax base. An improvement in the environmental situation can therefore be determined without additional information requirements other than those needed for evaluating the fiscal dividend.

strictive than the one formulated by Goulder. Thus the Pearce concept would dominate the Goulder concept with respect to practicability, at least as long as a decision by vote is costless.

But to go even further, the question whether or not to marginally raise the pollution tax rate will be answered in the affirmative if the tax reform as a whole is welfare-increasing. An isolated vote on only one issue, such as the first dividend, will not be possible since individuals take into consideration all effects on their utility induced by the tax reform. This means that they will weigh the possibly opposite signs of both dividends against each other in order to vote for a reform that is welfare-enhancing. Individual calculation again is the same as that of a benevolent central planner. This of course means that there is no real information hurdle where individuals are all the same. Splitting up the global welfare effect into different dividends, then, is of only theoretical interest and cannot be motivated by practicability aspects. This statement applies to both concepts.

If individuals are not completely identical but differ with respect to their preferences or their factor incomes, the voting process will no longer necessarily approach the second-best optimal allocation since there will be losers and winners in a marginal pollution tax reform. In this case the Pearce concept – similar to the Goulder concept – is not appropriate to provide a guide for policy-makers.

4.5   SECOND-BEST OPTIMAL POLLUTION TAX

Referring to the decomposition of the overall welfare effect according to the Pearce concept, the first-order conditions for a second-best optimal pollution tax will now be derived. For multiplier (4.103) equal to zero and isolating τ the result is

$$\frac{\partial e}{\partial u}\frac{du}{d\tau} \overset{!}{=} 0 \quad \Longrightarrow \quad \tau^* = \frac{\partial e}{\partial \varepsilon} - t\frac{\frac{dm}{d\tau}}{\frac{d\varepsilon}{d\tau}} \qquad (4.118)$$

Written in elasticity notation this leads to

$$\tau^* \cdot \left(1 + \frac{\alpha}{\beta} \cdot \eta_{(m,\varepsilon)}\right) = \frac{\partial e}{\partial \varepsilon} \qquad (4.119)$$

It can be seen very clearly that asking for the second-best optimal pollution tax level relative to the Pigou level is implicitly connected with an application of the Pearce concept. This means that the discussion whether or not the optimal environmental tax lies below or above marginal environmental damage (see, for example, Bovenberg and de Mooij 1994a or even Goulder 1995) is implicitly based on the application of the Pearce concept.[24] If the proceeds of the environmental tax are sufficient for balancing the public budget (i.e. $t = 0$ on the RHS of (4.118)) or if the tariff is a lump-sum tax, i.e. $dm/d\tau = \eta_{(m,\varepsilon)} = 0$, the analysis takes place in a first-best setting and the optimal environmental tax is the Pigou tax (i.e. $\tau^* = \partial e/\partial \varepsilon$). It can further be stated that *ceteris paribus* the deviation of the second-best optimal environmental tax from the shadow price of the environment $\partial e/\partial \varepsilon$ is the larger

- the larger the share of tariff income in total tax income or
- the larger the tax base elasticity of the tax which is substituted for the pollution tax compared to that of the environmental tax in reaction to a rise in the pollution tax rate.

A *ceteris paribus* high elasticity of the environmental tax base indicates that the internalization of the externality is connected with relatively low costs, whereas a high elasticity of the other tax base with respect to pollution tax changes indicates considerable spill-over effects caused by the pollution tax which – if positive – lower internalization costs or vice versa. In the Bovenberg case (for example, Bovenberg and de Mooij 1994a)

---

[24]Indeed, this statement made earlier by Killinger (1997) has been confirmed in the meantime: Bovenberg and van Hagen (1999) came up with an equivalent decomposition of the total welfare effect and conclude that they 'believe this second term in [equation] (12) [identical to the second dividend in decomposition (4.103)] is the most natural way to define the second dividend because it represents the impact of an environmental tax reform on non-environmental distortions' (p. 37). Contrasting this statement with the Bovenberg citations listed on p. 80 as examples of the application of the Goulder concept reveals that not only Goulder but also Bovenberg makes the confusing implicit switch from one double-dividend concept to the other.

where the green tax reform leads not only to a diminution in pollution but also in the base of the other tax (i.e. the second dividend according to the Pearce concept is negative), it becomes obvious that the optimal environmental tax is lower than the marginal environmental damage due to $\eta_{(m,\varepsilon)} > 0$.[25] If however only pollution diminishes in the course of an environmental tax reform, but the tax base of the other tax expands ($\eta_{(m,\varepsilon)} < 0$), there is a double dividend according to the Pearce concept, and the second-best optimal environmental tax lies above the marginal environmental damage. It should be added that in this case the fiscal dividend according to the Goulder concept does not necessarily have to be positive, too. This hinges crucially on the direct cost of internalization (DCI) caused by either tax. If the second dividend according to the Pearce concept is positive (i.e. $dm/d\tau > 0$), but the environmental one is negative ($d\varepsilon/d\tau > 0$) so that $\eta_{(m,\varepsilon)} > 0$, the second-best optimal environmental tax lies below the marginal environmental damage due to its negative general equilibrium impact on the environment.

In order to facilitate a comparison between Bovenberg and de Mooij's presentation of the optimal tax condition (for example, Bovenberg and de Mooij 1996, p. 13, eq. (3.2)) and the above result, condition (4.119) is reformulated by making use of the 'marginal cost of funds' concept defined in (4.84) and (4.87), respectively. Again written in elasticity notation, it follows that

$$\tau^* \cdot \left(1 + \frac{\text{MCF}_t}{\text{MCF}_\tau} \cdot \frac{\eta_{(B,t)}}{\eta_{(B,\tau)}} \cdot \eta_{(m,\varepsilon)} \right) = \frac{\partial e}{\partial \varepsilon} \qquad (4.120)$$

It can be seen that, different from their result, condition (4.120) depends on the ratio of the MCF of either tax instrument and not solely on the absolute value of the MCF of the tax that is being substituted. The higher, *ceteris paribus*, the MCF of the tariff, the larger the deviation of the optimal pollution tax from marginal environmental damage. High MCF of the pollution tax, however, corresponds to low internalization cost and hence calls for an internalization strategy similar to that in a first-best setting. The condition for the optimal pollution tax is also

---

[25] In their model the environmental tax reform leads to a decrease in labour supply since the implicit (green) tax on labour is a less efficient device for taxing labour than the explicit labour tax.

influenced by the ratio of tax revenue elasticities. A high elasticity of tax revenues of the pollution tax *ceteris paribus* calls for an optimal tax level close to the marginal environmental damage, whereas a high revenue elasticity of the tariff is in favour of a larger deviation from the marginal environmental damage. The ratio hence reflects the relative importance of either tax instrument for revenue-raising purposes.

In contrast to the comments found in the literature, there is no compelling interdependence between the existence of a double dividend and the level of the second-best optimal pollution tax with respect to marginal environmental damage.[26] This is because both double-dividend concepts are focused on the evaluation of marginal policy reforms. Even if a double dividend could be raised in some particular cases by starting the reform from an appropriate initial pollution tax level, it may well be that the optimal tax level is below the marginal environmental damage. What can be said is that, if an environmental tax reform starting from an initial pollution tax level that exactly corresponds to the marginal environmental damage – i.e. the first dividend according to the Pearce concept would be zero – raises a double dividend in Goulder's definition, the second-best optimal tax level will definitely lie above the marginal environmental damage. But even if his double-dividend hypothesis fails, the second-best optimal pollution tax level can still lie above marginal environmental damage. This is due to the fact that the gross cost of the tax reform may be positive, but still lower in absolute figures than the

---

[26]See for respective statements Goulder (1995, p. 176), or Schöb (1997, p. 167). Bovenberg and his co-authors in numerous analyses (e.g. Bovenberg and de Mooij 1994a,c) likewise acknowledge the double-dividend characteristic of an environmental tax reform if the second-best environmental tax is higher than the Pigou level at which the environmental tax exactly balances the marginal environmental damage. Specifically, by assuming an initial level of the environmental tax at the Pigou level, they reject the double-dividend hypothesis if a marginal tax swap of the environmental tax for another, distortionary tax is welfare-improving. In any case, this kind of analysis can be problematic since, different from the first-best setting when functions are probably monotonous, in the second-best framework functions may lose their well-behaved characteristics. It then follows that an arbitrarily chosen Pigou level does not necessarily have to be unique, but that there may exist several points where the environmental tax exactly equals the marginal environmental damage. Using it as a benchmark for assessing ecological tax reforms does not seem to be very sensible.

welfare gain from a cleaner environment. This scenario can be observed in Figure 3.4, p. 39, if at the Pigou level A^P TIE$_3$ are compared to the marginal cost of abatement.

In order to get a better idea of what it really means to have a second-best optimal pollution tax below or above the marginal environmental damage, the analysis should come back to the models of Bovenberg and de Mooij (1994a,c) extensively discussed in section 3.3, p. 40. A fiscally optimal consumption tax in their models is a flat rate across all goods. An environmental tax which is additionally introduced into the system exclusively burdens consumption of the dirty good – on top of the consumption tax. Due to the price increase, demand for the dirty good falls. This effect not only erodes the tax base of the pollution tax, but also that of the consumption tax since distortion of the consumption–leisure decision is further aggravated. This is because the opportunity cost of leisure has decreased and therefore less income is generated for consumption purposes. The first-order condition for the optimal pollution tax accounts for this negative spill-over effect and hence, as a compromise between the Ramsey and the Pigou rules, lies below the marginal environmental damage. But it has to be kept in mind that due to the environmental component the total tax burden on the dirty good in this second-best equilibrium is of course higher than that on the clean good.

4.6 CONCLUDING REMARKS

In this chapter the two most important double-dividend concepts to be found in the literature have been formalized within the same model framework in order to thoroughly analyse and compare them. It has been shown that both concepts refer to the first-best case as a benchmark and that they go back to a different interpretation of it. The Goulder concept interprets the first-best Pigouvian first-order conditions as a comparison between the marginal social utility from improved environment as the environmental dividend and the change in the marginal cost of funds of the ecological and the substituted tax as the fiscal one. This comparison is then applied to the second-best scenario of an ecological tax reform. It is obvious that such a reform can only raise a fiscal dividend if the environmental tax opens a new tax base which has been unexploited before due to, e.g., political restrictions. In this case the environmental tax would also be different from zero in a tax system that is optimized solely from a fiscal point of view. The Pearce concept, however, regards the same first-order Pigou conditions in the first-best setting as a comparison between – once again – the marginal environmental damage and – this time – the direct cost of internalization. In contrast to the Goulder concept, this comparison applied to an ecological tax reform in a second-best setting is defined as the first dividend whereas the additional effects emerging in the second-best world are ascribed to the second dividend which turned out to represent the tax interaction effect.

An important aim of the double-dividend concept is to decompose the overall welfare effect resulting from an ecological tax reform. This is done in order to provide an idea in which additional effects appear that have to be considered if environmental policy is undertaken within a second-best setting where additional distortions exist apart from the environmental one. In this respect the various concepts all have their own legitimacy. They decompose the same overall welfare effect in different ways. Consequently, in the second-best optimum all concepts must have the feature that either both dividends are equal to zero, or one is positive and the other negative, together summing to zero. A double dividend is therefore not a sensible policy goal under full information. Furthermore, it was outlined that the general equilibrium effect on the environment in the course of a revenue-neutral green tax reform in a second-best setting may even be negative.

A feature which has been attributed to the Goulder concept and which is of more practical use is that this concept would help policy-makers decide upon a tax reform where they do not have full information about the social marginal utility with respect to the environment. In the preceding analysis it was shown that the informational requirements for Goulder's concept are in fact not significantly lower than those for the Pearce concept. The possibility of a real no-regret policy in the case of a double dividend is only given against the backdrop of identical individuals. But in this case a vote would even lead to the second-best optimum, so that there is no need for a decomposition of the overall welfare effect into different dividends. If, on the other hand, individuals are not identical, Goulder's concept would not pave the way to a no-regret policy decision. The decisive criticism of his concept is that it does not meet its own high demands to provide a relevant since practicable policy rule with respect to green tax reforms. Additionally, the most probable outcome of a double-dividend scrutiny according to this concept is that the hypothesis fails due to at least one negative dividend and that a tax reform will not be undertaken.

A different argument against Goulder's decomposition is that Ruocco and Wiegard (1997) derive the peculiar result that the fiscal dividend becomes negative even in a setting where a pollution tax and a lump-sum tax simultaneously and optimally substitute for a distortionary tax on labour. The reason is that the negative tax base erosion effect on the tax base of the environmental tax cannot be overcompensated by the efficiency gains arising from the introduction of the lump-sum tax. The fiscal dividend is hence negative even though the system is transformed from a second-best to a first-best setting.

The discussion of the second-best optimal pollution tax level has shown that, in contrast to the results of Bovenberg et al., it is not only the marginal cost of public funds (MCF) of the tax to be replaced that matters, but also that of the pollution tax. Furthermore, it has been argued that there is no tight connection between Goulder's double dividend in the strong form and the level of the second-best optimal pollution tax with respect to the marginal environmental damage.

The conceptual analysis in this chapter provides the double-dividend issue in the context of ecological tax reforms with more clarity. Additionally, it makes possible an evaluation of the central result of the DIW report, namely that the proposed ecological tax reform would have a positive net impact on employment in Germany. Now the other weaknesses of the report must be analysed; *inter alia* it deals insufficiently with the external effects resulting from an ecological tax reform scenario. The next chapter therefore presents additional theoretical work which is needed for an inclusion of such aspects in econometric model analysis.

Chapter 5

Indirect internalization and international capital mobility

5.1 INTRODUCTION

As pointed out in Chapter 3, international environmental externalities are gaining growing attention due to their foreseeable or feared irreversibility. The main characteristic of, for instance, global warming or acid rain is that damages are imposed not only on the country of origin but also across borders. In the absence of a supranational authority with the competence to internalize the externalities efficiently by means of, for example, a Pigou tax, a prisoner's dilemma arises. Rationally acting national governments that wish to maximize utility of their consumers do not take into consideration damages the country imposes on others. Consequently, environmental externalities are generated at a level which is too high under global efficiency considerations. The failure of the European Union to implement a common energy tax in its member states, as was discussed for a long time, as well as the inability of the participating countries to agree on binding and coordinated actions against environmental degradation at the conferences succeeding Rio in Berlin and Kyoto, show that decentralized solutions are moving increasingly into the centre of interest again. The advancing integration of the world economy has directed the public debate as well as economic analysis to additional considerations of how to design national environmental tax policies.[1]

- *The interaction of international trade and the environment*
  Can environmental regulations serve as a substitute for trade policy? Do polluting industries move to areas with low environmental standards? Due to the increasing integration, national internalization instruments lose their first-best feature since environment-depleting industries can circumvent these taxes by leaving the country. As already discussed in Chapter 3, the global character of the externality implies that the environmental situation of an internalizing country does not necessarily improve.[2]
- *The interaction of factor mobility and environmental regulation*
  Does competition for internationally mobile factors lead to a downward regulation of environmental standards?
- *The possibility of indirectly internalizing externalities generated by a foreign country*
  International integration enables a big country as a victim of cross-border externalities to direct a lever towards the foreign externality generation and at least partly to internalize it by manipulating world market prices. In contrast to this, a small country that faces fixed prices on the world market can only internalize domestically generated externalities. Due to higher costs connected with a tighter environmental policy, production will be driven out of the country if other countries do not also implement an environmental policy. If the externality has the characteristic of an international public good (as is the case, for example, for carbon dioxide), environmental quality will not significantly change in the internalizing country, but its income situation will deteriorate due to lower production possibilities.

---

[1]Policy instruments considered in this chapter are restricted to taxes – regulations or emission permit schemes are excluded.

[2]Snape (1992) analyses the characteristics and particularities of international environmental externalities in detail.

In this chapter national gradual environmental tax reforms as well as optimal tax structures are analysed in the presence of cross-border externalities and international capital mobility.[3] The insights gained are then used to evaluate ecological tax reforms in an extended second-best framework. As was outlined in Chapter 3, the double-dividend quality of environmental taxes has so far mainly been analysed for closed economies without international factor mobility. Thus, further illumination is needed in an open economy where environmental damage is caused across national borders, when tax bases can erode due to international factor movements, and when strategic considerations are also relevant.

This chapter is based on Killinger (1996) but elaborates more intensively the double-dividend issues. A two-country model is used, with both countries connected by international capital movements and a cross-border externality. The analysis mainly focuses on welfare effects resulting from unilateral actions, as shown on the right of the right branch of Figure 3.1, p. 18. Aspects of retaliation are neglected by assuming that the countries do not react to the measures undertaken by another. The double-dividend analysis takes place against the background of distorted international allocation of capital through the existence of capital taxes.

When lump-sum taxes are available to the government for financing the budget, both pollution taxes and capital taxes aim at manipulating world market prices and additionally at directly and indirectly internalizing the externality. The targeting of the aims is more effective if both tax instruments are simultaneously implemented. Optimal environmental tax rates as well as optimal capital tax levels tend to be qualitatively higher in the case of joint implementation.[4] If lump-sum taxes are not

---

[3]Rauscher (1997) derives optimal policy reforms in a model with internationally mobile capital. His analysis is based on the standard approach to international factor mobility developed by MacDougall (1960) and Kemp (1964). A survey of this and other approaches to international factor mobility is given by Ruffin (1984). Rauscher's model is extended by an international externality. Oates and Schwab (1988) embed the problem in the local public finance literature. They analyse how jurisdictions within a federal state will optimally set capital taxes as well as environmental standards so as to maximize the utility of the representative consumer.

[4]The term 'qualitatively' indicates that this is not a statement with respect to absolute tax levels but rather that additional marginal effects are included in the

available to the government, conditions for the existence of a double dividend of environmental taxes are derived with reference to the concepts worked out and analysed in Chapter 4. The consideration will cover the case when the distortionary capital tax is cut back by means of the environmental tax proceeds.

The chapter proceeds as follows. In section 5.2 the model, which is an extension of the model used in Chapter 4, will be laid out. Section 5.3 then deals with aspects of gradual and optimal national internalization policies in the case of lump-sum taxes. The results are used as a reference point for section 5.4, where the question of whether a double dividend can be reaped from environmental taxes will be addressed. Section 5.5 concludes.

5.2   THE MODEL

The analysis refers to a two-country model based on Rauscher (1997) with international factor mobility, where country A is the home country and country B is the foreign country. In the following, lower-case letters or superscript A are used for country A, upper-case letters or superscript B for country B. Each economy is endowed with m factors of production. Among these are capital, an environmental resource,[5] and a third one which can be thought of as labour. Factor supplies of capital and labour are assumed to be inelastic. Capital is taken to be internationally mobile, which means that it flows towards the most attractive use across countries and therefore balances differences in the marginal productivity of capital. In the presence of international mobility, national capital supply is endogenous even if international capital supply is fixed. Both countries produce n goods. Without loss of generality, one good is chosen as numéraire, with its price normalized to unity. The production of goods in each country is connected with the generation of a cross-border externality. These national externality productions add up to a global externality level which lowers the utility of individuals in each country.

---

first-order conditions for optimal tax rates.
   [5] For instance clean air or drinking water reservoirs.

5.2.1   Consumer Behaviour

In both countries there is only one representative consumer, so that distributional aspects are ignored. The utility function of the representative individual in country A is $u(\boldsymbol{c}, \varepsilon)$, with $\boldsymbol{c}$ as the consumption vector being a choice variable for the consumer. Pollution ε by contrast takes the form of a public bad, and hence the level of its consumption is beyond the consumer's control. Preferences in the home country may then be represented by the expenditure function

$$e(\boldsymbol{p}, u_0, \varepsilon) = \min_{\boldsymbol{c}} \left\{ \boldsymbol{p}^T \cdot \boldsymbol{c} \ : \ u \geq u_0 \right\}$$

As in Chapter 4, $e(\cdot)$ is increasing in u and ε and is defined as the minimum cost of attaining utility level u_0 given the vector of prices of the consumption goods $\boldsymbol{p}$ and the current pollution level ε. An increase in the level of the pollutant harms the representative consumer and therefore raises the minimum cost of attaining a given utility level. The partial derivative of the expenditure function with respect to the level of pollution ($\partial e / \partial \varepsilon$) is the marginal willingness to pay for reductions in pollution and equals marginal environmental damage. The optimization problem for the household in country B is analogous.

5.2.2   Firm Behaviour

To model the production side of the economy, the aggregate revenue function is used again. Given the price of the consumption good and the level of either pollution taxes or capital taxes to be analysed in the following sections, firms maximize their individual profits. In doing so they collectively maximize GNP at domestic prices, which in this setting are equal to prices in the world market, i.e. $\boldsymbol{p} = \boldsymbol{P}$. The private sector of the economy thus acts as if it solves the problem

$$r(\boldsymbol{p}, \boldsymbol{v}, \varepsilon^A, k) = \max_{\boldsymbol{x}} \left\{ \boldsymbol{p}^T \cdot \boldsymbol{x} \ : \ \boldsymbol{x} \in T^A(\boldsymbol{v}, k, \varepsilon^A) \right\}$$
$$R(\boldsymbol{P}, \boldsymbol{V}, \varepsilon^B, K) = \max_{\boldsymbol{X}} \left\{ \boldsymbol{P}^T \cdot \boldsymbol{X} \ : \ \boldsymbol{X} \in T^B(\boldsymbol{V}, K, \varepsilon^B) \right\}$$

in the home and in the foreign country, respectively. v and V describe
the vectors of factor endowments.[6] The resource inputs ε^A and ε^B used
in country A and in country B, respectively, are defined as the share in
the global resource stock which is used up during the production process. Again, the input of an environmental resource into production can
alternatively be interpreted as emissions resulting from the production
process – the pollution levels of both countries contributing to the global
externality level $\varepsilon = \varepsilon\left(\varepsilon^A, \varepsilon^B\right)$, which is negatively perceived by the individuals.[7] The assumed substitutability of emissions and capital implies
that there is a capital-intensive pollution abatement technology which is
not modelled explicitly. However, the substitutability is restricted to a
certain range only, which implies that the costless factor environmental
resource cannot alone produce consumption goods. The initial capital
endowments in both countries are denoted by k^0 and K^0, respectively,
and the amount of capital exported from country A to country B by ξ.[8]
The amounts of capital k and K used in the production process in each
country consist of the countries' initial endowments with capital k^0 and
K^0, altered by the inflow of foreign capital and the outflow of domestic
capital, respectively

$$k = k^0 \pm \xi$$
$$K = K^0 \mp \xi$$

(5.1)

where the upper signs correspond to the case that country A is a net capital importer, and the lower signs represent the case that country A is a
net capital exporter.[9] T^A and T^B are the technology sets in both coun-
tries, x and X are the vectors of output. Partial derivatives $(\partial r/\partial \varepsilon^A)$
and $(\partial R/\partial \varepsilon^B)$ represent the marginal product of pollution in the production process, which is positive. The production function underlying
the GNP function in both countries is linearly homogeneous, concave,

---

[6]The other factors of production, i.e. capital and environmental resource, are also
made explicit for reasons of clarity.

[7]For example McGuire (1982) and Rauscher (1997) model emissions as an input
into the production process rather than as a joint output.

[8]$-\xi$ indicates exports from B to A.

[9]The notation that the upper line refers to the case of country A as a capital
importer will from now on be generally applied.

and non-decreasing.[10] For solutions to be unique, decreasing returns to scale are needed in the factors capital and environmental resource at the level of the GNP function (as will be seen later). This is achieved by assuming a third factor of production – as already mentioned, labour – to be fixed in supply. The environmental resource is a public domain and therefore, if there is no environmental regulation, it is used up to the point where its marginal product is zero. Since the externality, as in Chapter 4, is assumed to be of an eyesore type, it only enters the utility function and does not generate detrimental effects on the countries' production possibilities. An increase in the level of pollution produced by one firm does not affect the cost to any other firm.

5.2.3   Government Behaviour

The government of each country is assumed to maximize utility of its representative consumer by means of the policy instruments at hand. Its policy is constrained by the need to raise public funds, for example in order to finance the provision of public goods. Again, the provision will not be modelled explicitly so that the budget constraint is assumed to be exogenously fixed at the level B. The budget constraint B has to be financed by the country's tax proceeds it reaps from three different sources

$$B = h + \tau^A \cdot \varepsilon^A + \theta^A \cdot \xi \tag{5.2}$$

where h is a non-distortionary head tax, τ^A a pollution tax and θ^A a tax on repatriated capital rents.[11] The head tax serves to fill the gap between the tax proceeds of the two other tax instruments implemented at their optimal levels and the governmental budgetary needs. This scenario will be used as a benchmark case. Section 5.4 will ignore lump-sum taxes in order to analyse the double-dividend character of environmental taxes. The implementation of tax instruments will only be considered for the home country. In country B tax instruments are available for

---

[10]This means that $\partial^2 r / \left(\partial \varepsilon^A \right)^2 < 0$ and $\partial^2 r / \partial k^2 < 0$. Further, it is assumed that $\partial^2 r / \left(\partial \varepsilon^A \partial k \right) = \partial^2 r / \left(\partial k \partial \varepsilon^A \right) > 0$. For further discussion of the GNP function, see e.g. Cornes (1992) and Dixit and Norman (1980).

[11]The last of the taxes may also be negative, i.e. a subsidy.

neither strategic nor environmental ends. Consequently, the question of retaliation is excluded from the analysis.

The internationally mobile capital provides country A with leverage strategically to influence the factor reward for the capital it lends to or borrows from the rest of the world and to influence the foreign production of cross-border externalities. With its policy tools the government hence pursues three aims in favour of the representative consumer:

- first, influencing the capital rent on the world market through the strategic control of domestic capital supply or demand;
- second, internalizing the domestically produced externalities so as to improve environmental quality;
- third, indirectly internalizing the externalities caused abroad which are also perceived in the home country by manipulating the international allocation of mobile capital.

5.3 INDIRECT INTERNALIZATION AND LUMP-SUM TAXES

In order to keep the analysis tractable and to concentrate exclusively on the specifics of international capital mobility, the following deliberations will ignore changes in good prices. It is assumed that both countries produce only one composite good which is chosen as numéraire, with its price normalized to unity. Trade in the good serves to pay factor rewards to the mobile factor capital. The production of the composite good in each country generates a cross-border externality.[12]

The analysis is now restricted to only three factors of production: capital, the environmental resource, and labour. The last is analytically taken to be hidden, which means that it is not made explicit in the

---

[12] Although private consumption is restricted to only one composite consumption good, the dual approach is useful also to illustrate the effects of environmental degradation which enters the expenditure function of the representative consumer as a quantity constraint. The analysis of 'consumer choice' between the consumption good and environmental quality which will be optimized by the national government is facilitated, and general equilibrium effects on all variables such as for instance the level of pollution can easily be determined.

revenue function.

Considering a standard model of two perfectly competitive open economies which have the market power to influence factor prices on the world markets, the analysis will take the stance of country A and will hence assess its policy measures, whereas country B can be regarded as the rest of the world.

5.3.1   Pollution Taxes

First, the general equilibrium effects of a marginal introduction or rise of a pollution tax in country A will be investigated as the only policy instrument available to the government apart from the head tax. The pollution tax is designed to be levied proportionately on the input of the externality in the production process. Given a pollution tax only in country A, with country A as a net capital importer or exporter, the conditions for an international equilibrium are

$$e(1, u, \varepsilon) = r\left(1, \varepsilon^A, k\right) \mp \xi \cdot \frac{\partial R\left(1, \varepsilon^B, K\right)}{\partial K} - B \qquad (5.3a)$$

$$E(1, U, \varepsilon) = R\left(1, \varepsilon^B, K\right) \pm \xi \cdot \frac{\partial R\left(1, \varepsilon^B, K\right)}{\partial K} \qquad (5.3b)$$

$$\varepsilon = \varepsilon\left(\varepsilon^A, \varepsilon^B\right) \qquad (5.3c)$$

$$\frac{\partial r\left(1, \varepsilon^A, k\right)}{\partial \varepsilon^A} = \tau^A \qquad (5.3d)$$

$$\frac{\partial R\left(1, \varepsilon^B, K\right)}{\partial \varepsilon^B} = 0 \qquad (5.3e)$$

$$\frac{\partial r\left(1, \varepsilon^A, k\right)}{\partial k} = \frac{\partial R\left(1, \varepsilon^B, K\right)}{\partial K} \qquad (5.3f)$$

$$h + \tau^A \cdot \varepsilon^A = B \qquad (5.3g)$$

Subequations (5.3a) and (5.3b) reflect the national income identity for each country with $(\partial R/\partial K) \cdot \xi$ as the factor reward for imported or exported capital, respectively. If country A is a net capital importer, only revenue from domestic production net of after-tax capital reward to the other country and net of public budgetary needs can be used for consumption purposes. (5.3c) illustrates that the aggregate externality level perceived by the representative consumers in both countries consists of the discharge of pollutants arising from production in either country. Conditions (5.3d) and (5.3e) determine the marginal product of the environmental resource in equilibrium. Since the resource (or, in the alternative interpretation, pollution) is not privately owned, it will be used in the production process up to the point where its marginal productivity equals zero (as in condition (5.3e) for country B). Alternatively, in the case where a price is assigned to the resource by means of an environmental tax, its rate constitutes the lower bound of the resource's productivity in production. (5.3f) is an arbitrage condition which indicates that capital is reallocated until its marginal productivity is internationally equalized. (5.3g) reflects that only the head tax and the pollution tax contribute to financing the public budget B. If B is equal to zero, the analysis is analogous to the common assumption of a lump-sum redistribution of Pigou tax receipts. Assume that in the initial equilibrium B is completely financed with the help of head taxes. The marginal introduction of a pollution tax with B remaining unchanged implies that the contribution of the head tax must diminish. The endogenous determination of the head tax also applies to the case where the pollution tax is already in place in the initial equilibrium. Thus, system (5.3) determines $u, U, \xi, \varepsilon, \varepsilon^A, \varepsilon^B$ and h.

For the comparative static analysis, equation system (5.3) is totally differentiated. According to (5.1) the result is

$$\pm \, dk = \mp \, dK = d\xi \tag{5.4}$$

The variable exogenous to the system is country A's pollution tax τ^A. Written in matrix notation

$$D \begin{bmatrix} \partial e/\partial u \cdot du/d\tau^A \\ \partial E/\partial U \cdot dU/d\tau^A \\ d\varepsilon/d\tau^A \\ d\varepsilon^A/d\tau^A \\ d\varepsilon^B/d\tau^A \\ d\xi/d\tau^A \\ dh/d\tau^A \end{bmatrix} = \begin{bmatrix} 0 \\ 0 \\ 0 \\ 1 \\ 0 \\ 0 \\ -\varepsilon^A \end{bmatrix} \tag{5.5}$$

where matrix D is

$$
D \stackrel{\text{def}}{=}
\begin{bmatrix}
1 & 0 & \dfrac{\partial e}{\partial \varepsilon} & -\tau^A & \pm\,\xi\,\dfrac{\partial^2 R}{\partial K \partial \varepsilon^B} & -\xi\,\dfrac{\partial^2 R}{\partial K^2} & 0 \\[2ex]
0 & 1 & \dfrac{\partial E}{\partial \varepsilon} & 0 & \mp\,\xi\,\dfrac{\partial^2 R}{\partial K \partial \varepsilon^B} & \xi\,\dfrac{\partial^2 R}{\partial K^2} & 0 \\[2ex]
0 & 0 & 1 & -\dfrac{\partial \varepsilon}{\partial \varepsilon^A} & -\dfrac{\partial \varepsilon}{\partial \varepsilon^B} & 0 & 0 \\[2ex]
0 & 0 & 0 & \dfrac{\partial^2 r}{\partial (\varepsilon^A)^2} & 0 & \pm\,\dfrac{\partial^2 r}{\partial \varepsilon^A \partial k} & 0 \\[2ex]
0 & 0 & 0 & 0 & \dfrac{\partial^2 R}{\partial (\varepsilon^B)^2} & \mp\,\dfrac{\partial^2 R}{\partial \varepsilon^B \partial K} & 0 \\[2ex]
0 & 0 & 0 & \pm\,\dfrac{\partial^2 r}{\partial k \partial \varepsilon^A} & \mp\,\dfrac{\partial^2 R}{\partial K \partial \varepsilon^B} & \left(\dfrac{\partial^2 r}{\partial k^2}+\dfrac{\partial^2 R}{\partial K^2}\right) & 0 \\[2ex]
0 & 0 & 0 & \tau^A & 0 & 0 & 1
\end{bmatrix}
$$

$$(5.6)$$

with $(\partial r/\partial k - \partial R/\partial K)$ equal to zero according to (5.3f), and $\partial r/\partial \varepsilon^A$ equal to τ^A, the tax on pollution.

To derive the effect of raising the environmental tax on utility in country A, first the sign of the determinant of matrix D has to be determined

$$
|D| = \frac{\partial^2 R}{\partial (\varepsilon^B)^2}\,H^A + \frac{\partial^2 r}{\partial (\varepsilon^A)^2}\,H^B \quad < 0 \tag{5.7}
$$

with

$$
H^A = \frac{\partial^2 r}{\partial (\varepsilon^A)^2}\,\frac{\partial^2 r}{\partial k^2} - \frac{\partial^2 r}{\partial \varepsilon^A \partial k}\,\frac{\partial^2 r}{\partial k \partial \varepsilon^A} > 0 \quad \text{and}
$$

$$
H^B = \frac{\partial^2 R}{\partial (\varepsilon^B)^2}\,\frac{\partial^2 R}{\partial K^2} - \frac{\partial^2 R}{\partial \varepsilon^B \partial K}\,\frac{\partial^2 R}{\partial K \partial \varepsilon^B} > 0 \tag{5.8}
$$

Both terms H^A and H^B reflect the diminishing marginal products of the hidden factor in production of country A and B, respectively.[13] Determi-

---

[13] If capital and the externality were the only factors of production, both terms H^A and H^B would be equal to zero for the revenue function being linearly homogeneous in inputs. Under this assumption a unique solution would not exist, as can be seen from the determinant of matrix D being then equal to zero. For τ^A deviating from zero, all capital would flow out of the country and be invested in country B, and the system would no longer be differentiable.

nant $|D|$ of system (5.5) is the same for both scenarios, with country A importing or exporting capital.

Now the welfare multiplier of a marginal rise in the pollution tax rate is determinable. Its different effects can be isolated and their implications on welfare in the country under consideration can be determined

$$
\frac{\partial e}{\partial u}\frac{du}{d\tau^A} = - \underbrace{\left(\underbrace{\frac{\partial e}{\partial \varepsilon}\frac{\partial \varepsilon}{\partial \varepsilon^A}}_{(1)} - \underbrace{\tau^A}_{(2)} \right)} \frac{1}{\dfrac{\partial^2 r}{\partial (\varepsilon^A)^2}}
$$

$$
+ \frac{1}{|D|} \left(- \underbrace{\left(\underbrace{\frac{\partial e}{\partial \varepsilon}\frac{\partial \varepsilon}{\partial \varepsilon^A}}_{(3)} - \underbrace{\tau^A}_{(5)} \right)} \dfrac{\dfrac{\partial^2 r}{\partial \varepsilon^A \partial k}}{\dfrac{\partial^2 r}{\partial (\varepsilon^A)^2}} \right.
$$

$$
\left. + \underbrace{\left(\underbrace{\frac{\partial e}{\partial \varepsilon}\frac{\partial \varepsilon}{\partial \varepsilon^B}\frac{\partial^2 R}{\partial \varepsilon^B \partial K}}_{(4)} \mp \underbrace{\xi H^B}_{(6)} \right)} \frac{1}{\dfrac{\partial^2 R}{\partial (\varepsilon^B)^2}} \dfrac{\partial^2 r}{\partial k \partial \varepsilon^A} \dfrac{\partial^2 R}{\partial (\varepsilon^B)^2} \right)
$$

$$(5.9)$$

Terms (1) and (2) reflect the direct impact of an environmental tax: since the tax attaches a positive price to the externality, its use in domestic production diminishes. The first term (1) represents a direct positive effect on the domestic environmental situation with regard to domestic externality production. For $\tau^A = \left(\partial r / \partial \varepsilon^A \right)$ being positive, term (2) reflects the loss in domestic production which results from the positive price now being attached to pollution as an input. Consequently it is used less intensively in the production process. The effect on domestic utility is negative and can alternatively be interpreted as a direct tax base erosion effect. Terms (3) to (6) reflect the effects resulting from the induced reallocation of the internationally mobile capital: the diminished input of pollution into domestic production *ceteris paribus* means a decrease in the marginal productivity of capital invested in country A. Capital is driven out of the country and marginal productivity of the factor pollution in country A diminishes, that in country B rises. Hence there is an additional positive environmental effect in the home country (term (3)), whereas term (4) reflects the corresponding change in foreign pollution due to a reallocation of internationally mobile capital. The generation of foreign pollution consequently increases and will also be perceived in country A because of the international dimension of the externality. Since there is substitutability between capital and pollution in both countries, a marginal rise in the domestic environmental tax with respect to the reaction of foreign pollution hence lowers domestic utility. Term (5) again is a negative tax base erosion effect on the environmental tax induced by the international capital reallocation. The negative sign of the last term (6) in equation (5.9) (taking account of the sign of $|D|$) reveals that an increase in the pollution tax rate in a capital-exporting country runs counter to the reduction of capital supply on the world capital market in order strategically to increase the factor reward. The opposite applies to a country which is a net borrower on the world capital market with the effect hence being positive. For a capital-exporting country, the strategic component in national calculations points in the same direction as the aspects of an indirect internalization of cross-border externalities (4).

Summing up, terms (1) and (3) reflect the valuation of a change in the global pollution level due to the change in the domestic externality contribution, induced by the marginal augmentation in the pollution tax. With respect to this effect the environmental tax raises utility of the representative consumer. Term (4) reflects the valuation of a change in foreign externality generation. Terms (2) and (5) are only different from zero if there is a pollution tax already in place in the initial equilibrium.

First-order conditions for an optimal pollution tax of a capital-importing or capital-exporting country in a setting with internationally mobile capital and cross-border externalities can be derived by setting the respective equations in (5.9) equal to zero, and solving for pollution tax τ^A. This condition for the tax rate only consists of endogenous variables. In combination with equation system (5.3), together with potential other conditions which guarantee the whole system to be sufficient for the derivation of an optimum, the optimal level of the pollution tax can be determined.

The above-derived result in an open setting proves that the environmental tax loses its first-best character if the jurisdiction is smaller than the area where the externality is perceived. In the present case this is due to two reasons:

- Countries maximize utility of their own representative consumer and hence ignore the detrimental effects of their externality generation on consumers abroad.
- By the same reasoning they exploit the ability of a big country strategically to alter prices on world markets in their own favour.

The implementation of an optimal tax rate that can be derived from multiplier (5.9) thus leads to a *national* second-best result. It is only *second-best* in nature because the various national aims concerning the strategic exploitation of a country's market power on the world capital market as well as the direct and indirect internalization of the cross-border externality are attacked with only one policy instrument – the pollution tax.[14]

As indicated, in a closed-economy setting with a sufficiently rich set of instruments available to the government, the optimal environmental tax, the so-called Pigou tax, demands levying a tax on the externality equal to the marginal damage it generates globally in the optimum. This result can be reproduced in a world with two or more countries without a supranational authority being in place if countries agree upon perfect cooperation – a scenario that is not very realistic and which in Chapter 3 has therefore only been dealt with as a benchmark case. Such cooperation aiming at maximizing global utility is tantamount to a complete internalization of all technological as well as fiscal externalities, as will now be seen.

A globally Pareto-efficient result by means of taxes can only be reached if both countries jointly implement a pollution tax. In this case there is only one change in equation system (5.3):[15] when the foreign

---

[14]This reasoning is known as 'target principle'.

[15]The analysis is restricted to the case of country A as a capital-exporting country.

environmental tax is denoted with τ^B, equation (5.3e) changes to

$$\frac{\partial R\left(1, \varepsilon^B, K\right)}{\partial \varepsilon^B} = \tau^B \tag{5.3e$'$}$$

By totally differentiating the equilibrium conditions the result achieved is

$$D_{\mathrm{P}} \begin{bmatrix} \partial e/\partial u \cdot du \\ \partial E/\partial U \cdot dU \\ d\varepsilon \\ d\varepsilon^A \\ d\varepsilon^B \\ d\xi \\ dh \end{bmatrix} = \begin{bmatrix} 0 \\ 0 \\ 0 \\ d\tau^A \\ d\tau^B \\ 0 \\ -\varepsilon^A \cdot d\tau^A \end{bmatrix} \tag{5.10}$$

where matrix D_{P} is

$$D_{\mathrm{P}} \overset{\text{def}}{=} \begin{bmatrix} 1 & 0 & \dfrac{\partial e}{\partial \varepsilon} & -\tau^A & -\xi\dfrac{\partial^2 R}{\partial K \partial \varepsilon^B} & -\xi\dfrac{\partial^2 R}{\partial K^2} & 0 \\[2mm] 0 & 1 & \dfrac{\partial E}{\partial \varepsilon} & 0 & \xi\dfrac{\partial^2 R}{\partial K \partial \varepsilon^B} - \tau^B & \xi\dfrac{\partial^2 R}{\partial K^2} & 0 \\[2mm] 0 & 0 & 1 & -\dfrac{\partial \varepsilon}{\partial \varepsilon^A} & -\dfrac{\partial \varepsilon}{\partial \varepsilon^B} & 0 & 0 \\[2mm] 0 & 0 & 0 & \dfrac{\partial^2 r}{\partial\left(\varepsilon^A\right)^2} & 0 & -\dfrac{\partial^2 r}{\partial \varepsilon^A \partial k} & 0 \\[2mm] 0 & 0 & 0 & 0 & \dfrac{\partial^2 R}{\partial\left(\varepsilon^B\right)^2} & \dfrac{\partial^2 R}{\partial \varepsilon^B \partial K} & 0 \\[2mm] 0 & 0 & 0 & \dfrac{\partial^2 r}{\partial k \partial \varepsilon^A} & \dfrac{\partial^2 R}{\partial K \partial \varepsilon^B} & \dfrac{\partial^2 r}{\partial k^2} + \dfrac{\partial^2 R}{\partial K^2} & 0 \\[2mm] 0 & 0 & 0 & \tau^A & 0 & 0 & 1 \end{bmatrix} \tag{5.11}$$

with $(\partial r/\partial k - \partial R/\partial K)$ being equal to zero according to (5.3f). There is still $-dk = dK = d\xi$. The determinant of matrix D_{P} is equal to $|D|$ derived in (5.7).

Now the effects of both tax instruments on domestic and foreign

---

For a capital-importing country it is analogous.

utility can be determined in the case of simultaneous implementation

$$\frac{\partial e}{\partial u}\frac{du}{d\tau^A} = -\left(\frac{\partial e}{\partial \varepsilon}\frac{\partial \varepsilon}{\partial \varepsilon^A} - \tau^A\right)\frac{1}{\frac{\partial^2 r}{\partial(\varepsilon^A)^2}}$$

$$+\frac{1}{|D_P|}\left(-\left(\frac{\partial e}{\partial \varepsilon}\frac{\partial \varepsilon}{\partial \varepsilon^A} - \tau^A\right)\frac{\frac{\partial^2 r}{\partial \varepsilon^A \partial k}}{\frac{\partial^2 r}{\partial(\varepsilon^A)^2}}\right.$$

$$\left.+\left(\frac{\partial e}{\partial \varepsilon}\frac{\partial \varepsilon}{\partial \varepsilon^B}\frac{\partial^2 R}{\partial \varepsilon^B \partial K} + \xi H^B\right)\frac{1}{\frac{\partial^2 R}{\partial(\varepsilon^B)^2}}\right)\frac{\partial^2 r}{\partial k \partial \varepsilon^A}\frac{\partial^2 R}{\partial(\varepsilon^B)^2}$$

$$\tag{5.12}$$

$$\frac{\partial E}{\partial U}\frac{dU}{d\tau^A} = \frac{1}{|D_P|}\left[-\frac{\partial E}{\partial \varepsilon}\frac{\partial \varepsilon}{\partial \varepsilon^A}\left(\frac{\partial^2 r}{\partial k^2}\frac{\partial^2 R}{\partial(\varepsilon^B)^2} - H^B\right)\right.$$

$$\left.+\left(\frac{\partial E}{\partial \varepsilon}\frac{\partial \varepsilon}{\partial \varepsilon^B} - \tau^B\right)\frac{\partial^2 r}{\partial k \partial \varepsilon^A}\frac{\partial^2 R}{\partial \varepsilon^B \partial K} - \frac{\partial^2 r}{\partial k \partial \varepsilon^A}\xi H^B\right]$$

$$\tag{5.13}$$

$$\frac{\partial E}{\partial U}\frac{dU}{d\tau^B} = -\left(\frac{\partial E}{\partial \varepsilon}\frac{\partial \varepsilon}{\partial \varepsilon^B} - \tau^B\right)\frac{1}{\frac{\partial^2 R}{\partial(\varepsilon^B)^2}}$$

$$+\frac{1}{|D_P|}\left(\frac{\partial E}{\partial \varepsilon}\frac{\partial \varepsilon}{\partial \varepsilon^A}\frac{\frac{\partial^2 r}{\partial \varepsilon^A \partial k}}{\frac{\partial^2 r}{\partial(\varepsilon^A)^2}}\right.$$

$$\left.-\left(\frac{\partial E}{\partial \varepsilon}\frac{\partial \varepsilon}{\partial \varepsilon^B} - \tau^B\right)\frac{\frac{\partial^2 R}{\partial \varepsilon^B \partial K}}{\frac{\partial^2 R}{\partial(\varepsilon^B)^2}} - \frac{1}{\frac{\partial^2 r}{\partial(\varepsilon^A)^2}}\xi H^A\right)\tag{5.14}$$

$$\frac{\partial e}{\partial u}\frac{du}{d\tau^B} = \frac{1}{|D_P|}\left[\left(\frac{\partial e}{\partial \varepsilon}\frac{\partial \varepsilon}{\partial \varepsilon^A} - \tau^A\right)\frac{\partial^2 r}{\partial \varepsilon^A \partial k}\frac{\partial^2 R}{\partial K \partial \varepsilon^B}\right.$$

$$\left. - \frac{\partial e}{\partial \varepsilon}\frac{\partial \varepsilon}{\partial \varepsilon^B}\left(\frac{\partial^2 r}{\partial (\varepsilon^A)^2}\frac{\partial^2 R}{\partial K^2} + H^A\right) + \frac{\partial^2 R}{\partial K \partial \varepsilon^B}\xi H^A\right] \quad (5.15)$$

For the result to be Pareto-efficient the impacts of a country's policy measures on the other country must also be taken into account. Therefore, multipliers (5.12) and (5.13) as well as (5.14) and (5.15) must sum to zero

$$\frac{\partial e}{\partial u}\frac{du}{d\tau^A} + \frac{\partial E}{\partial U}\frac{dU}{d\tau^A} =$$

$$\frac{1}{|D_P|}\left[-\left(\left(\frac{\partial e}{\partial \varepsilon} + \frac{\partial E}{\partial \varepsilon}\right)\frac{\partial \varepsilon}{\partial \varepsilon^A} - \tau^A\right)\left(\frac{\partial^2 r}{\partial k^2}\frac{\partial^2 R}{\partial (\varepsilon^B)^2} + H^B\right)\right.$$

$$\left. + \left(\left(\frac{\partial e}{\partial \varepsilon} + \frac{\partial E}{\partial \varepsilon}\right)\frac{\partial \varepsilon}{\partial \varepsilon^B} - \tau^B\right)\frac{\partial^2 r}{\partial k \partial \varepsilon^A}\frac{\partial^2 R}{\partial \varepsilon^B \partial K}\right] \overset{!}{=} 0 \quad (5.16)$$

$$\frac{\partial e}{\partial u}\frac{du}{d\tau^B} + \frac{\partial E}{\partial U}\frac{dU}{d\tau^B} =$$

$$\frac{1}{|D_P|}\left[-\left(\left(\frac{\partial e}{\partial \varepsilon} + \frac{\partial E}{\partial \varepsilon}\right)\frac{\partial \varepsilon}{\partial \varepsilon^B} - \tau^B\right)\left(\frac{\partial^2 r}{\partial (\varepsilon^A)^2}\frac{\partial^2 R}{\partial K^2} + H^A\right)\right.$$

$$\left. + \left(\left(\frac{\partial e}{\partial \varepsilon} + \frac{\partial E}{\partial \varepsilon}\right)\frac{\partial \varepsilon}{\partial \varepsilon^A} - \tau^A\right)\frac{\partial^2 r}{\partial \varepsilon^A \partial k}\frac{\partial^2 R}{\partial K \partial \varepsilon^B}\right] \overset{!}{=} 0 \quad (5.17)$$

Solving both conditions simultaneously determines first-order conditions for optimal pollution tax rates in both countries that guarantee global efficiency

$$\tau^{A*} = \frac{\partial r}{\partial \varepsilon^A} \quad = \left(\frac{\partial e}{\partial \varepsilon} + \frac{\partial E}{\partial \varepsilon}\right)\frac{\partial \varepsilon}{\partial \varepsilon^A}$$

$$(5.18)$$

$$\tau^{B*} = \frac{\partial R}{\partial \varepsilon^B} \quad = \left(\frac{\partial e}{\partial \varepsilon} + \frac{\partial E}{\partial \varepsilon}\right)\frac{\partial \varepsilon}{\partial \varepsilon^B}$$

$$(5.19)$$

This is precisely the Pigou tax which in the optimum should equal *global* marginal environmental damage caused by either country. One tax instrument in each country is hence sufficient to yield Pareto optimality since strategic aspects are no longer considered. The resulting allocation is first-best from the global perspective. In Figure 3.1, p. 18, this result is reflected by the left of the inner branches. If the externality is of a pure public-good type and pollution is the only distortion, optimal rates of the environmental tax must be identical across countries.

5.3.2   Capital Taxes

In this section the effects of marginally increasing a tax on repatriated capital rents are analysed. System (5.3) of equilibrium conditions depicted in subsection 5.3.1 for country A as a capital importer and exporter remains unchanged except for conditions (5.3d), (5.3f) and (5.3g) which change to (5.20d), (5.20f) and (5.20g), respectively:

$$\frac{\partial r\left(1, \varepsilon^A, k\right)}{\partial \varepsilon^A} = 0 \tag{5.20d}$$

$$\frac{\partial r\left(1, \varepsilon^A, k\right)}{\partial k} \mp \theta^A = \frac{\partial R\left(1, \varepsilon^B, K\right)}{\partial K} \tag{5.20f}$$

$$h + \theta^A \xi = B \tag{5.20g}$$

The variable that is exogenous to the system is country A's capital tax θ^A which drives a wedge between domestic and foreign marginal productivity of capital, as can be seen from (5.20f). Due to the lack of an environmental tax, the price attached to the environmental input equals zero.

Totally differentiating the equation system composed of (5.3) and (5.20) and accounting for (5.4) yields in matrix notation

$$D_{\theta^A} \begin{bmatrix} \partial e/\partial u \cdot du/d\theta^A \\ \partial E/\partial U \cdot dU/d\theta^A \\ d\varepsilon/d\theta^A \\ d\varepsilon^A/d\theta^A \\ d\varepsilon^B/d\theta^A \\ d\xi/d\theta^A \\ dh/d\theta^A \end{bmatrix} = \begin{bmatrix} 0 \\ 0 \\ 0 \\ 0 \\ 0 \\ 1 \\ -\xi \end{bmatrix} \tag{5.21}$$

where matrix D_{θ^A} is

$$
D_{\theta^A} \stackrel{\text{def}}{=}
\begin{bmatrix}
1 & 0 & \dfrac{\partial e}{\partial \varepsilon} & 0 & \pm\,\xi\dfrac{\partial^2 R}{\partial K \partial \varepsilon^B} & -\theta - \xi\dfrac{\partial^2 R}{\partial K^2} & 0 \\[2ex]
0 & 1 & \dfrac{\partial E}{\partial \varepsilon} & 0 & \mp\,\xi\dfrac{\partial^2 R}{\partial K \partial \varepsilon^B} & \xi\dfrac{\partial^2 R}{\partial K^2} & 0 \\[2ex]
0 & 0 & 1 & -\dfrac{\partial \varepsilon}{\partial \varepsilon^A} & -\dfrac{\partial \varepsilon}{\partial \varepsilon^B} & 0 & 0 \\[2ex]
0 & 0 & 0 & \dfrac{\partial^2 r}{\partial (\varepsilon^A)^2} & 0 & \pm\,\dfrac{\partial^2 r}{\partial \varepsilon^A \partial k} & 0 \\[2ex]
0 & 0 & 0 & 0 & \dfrac{\partial^2 R}{\partial (\varepsilon^B)^2} & \mp\,\dfrac{\partial^2 R}{\partial \varepsilon^B \partial K} & 0 \\[2ex]
0 & 0 & 0 & \pm\,\dfrac{\partial^2 r}{\partial k \partial \varepsilon^A} & \mp\,\dfrac{\partial^2 R}{\partial K \partial \varepsilon^B} & \dfrac{\partial^2 r}{\partial k^2} + \dfrac{\partial^2 R}{\partial K^2} & 0 \\[2ex]
0 & 0 & 0 & 0 & 0 & \theta^A & 1
\end{bmatrix}
$$

$$(5.22)$$

with τ^A equal to zero according to (5.20d). The determinant of matrix D_{θ^A} is equal to $|D|$ derived in (5.7).

The influence of a marginal rise in the tax on repatriated capital rents on domestic utility in country A can now be calculated

$$
\frac{\partial e}{\partial u}\frac{du}{d\theta^A} = \frac{1}{|D_{\theta^A}|}\left(\underbrace{\pm\,\frac{\partial e}{\partial \varepsilon}\frac{\partial \varepsilon}{\partial \varepsilon^A}\frac{\dfrac{\partial^2 r}{\partial \varepsilon^A \partial k}}{\dfrac{\partial^2 r}{\partial (\varepsilon^A)^2}}}_{(1)} \underbrace{-\,\frac{\partial e}{\partial \varepsilon}\frac{\partial \varepsilon}{\partial \varepsilon^B}\frac{\dfrac{\partial^2 R}{\partial \varepsilon^B \partial K}}{\dfrac{\partial^2 R}{\partial (\varepsilon^B)^2}}}_{(2)} \right.
$$

$$
\left. \underbrace{+\; \theta^A}_{(3)} \underbrace{+\,\xi H^B\,\frac{1}{\dfrac{\partial^2 R}{\partial (\varepsilon^B)^2}}}_{(4)} \right)\frac{\partial^2 r}{\partial (\varepsilon^A)^2}\frac{\partial^2 R}{\partial (\varepsilon^B)^2}
\qquad (5.23)
$$

with $(\partial r/\partial k - \partial R/\partial K)$ being equal to $\left(\pm\,\theta^A\right)$ according to (5.20f).

The multipliers reveal that in contrast to multipliers (5.9) for the pollution tax there are no direct effects. Effects (1) to (4) all result from an induced reallocation of the internationally mobile capital. The first underbraced term (1) is the valuation of an induced change in domestic externality generation as already known from effect (3) for the pollution tax in multiplier (5.9). For country A, as a capital exporter, the introduction of the tax lowers net factor rewards to capital invested abroad. Consequently less capital will be invested in country B, which *ceteris paribus* lowers capital productivity but raises pollution productivity in the home country. More pollution will hence be generated in the home country, which lowers domestic utility. Therefore, the sign of effect (1) in contrast to effect (3) for the environmental tax is negative, taking account of the negative sign of $|D_{\theta^A}|$. Term (2) corresponds to term (4) in multiplier (5.9), its sign this time being positive due to the induced diminution of foreign pollution for country A as a net capital exporter. The effects are reverted if country A is a net capital-importing country. In this case the tax on capital rents repatriated to country B drives foreign direct investment out of the country, which implies a positive effect on domestic externality generation, but a negative one on foreign externality generation. The third underbraced term (3) in both multipliers (5.23) reflects the erosion of the capital tax base because of an increase in the tax rate and corresponds to effect (5) in the multiplier for the pollution tax. This effect is only different from zero if the tax was already in place in the initial equilibrium. For θ^A being positive, the effect has a negative impact on domestic utility. The last term (4) for both a capital-exporting and importing country is a positive tax rate effect. It is the counterpart to effect (3) and embodies the rise in tax revenue because of the increase in the tax rate. Strategically speaking, the country as a capital exporter tries to create an excess demand for capital on the world capital market in order to raise the return on capital. As a capital importer the country instead tries to induce an excess supply of capital on the world capital market in order to lower the return on borrowed capital.

It is evident that the capital tax again serves to exploit the country's power in the world capital market and additionally to internalize externalities within the own country as well as in the foreign country. However, internalization is only achieved indirectly via the manipulation of international capital allocation.

To derive first-order conditions for an optimal capital tax rate, expressions in square brackets in (5.23) have to be set equal to zero. This means that an optimal tax on repatriated capital rents balances both positive and negative effects on the environment as well as on the country's income situation. Due to the pursuit of the strategic aspects and the neglect of environmental damages imposed on country B, the tax rate again is only (second-best) optimal from a *national* point of view.

Global efficiency with a tax on repatriated capital rents available to the governments in both countries is not achievable because the effects are just diametral. A tax on repatriated capital rents is hence not a perfect substitute for a pollution tax.

5.3.3   Pollution Taxes and Capital Taxes

After separate analysis of the two tax instruments for the government in country A, the effects of a joint application of both taxes will be under scrutiny. The equilibrium conditions in this case are a synthesis of both former scenarios, and in equation system (5.3) conditions (5.3f) and (5.3g) change to

$$\frac{\partial r\left(1,\varepsilon^A,k\right)}{\partial k} \mp \theta^A = \frac{\partial R\left(1,\varepsilon^B,K\right)}{\partial K} \tag{5.24f}$$

$$h + \tau^A\,\varepsilon^A + \theta^A\,\xi = B \tag{5.24g}$$

respectively. The government in country A can directly affect domestically generated externalities as well as the return to capital investment abroad undertaken by its representative consumer (or by the foreign representative consumer for country A as a capital importer). The interesting point is how an optimal tax policy can be characterized under the interdependencies arising from the joint implementation of both instruments.

The new system again is totally differentiated, with θ^A and τ^A as policy instruments for country A, and the head tax is endogenously determined. In matrix notation

$$
D_{\tau^A,\theta^A}
\begin{bmatrix}
\partial e/\partial u \cdot du \\
\partial E/\partial U \cdot dU \\
d\varepsilon \\
d\varepsilon^A \\
d\varepsilon^B \\
d\xi \\
dh
\end{bmatrix}
=
\begin{bmatrix}
0 \\
0 \\
0 \\
d\tau^A \\
0 \\
d\theta^A \\
-\varepsilon^A \cdot d\tau^A - \xi \cdot d\theta^A
\end{bmatrix}
\tag{5.25}
$$

where matrix D_{τ^A,θ^A} is

$$
D_{\tau^A,\theta^A} \stackrel{\text{def}}{=}
\begin{bmatrix}
1 & 0 & \dfrac{\partial e}{\partial \varepsilon} & -\tau^A & \pm\,\xi\dfrac{\partial^2 R}{\partial K \partial \varepsilon^B} & -\theta - \xi\dfrac{\partial^2 R}{\partial K^2} & 0 \\[2ex]
0 & 1 & \dfrac{\partial E}{\partial \varepsilon} & 0 & \mp\,\xi\dfrac{\partial^2 R}{\partial K \partial \varepsilon^B} & \xi\dfrac{\partial^2 R}{\partial K^2} & 0 \\[2ex]
0 & 0 & 1 & -\dfrac{\partial \varepsilon}{\partial \varepsilon^A} & -\dfrac{\partial \varepsilon}{\partial \varepsilon^B} & 0 & 0 \\[2ex]
0 & 0 & 0 & \dfrac{\partial^2 r}{\partial(\varepsilon^A)^2} & 0 & \pm\dfrac{\partial^2 r}{\partial\varepsilon^A \partial k} & 0 \\[2ex]
0 & 0 & 0 & 0 & \dfrac{\partial^2 R}{\partial(\varepsilon^B)^2} & \mp\dfrac{\partial^2 R}{\partial\varepsilon^B \partial K} & 0 \\[2ex]
0 & 0 & 0 & \pm\dfrac{\partial^2 r}{\partial k \partial\varepsilon^A} & \mp\dfrac{\partial^2 R}{\partial K \partial\varepsilon^B} & \dfrac{\partial^2 r}{\partial k^2}+\dfrac{\partial^2 R}{\partial K^2} & 0 \\[2ex]
0 & 0 & 0 & \tau^A & 0 & \theta^A & 1
\end{bmatrix}
$$
$$\tag{5.26}$$

The determinant of matrix D_{τ^A,θ^A} is equal to $|D|$ derived in (5.7). As multipliers for the pollution tax and the tax on repatriated capital rents, respectively, we obtain

$$
\frac{\partial e}{\partial u}\frac{du}{d\tau^A} = -\left(\frac{\partial e}{\partial \varepsilon}\frac{\partial \varepsilon}{\partial \varepsilon^A} - \tau^A\right)\frac{1}{\dfrac{\partial^2 r}{\partial(\varepsilon^A)^2}}
$$

$$
+ \frac{1}{|D_{\tau^A,\theta^A}|}\cdot\left(-\left(\frac{\partial e}{\partial \varepsilon}\frac{\partial \varepsilon}{\partial \varepsilon^A} - \tau^A\right)\frac{\dfrac{\partial^2 r}{\partial \varepsilon^A \partial k}}{\dfrac{\partial^2 r}{\partial(\varepsilon^A)^2}} \mp \theta^A \right.
$$

$$
\left. + \left(\frac{\partial e}{\partial \varepsilon}\frac{\partial \varepsilon}{\partial \varepsilon^B}\frac{\partial^2 R}{\partial \varepsilon^B \partial K} \mp \xi H^B\right)\frac{1}{\dfrac{\partial^2 R}{\partial(\varepsilon^B)^2}}\right)\frac{\partial^2 r}{\partial k \partial \varepsilon^A}\frac{\partial^2 R}{\partial(\varepsilon^B)^2}
$$

$$(5.27)$$

$$
\frac{\partial e}{\partial u}\frac{du}{d\theta^A} = \mp\frac{1}{|D_{\tau^A,\theta^A}|}\cdot\left(-\left(\frac{\partial e}{\partial \varepsilon}\frac{\partial \varepsilon}{\partial \varepsilon^A} - \tau^A\right)\frac{\dfrac{\partial^2 r}{\partial \varepsilon^A \partial k}}{\dfrac{\partial^2 r}{\partial(\varepsilon^A)^2}} \mp \theta^A \right.
$$

$$
\left. + \left(\frac{\partial e}{\partial \varepsilon}\frac{\partial \varepsilon}{\partial \varepsilon^B}\frac{\partial^2 R}{\partial \varepsilon^B \partial K} \mp \xi H^B\right)\frac{1}{\dfrac{\partial^2 R}{\partial(\varepsilon^B)^2}}\right)\frac{\partial^2 r}{\partial(\varepsilon^A)^2}\frac{\partial^2 R}{\partial(\varepsilon^B)^2}
$$

$$(5.28)$$

with $(\partial r/\partial k - \partial R/\partial K)$ being equal to $\left(\pm\,\theta^A\right)$ according to (5.24f).

As can be seen from multipliers (5.27) and (5.28), both tax instruments are interconnected since the pollution tax rate appears in the multiplier of the capital tax and vice versa. By exactly these tax interaction effects the above multipliers deviate from those derived in subsections 5.3.1 and 5.3.2. They are different from zero only if the taxes are already in place in the initial equilibrium.

Setting multipliers (5.27) and (5.28) of both instruments equal to zero and simulataneously solving for τ^A and θ^A determines the first-order conditions for optimal values of both tax instruments

$$\tau^{A*} = \frac{\partial e}{\partial \varepsilon} \frac{\partial \varepsilon}{\partial \varepsilon^A} \tag{5.29}$$

$$\theta^{A*} = \left(\pm \frac{\partial e}{\partial \varepsilon} \frac{\partial \varepsilon}{\partial \varepsilon^B} \frac{\partial^2 R}{\partial \varepsilon^B \partial K} - \xi H^B \right) \frac{1}{\frac{\partial^2 R}{\partial (\varepsilon^B)^2}} \tag{5.30}$$

The optimal level of the domestic pollution tax for both a capital-importing and exporting country is precisely the well-known Pigou tax. The reason why this first-best tax instrument regains its efficiency quality is that now the capital tax shields the home country by offsetting the negative effects the pollution tax induces with respect to foreign externality generation and to the cost of capital in the world capital market. Hence each instrument has to pursue a specific objective. Since the first-order condition for the optimal domestic pollution tax accounts only for domestic damages generated by domestic production, the Pigou tax is qualitatively lower than that guaranteeing global efficiency and can only lead to a *national* first-best solution. This result is depicted on the right of the right branch of Figure 3.1, p. 18. For the home country as a net capital-exporting country, the optimal capital tax rate is unambiguously positive, i.e. capital exports are restricted via tax policy for environmental and strategic ends. A positive tax rate on repatriated capital rents serves as a means to generate an excess demand for capital on the world capital market. For the country as a capital importer, counteracting effects are observed with regard to the optimal tax rate since foreign externality generation demands that the tax be negative (i.e. the domestic government subsidizes foreign investors), whereas strategic considerations ask for an excess supply of capital in the world market to be induced by a positive tax on repatriated capital rents. A comparison of the first-order condition for an optimal environmental tax (5.29) with the situation when the pollution tax is the only available tax instrument is difficult. The latter can be derived by setting multiplier (5.9) equal to zero and solving for the pollution tax. The additional effects compared to those contained in (5.29) are counteracting; a comparison is hence not straightforward. Furthermore, the underlying equilibria are different, which means that the comparison of the tax rates in both scenarios can only be a qualitative one. For the case of country A as a capital exporter, it can be said that the optimal environmental tax is higher in the case of joint implementation if the negative effects (4) to (6) in multiplier (5.9) offset the positive environmental effect (3).

5.3.4   Interpretation of the Results

From the first-order conditions for the optimal tax rates derived in this section it can be seen that in an open-economy setting with cross-border externalities the traditional Pigou tax loses its characteristic feature as a first-best instrument. Countries maximize national welfare and neglect both fiscal and technological externalities that they impose on other countries. In the decentralized equilibrium, global pollution generation is too high and the amount of international capital movements deviates from its global optimum. In this case the isolated use of a tax on repatriated capital rents has similar effects on a country's welfare as the implementation solely of a pollution tax. Both instruments are appropriate to effect both ends at the same time: internalization and exploitation of market power. Only if joint implementation of both instruments is possible does the traditional Pigou tax (though restricted to national considerations) regain its optimality character. But again it must be emphasized that the resulting allocation is only first-best from the *national* point of view, not from the global one.

On the other hand, if countries agree upon a cooperative internalization of cross-border externalities, the global first-best result can only be reached by means of national Pigou taxes that also take into account the environmental damages from domestic production imposed on other countries. As outlined in Chapter 3, efforts to reach cooperation between countries are associated with considerable impediments, since the treaties have to be designed in an incentive-compatible manner. A tax on repatriated capital rents – even if implemented in both countries at the same time – is not appropriate to achieve global efficiency.

In the following section the assumption will be made that lump-sum taxes are no longer available to the government. The analysis focuses on the question of how matters change if the proceeds of a marginal introduction or increase of a pollution tax are used to drive back tax revenue generated by means of the distortionary tax on repatriated capital rents. In order to get a better understanding of what the actual changes are, use is made of both double-dividend concepts that were defined in Chapter 4.

5.4   INDIRECT INTERNALIZATION AND DOUBLE DIVIDEND

In this setting two distortions prevail: the misallocation of factors because of environmental externalities which are not internalized, and also that due to the taxation of repatriated capital rents as a revenue-raising device. The capital tax is a distortionary way to close the gap between the proceeds stemming from the environmental tax and the budgetary needs. Consequently, the capital tax is not primarily focused on the exploitation of the country's market power but must help to finance the public budget. The marginal implementation or rise of a pollution tax in this framework can yield a double dividend by alleviating both distortions. Alternatively – if expressed in terms of the Goulder concept – it can yield only one dividend, which most likely is an improvement in the country's environmental situation, and thereby simultaneously generates a negative fiscal dividend by increasing the other distortion. But, as already seen in Chapter 4, even a negative environmental dividend accompanied by a positive second dividend or a double negative dividend are possible outcomes of the analysis. The results of such second-best considerations hinge entirely on the specific formulation of the model as well as on the underlying double-dividend concept.

Compared to equation system (5.3), only equations (5.3f) and (5.3g) change

$$\frac{\partial r\left(1, \varepsilon^A, k\right)}{\partial k} \mp \theta^A = \frac{\partial R\left(1, \varepsilon^B, K\right)}{\partial K} \tag{5.31f}$$

$$\theta^A \xi + \tau^A \varepsilon^A = B \tag{5.31g}$$

Equation (5.31g) reflects that τ^A and θ^A are now the only tax instruments available to the government.

Totally differentiating equation systems (5.3) and (5.31) in the case that country A is a capital importer or exporter, respectively, when θ^A is endogenously determined and the pollution tax τ^A as the policy instrument is exogenously altered, the result is

$$
D^*_{I,E}
\begin{bmatrix}
\partial e/\partial u \cdot du/d\tau^A \\
\partial E/\partial U \cdot dU/d\tau^A \\
d\varepsilon/d\tau^A \\
d\varepsilon^A/d\tau^A \\
d\varepsilon^B/d\tau^A \\
d\xi/d\tau^A \\
d\theta^A/d\tau^A
\end{bmatrix}
=
\begin{bmatrix}
0 \\
0 \\
0 \\
1 \\
0 \\
0 \\
-\varepsilon^A
\end{bmatrix}
\tag{5.32}
$$

where matrix $D^*_{I,E}$ is

$$
D^*_{I,E} \overset{\text{def}}{=}
\begin{bmatrix}
1 & 0 & \dfrac{\partial e}{\partial \varepsilon} & -\tau^A & \pm\, \xi\dfrac{\partial^2 R}{\partial K \partial \varepsilon^B} & -\theta^A - \xi\dfrac{\partial^2 R}{\partial K^2} & 0 \\[2ex]
0 & 1 & \dfrac{\partial E}{\partial \varepsilon} & 0 & \mp\, \xi\dfrac{\partial^2 R}{\partial K \partial \varepsilon^B} & \xi\dfrac{\partial^2 R}{\partial K^2} & 0 \\[2ex]
0 & 0 & 1 & -\dfrac{\partial \varepsilon}{\partial \varepsilon^A} & -\dfrac{\partial \varepsilon}{\partial \varepsilon^B} & 0 & 0 \\[2ex]
0 & 0 & 0 & \dfrac{\partial^2 r}{\partial (\varepsilon^A)^2} & 0 & \pm\dfrac{\partial^2 r}{\partial \varepsilon^A \partial k} & 0 \\[2ex]
0 & 0 & 0 & 0 & \dfrac{\partial^2 R}{\partial (\varepsilon^B)^2} & \mp\dfrac{\partial^2 R}{\partial \varepsilon^B \partial K} & 0 \\[2ex]
0 & 0 & 0 & \pm\dfrac{\partial^2 r}{\partial k \partial \varepsilon^A} & \mp\dfrac{\partial^2 R}{\partial K \partial \varepsilon^B} & \dfrac{\partial^2 r}{\partial k^2} + \dfrac{\partial^2 R}{\partial K^2} & -1 \\[2ex]
0 & 0 & 0 & \tau^A & 0 & \theta^A & \xi
\end{bmatrix}
\tag{5.33}
$$

with $(\partial r/\partial k - \partial R/\partial K)$ being equal to $\left(\pm\ \theta^A\right)$ according to (5.31f) and $\partial r/\partial \varepsilon^A$ equal to τ^A, the tax on pollution.

The determinant of matrix $D^*_{I,E}$ is different from that of matrix D in equation system (5.3) (see equation (5.7)). For the home country as a net capital importer or exporter, the determinant is equal to

$$|D^*_{I,E}| = \theta^A \underbrace{\frac{\partial^2 r}{\partial (\varepsilon^A)^2} \frac{\partial^2 R}{\partial (\varepsilon^B)^2}}_{(+)} \mp \underbrace{\tau^A \frac{\partial^2 r}{\partial \varepsilon^A \partial k} \frac{\partial^2 R}{\partial (\varepsilon^B)^2}}_{\left(\pm\right)} + \underbrace{\xi \cdot |D|}_{(-)} \quad (5.34)$$

where the last term is expressed in terms of the determinant of matrix D in equation system (5.3). The first two terms reflect the impacts of revenue-recycling on the base of the capital tax and on that of the environmental tax, respectively. The tax base effect on the capital tax in both cases is positive due to the implicit diminution of its tax rate. The tax base effect on the environmental tax is only positive in the case of country A being a capital-importing country. In this case the diminution of the tax rate on repatriated capital rents resulting from revenue-recycling induces an inflow of capital into the home country which in turn increases the tax base of the environmental tax. The last term represents the negative tax rate effect attached to the decrease in the capital tax.

In order to determine the sign of determinant $|D^*_{I,E}|$, it is assumed that the capital tax is on the increasing branch of its Laffer curve (i.e. $dB/d\theta^A > 0$). This assumption with respect to the tax instrument, the proceeds of which are being substituted for pollution tax revenue, corresponds to the stability conditions derived in Chapter 4. Determining $dB/d\theta^A$ from a setting similar to system (5.32), but when θ^A changes, τ^A is fixed, and B is free to adapt, results in

$$I^*_{I,E} \begin{bmatrix} \partial e/\partial u \cdot du/d\theta^A \\ \partial E/\partial U \cdot dU/d\theta^A \\ d\varepsilon/d\theta^A \\ d\varepsilon^A/d\theta^A \\ d\varepsilon^B/d\theta^A \\ d\xi/d\theta^A \\ dB/d\theta^A \end{bmatrix} = \begin{bmatrix} 0 \\ 0 \\ 0 \\ 0 \\ 0 \\ 1 \\ -\xi \end{bmatrix} \quad (5.35)$$

where matrix $I_{I,E}^*$ is

$$
I_{I,E}^* \overset{\text{def}}{=}
\begin{bmatrix}
1 & 0 & \dfrac{\partial e}{\partial \varepsilon} & -\tau^A & \pm\,\xi\,\dfrac{\partial^2 R}{\partial K \partial \varepsilon^B} & -\theta^A - \xi\,\dfrac{\partial^2 R}{\partial K^2} & 1 \\[2ex]
0 & 1 & \dfrac{\partial E}{\partial \varepsilon} & 0 & \mp\,\xi\,\dfrac{\partial^2 R}{\partial K \partial \varepsilon^B} & \xi\,\dfrac{\partial^2 R}{\partial K^2} & 0 \\[2ex]
0 & 0 & 1 & -\dfrac{\partial \varepsilon}{\partial \varepsilon^A} & -\dfrac{\partial \varepsilon}{\partial \varepsilon^B} & 0 & 0 \\[2ex]
0 & 0 & 0 & \dfrac{\partial^2 r}{\partial (\varepsilon^A)^2} & 0 & \pm\,\dfrac{\partial^2 r}{\partial \varepsilon^A \partial k} & 0 \\[2ex]
0 & 0 & 0 & 0 & \dfrac{\partial^2 R}{\partial (\varepsilon^B)^2} & \mp\,\dfrac{\partial^2 R}{\partial \varepsilon^B \partial K} & 0 \\[2ex]
0 & 0 & 0 & \pm\,\dfrac{\partial^2 r}{\partial k \partial \varepsilon^A} & \mp\,\dfrac{\partial^2 R}{\partial K \partial \varepsilon^B} & \dfrac{\partial^2 r}{\partial k^2} + \dfrac{\partial^2 R}{\partial K^2} & 0 \\[2ex]
0 & 0 & 0 & \tau^A & 0 & \theta^A & -1
\end{bmatrix}
$$

$$(5.36)$$

with determinant

$$|I_{I,E}^*| = -|D| \tag{5.37}$$

the negative of the determinant of system (5.3) in the case where a lump-sum tax was available. From this follows

$$
\frac{dB}{d\theta^A} = \frac{1}{|D|}\left(\theta^A\,\frac{\partial^2 r}{\partial(\varepsilon^A)^2}\,\frac{\partial^2 R}{\partial(\varepsilon^B)^2} \mp \tau^A\,\frac{\partial^2 r}{\partial \varepsilon^A \partial k}\,\frac{\partial^2 R}{\partial(\varepsilon^B)^2} + \xi\,|D|\right)
$$

$$(5.38)$$

$$
= \frac{|D_{I,E}^*|}{|D|}
$$

Since $|D|$ is negative, multiplier $dB/d\theta^A$ to be positive requires that the determinant of $D_{I,E}^*$ be negative in sign.

It is now possible to determine the effects of a marginal alteration of the pollution tax on domestic welfare

$$\frac{\partial e}{\partial u}\frac{du}{d\tau^A} = -\left(\frac{\partial e}{\partial \varepsilon}\frac{\partial \varepsilon}{\partial \varepsilon^A} - \tau^A\right)\frac{1}{\frac{\partial^2 r}{\partial(\varepsilon^A)^2}}$$

$$+ \frac{1}{\left|D^*_{I,E}\right|} \cdot \left(-\left(\frac{\partial e}{\partial \varepsilon}\frac{\partial \varepsilon}{\partial \varepsilon^A} - \tau^A\right)\underbrace{\frac{\frac{\partial^2 r}{\partial \varepsilon^A \partial k}}{\frac{\partial^2 r}{\partial(\varepsilon^A)^2}}}_{(2)} \mp \underbrace{\theta^A}_{(3)} \right.$$

$$+ \left(\frac{\partial e}{\partial \varepsilon}\frac{\partial \varepsilon}{\partial \varepsilon^B}\frac{\partial^2 R}{\partial \varepsilon^B \partial K} \mp \xi H^B\right)\frac{1}{\frac{\partial^2 R}{\partial(\varepsilon^B)^2}}$$

$$\left. \cdot \left(\underbrace{\xi\frac{\partial^2 r}{\partial k \partial \varepsilon^A}}_{(1)} \pm \left(\underbrace{\varepsilon^A\frac{\partial^2 r}{\partial(\varepsilon^A)^2}}_{(4)} + \underbrace{\tau^A}_{(5)}\right)\right)\frac{\partial^2 R}{\partial(\varepsilon^B)^2} \right)$$

$$(5.39)$$

with $(\partial r/\partial k - \partial R/\partial K)$ being equal to $\left(\pm \theta^A\right)$ according to (5.31f).

The first line of both multipliers reflects the direct impact of the environmental tax on domestic utility through attaching a positive price to the environmental resource, i.e. to the externality. The remaining effects all result from an international reallocation of capital. Effect (1) in the multipliers for both scenarios reflects the isolated effect of a change in the environmental tax rate as already known from multiplier (5.9) in section 5.3 with effect (2) as the negative direct tax base erosion effect of the pollution tax on its own tax base. Since the capital tax is in place in the initial equilibrium, there is also a spill-over effect (3) which appeared already in multiplier (5.27) for the case of joint implementation. The effect is positive if country A exports and negative if it imports capital. The revenue-recycling effect (4) reflects the impact of an induced reduction in the capital tax rate since increased proceeds from the environmental tax lower the capital tax rate. The effects connected with (4) – taking care of the negative sign of the determinant – are hence inverse to those in multiplier (5.23) derived in section 5.3 for a marginal increase in the capital tax. Effect (5) finally reflects that the introduction of a pollution tax not only directly creates welfare losses through the direct tax base erosion effect; this erosion in turn diminishes the extent to which the capital tax can be replaced by the environmental tax and hence lessens the possibility for revenue-recycling. The net revenue-recycling effect resulting from (4) and (5), which leads to a change in the capital tax, in turn produces an erosion effect of the capital tax on its own base as well as a spill-over effect on the pollution tax (effects (3) and (2), respectively).

In order to get a better understanding of how the analysis has changed compared to the scenario where a lump-sum tax was available to the government, a return to the double-dividend concepts of Chapter 4 is helpful. Furthermore, by using these two concepts it will be possible to identify the additional aspects that arise (i) from the externality now being of a global type, (ii) from international factor mobility, as well as (iii) from strategic considerations. Finally, it will be possible to evaluate whether a double dividend can be raised from the introduction of environmental taxes.

5.4.1 The Goulder Concept

Decomposing the total welfare effect in the first line of equation system (5.32), that results from an ecological tax reform according to Goulder's concept, leads to

$$\frac{\partial e}{\partial u}\frac{du}{d\tau^A} = \left(-\frac{\partial e}{\partial \varepsilon}\frac{\partial \varepsilon}{\partial \varepsilon^A} \cdot \frac{d\varepsilon^A}{d\tau^A} - \frac{\partial e}{\partial \varepsilon}\frac{\partial \varepsilon}{\partial \varepsilon^B} \cdot \frac{d\varepsilon^B}{d\tau^A} \right)$$

$$- \left(\xi \cdot \frac{d\theta^A}{d\tau^A} + \varepsilon^A - \xi \frac{H^B}{\dfrac{\partial^2 R}{\partial \left(\varepsilon^B \right)^2}} \cdot \frac{d\xi}{d\tau^A} \right) \qquad (5.40)$$

The first two effects weighted with multipliers $(d\varepsilon^A/d\tau^A)$ and $(d\varepsilon^B/d\tau^A)$, respectively, reflect the global environmental effect and hence represent the environmental dividend. Compared to Chapter 4, the environmental effect is not only based on domestic changes in environmental depletion, but also accounts for the effects induced abroad. For CO_2 this is the 'carbon leakage effect' addressed in Chapter 3. The specialty of both effects is that they have opposite effects on domestic welfare. The last three effects in the second line of (5.40) represent Goulder's fiscal dividend. But apart from the revenue-recycling effect (first term in brackets) and the tax-withdrawing effect (second term in brackets) already known from Chapter 4, the last term reflects that an ecological tax reform also achieves strategic ends. Therefore it only shows up if the country which introduces an ecological tax reform is large enough to impose an impact on international prices. The effect should not be misinterpreted as a tax interaction effect, as will be seen in the following where the Pearce concept will be applied for decomposition purposes. As in Chapter 4, the tax interaction effect is not explicitly observable under the Goulder decomposition. For multiplier $d\xi/d\tau^A < 0$, i.e. for the ecological tax reform imposing a negative effect on cross-border capital flows, this last effect is positive. From system (5.32) it follows that

$$
\frac{d\xi}{d\tau^A} = \frac{-\dfrac{\partial^2 R}{\partial\left(\varepsilon^B\right)^2}}{\left|D^*_{E,I}\right|} \left(\underbrace{\tau^A}_{(-)} \underbrace{\pm\, \xi\,\frac{\partial^2 r}{\partial k \partial \varepsilon^A}}_{(\mp)} + \underbrace{\varepsilon^A\,\frac{\partial^2 r}{\partial\left(\varepsilon^A\right)^2}}_{(+)} \right) \tag{5.41}
$$

Taking into account the negative sign of the term in front of the brackets, the first term in brackets is negative and the third is positive. The second term is positive for a capital exporter, as a higher tax on the environment *ceteris paribus* causes more capital to leave the country, and negative otherwise. It hence follows that it is more likely for a capital-importing country that an ecological tax reform can partly be financed by an improvement in the country's terms of trade with respect to factor prices.

For the analysis it will again be useful to apply Schöb's decomposition of the total welfare effect. Hence the marginal social cost of public funds (MSCF) will be decomposed into a direct and an indirect effect caused by the change in either tax instrument, i.e. the marginal cost of public funds (MCF) and the marginal environmental impact (MEI), respectively.

Capital tax

To derive the MCF for the capital tax, system (5.32) is considered for the case of an incremental tax reform (i.e. B is endogenous) when the global externality level ε and the pollution tax τ^A are constant. The result is

$$
I_{I,E}
\begin{bmatrix}
\partial e/\partial u \cdot du/d\theta^A \\
\partial E/\partial U \cdot dU/d\theta^A \\
d\varepsilon^A/d\theta^A \\
d\varepsilon^B/d\theta^A \\
d\xi/d\theta^A \\
dB/d\theta^A
\end{bmatrix}
=
\begin{bmatrix}
0 \\ 0 \\ 0 \\ 0 \\ 1 \\ -\xi
\end{bmatrix}
\tag{5.42}
$$

where matrix I is

$$
I_{I,E} \stackrel{\text{def}}{=}
\begin{bmatrix}
1 & 0 & -\tau^A & \pm\,\xi\dfrac{\partial^2 R}{\partial K \partial \varepsilon^B} & -\left(\theta^A + \xi\dfrac{\partial^2 R}{\partial K^2}\right) & 1 \\[2mm]
0 & 1 & 0 & \mp\,\xi\dfrac{\partial^2 R}{\partial K \partial \varepsilon^B} & \xi\dfrac{\partial^2 R}{\partial K^2} & 0 \\[2mm]
0 & 0 & \dfrac{\partial^2 r}{\partial(\varepsilon^A)^2} & 0 & \pm\dfrac{\partial^2 r}{\partial \varepsilon^A \partial k} & 0 \\[2mm]
0 & 0 & 0 & \dfrac{\partial^2 R}{\partial(\varepsilon^B)^2} & \mp\dfrac{\partial^2 R}{\partial \varepsilon^B \partial K} & 0 \\[2mm]
0 & 0 & \pm\dfrac{\partial^2 r}{\partial k \partial \varepsilon^A} & \mp\dfrac{\partial^2 R}{\partial K \partial \varepsilon^B} & \left(\dfrac{\partial^2 r}{\partial k^2} + \dfrac{\partial^2 R}{\partial K^2}\right) & 0 \\[2mm]
0 & 0 & \tau^A & 0 & \theta^A & -1
\end{bmatrix}
\tag{5.43}
$$

with determinant

$$
|I_{E,I}| = -|D| \tag{5.44}
$$

where $-|D|$ again is the negative of the determinant of system (5.3) in the case where a lump-sum tax was available. From this follows

$$\frac{\partial e}{\partial u}\frac{du}{d\theta^A}\bigg|_{\bar{\varepsilon}} = -\xi\,\frac{\dfrac{\partial^2 R}{\partial(\varepsilon^B)^2}H^A}{|D|} \tag{5.45}$$

and the definition

$$\text{MCF}_{\theta^A} \overset{\text{def}}{=} -\frac{\partial e}{\partial u}\frac{du}{d\theta^A}\bigg|_{\bar{\varepsilon}}\cdot\frac{1}{\dfrac{dB}{d\theta^A}} = \xi\,\frac{\dfrac{\partial^2 R}{\partial(\varepsilon^B)^2}H^A}{|D|}\cdot\frac{1}{\dfrac{dB}{d\theta^A}} \tag{5.46}$$

where $dB/d\theta^A$ is known from (5.38).

For the MEI_{θ^A}, multiplier $d\varepsilon/d\theta^A$ is derived for the case of an incremental green tax reform (i.e. B is endogenous) with the pollution tax τ^A constant according to (5.35)

$$\frac{d\varepsilon}{d\theta^A}\bigg|_{\overline{\tau^A}} = \frac{1}{|D|}\left(\mp\,\frac{\partial\varepsilon}{\partial\varepsilon^A}\frac{\partial^2 r}{\partial\varepsilon^A\partial k}\frac{\partial^2 R}{\partial(\varepsilon^B)^2} \pm \frac{\partial\varepsilon}{\partial\varepsilon^B}\frac{\partial^2 r}{\partial(\varepsilon^A)^2}\frac{\partial^2 R}{\partial\varepsilon^B\partial K}\right) \tag{5.47}$$

Multiplier (5.47) weighted with the negative of the marginal willingness to pay for the environment then defines the marginal environmental impact (MEI) of the capital tax as

$$\text{MEI}_{\theta^A} \overset{\text{def}}{=} -\frac{\partial e}{\partial\varepsilon}\cdot\frac{d\varepsilon}{d\theta^A}\bigg|_{\overline{\tau^A}}\cdot\frac{1}{\dfrac{dB}{d\theta^A}}$$

$$= \frac{\partial e}{\partial\varepsilon}\left(\frac{\pm\dfrac{\partial\varepsilon}{\partial\varepsilon^A}\dfrac{\partial^2 r}{\partial\varepsilon^A\partial k}\dfrac{\partial^2 R}{\partial(\varepsilon^B)^2} \mp \dfrac{\partial\varepsilon}{\partial\varepsilon^B}\dfrac{\partial^2 r}{\partial(\varepsilon^A)^2}\dfrac{\partial^2 R}{\partial\varepsilon^B\partial K}}{|D|}\right)\frac{1}{\dfrac{dB}{d\theta^A}} \tag{5.48}$$

As direct cost of internalization (DCI) of the capital tax, multiplier $d\varepsilon^A/d\theta^A$ is derived for the case of an incremental tax reform where the public budget is free to adapt and the pollution tax is constant according to (5.35)

$$\frac{d\varepsilon^A}{d\theta^A}\bigg|_{\overline{\tau^A}} = \frac{1}{|D|}\left(\mp\,\frac{\partial^2 r}{\partial\varepsilon^A\partial k}\frac{\partial^2 R}{\partial(\varepsilon^B)^2}\right) \tag{5.49}$$

followed by the definition

$$\text{DCI}_{\theta^A} \stackrel{\text{def}}{=} -\tau^A \cdot \frac{d\varepsilon^A}{d\theta^A}\bigg|_{\tau^A} \cdot \frac{1}{\dfrac{dB}{d\theta^A}}$$

$$= \pm \tau^A \cdot \frac{\dfrac{\partial^2 r}{\partial \varepsilon^A \partial k} \dfrac{\partial^2 R}{\partial (\varepsilon^B)^2}}{|D|} \cdot \frac{1}{\dfrac{dB}{d\theta^A}} \qquad (5.50)$$

Environmental tax

For the MCF of the environmental tax, system (5.32) is considered for the case of an incremental tax reform (i.e. the public budget B is endogenous) when aggregate environmental degradation ε and the capital tax θ^A are constant

$$I \begin{bmatrix} \partial e/\partial u \cdot du/d\tau^A \\ \partial E/\partial U \cdot dU/d\tau^A \\ d\varepsilon^A/d\tau^A \\ d\varepsilon^B/d\tau^A \\ d\xi/d\tau^A \\ dB/d\tau^A \end{bmatrix} = \begin{bmatrix} 0 \\ 0 \\ 1 \\ 0 \\ 0 \\ -\varepsilon^A \end{bmatrix} \qquad (5.51)$$

where matrix I has already been defined in (5.43). From this it can be determined that

$$\frac{\partial e}{\partial u}\frac{du}{d\tau^A}\bigg|_{\bar{\varepsilon}} = -\varepsilon^A \mp \frac{\xi \dfrac{\partial^2 r}{\partial k \partial \varepsilon^A} H^B}{|D|} \qquad (5.52)$$

and

$$\text{MCF}_{\tau^A} \stackrel{\text{def}}{=} -\frac{\partial e}{\partial u}\frac{du}{d\tau^A}\bigg|_{\bar{\varepsilon}} \cdot \frac{1}{\dfrac{dB}{d\tau^A}} = \left(\varepsilon^A \pm \frac{\xi \dfrac{\partial^2 r}{\partial k \partial \varepsilon^A} H^B}{|D|} \right) \cdot \frac{1}{\dfrac{dB}{d\tau^A}} \qquad (5.53)$$

$dB/d\tau^A$ can be determined in a setting similar to system (5.32), but when τ^A changes, θ^A is fixed, and B is free to adapt so that the result is

$$
I_{I,E}^* \begin{bmatrix} \partial e/\partial u \cdot du/d\tau^A \\ \partial E/\partial U \cdot dU/d\tau^A \\ d\varepsilon/d\tau^A \\ d\varepsilon^A/d\tau^A \\ d\varepsilon^B/d\tau^A \\ d\xi/d\tau^A \\ dB/d\tau^A \end{bmatrix} = \begin{bmatrix} 0 \\ 0 \\ 0 \\ 1 \\ 0 \\ 0 \\ -\varepsilon^A \end{bmatrix} \tag{5.54}
$$

where matrix $I_{I,E}^*$ has been defined in (5.36). From this it follows that

$$
\frac{dB}{d\tau^A} = \frac{1}{|D|} \left(\mp \theta^A \frac{\partial^2 r}{\partial k \partial \varepsilon^A} \frac{\partial^2 R}{\partial (\varepsilon^B)^2} + \tau^A \left(\frac{\partial^2 r}{\partial k^2} \frac{\partial^2 R}{\partial (\varepsilon^B)^2} + H^B \right) \right.
$$

$$
\left. + \varepsilon^A |D| \right) \tag{5.55}
$$

For the environmental effect of the pollution tax, multiplier $d\varepsilon/d\tau^A$ is derived for the case of an incremental green tax reform when the public budget is free to adapt and the capital tax is exogenous according to (5.54)

$$
\frac{d\varepsilon}{d\tau^A}\bigg|_{\theta^A} = \frac{1}{|D|} \left(\frac{\partial \varepsilon}{\partial \varepsilon^A} \left(\frac{\partial^2 r}{\partial k^2} \frac{\partial^2 R}{\partial (\varepsilon^B)^2} + H^B \right) - \frac{\partial \varepsilon}{\partial \varepsilon^B} \frac{\partial^2 r}{\partial k \partial \varepsilon^A} \frac{\partial^2 R}{\partial \varepsilon^B \partial K} \right) \tag{5.56}
$$

Weighting multiplier (5.56) with the negative of the marginal willingness to pay for the environment again defines the marginal environmental impact (MEI) of the pollution tax

$$
\text{MEI}_{\tau^A} \stackrel{\text{def}}{=} -\frac{\partial e}{\partial \varepsilon} \cdot \frac{d\varepsilon}{d\tau^A}\bigg|_{\theta^A} \cdot \frac{1}{\frac{dB}{d\tau^A}}
$$

$$
= \frac{\partial e}{\partial \varepsilon} \cdot \frac{-\frac{\partial \varepsilon}{\partial \varepsilon^A} \left(\frac{\partial^2 r}{\partial k^2} \frac{\partial^2 R}{\partial (\varepsilon^B)^2} + H^B \right) + \frac{\partial \varepsilon}{\partial \varepsilon^B} \frac{\partial^2 r}{\partial k \partial \varepsilon^A} \frac{\partial^2 R}{\partial \varepsilon^B \partial K}}{|D|}
$$

$$
\cdot \frac{1}{\frac{dB}{d\tau^A}} \tag{5.57}
$$

For the DCI of the pollution tax, multiplier $d\varepsilon^A/d\tau^A$ is derived again for the case of an incremental green tax reform (i.e. B is endogenous) when the capital tax is exogenous according to (5.54)

$$\left.\frac{d\varepsilon^A}{d\tau^A}\right|_{\theta^A} = \frac{1}{|D|}\left(\frac{\partial^2 r}{\partial k^2}\frac{\partial^2 R}{\partial(\varepsilon^B)^2} + H^B\right) \qquad (5.58)$$

followed by the definition

$$\mathrm{DCI}_{\tau^A} \stackrel{\text{def}}{=} -\tau^A \cdot \left.\frac{d\varepsilon^A}{d\tau^A}\right|_{\theta^A} \cdot \frac{1}{\dfrac{dB}{d\tau^A}}$$

$$= -\tau^A \cdot \frac{\dfrac{\partial^2 r}{\partial k^2}\dfrac{\partial^2 R}{\partial(\varepsilon^B)^2} + H^B}{|D|} \cdot \frac{1}{\dfrac{dB}{d\tau^A}} \qquad (5.59)$$

By means of this rather technical analysis the tools have developed that will now be applied in order to derive conditions for a positive environmental or fiscal dividend, thereby giving a better insight into the decomposition in equation (5.40).

Condition for positive fiscal dividend

From the second line of multiplier (5.40), it follows as a necessary and sufficient condition for Goulder's fiscal dividend to be positive that

$$\xi\frac{H^B}{\dfrac{\partial^2 R}{\partial(\varepsilon^B)^2}} \cdot \frac{d\xi}{d\tau^A} - \left(\xi \cdot \frac{d\theta^A}{d\tau^A} + \varepsilon^A\right) \stackrel{!}{>} 0 \qquad (5.60)$$

which, when transformed into elasticity notation, is equivalent to

$$\frac{\eta_{(B,\tau^A)}}{\eta_{(B,\theta^A)}} \stackrel{!}{>} \frac{\beta}{\gamma}\left(-\frac{\xi}{\varepsilon^A}\frac{H^B}{\dfrac{\partial^2 R}{\partial(\varepsilon^B)^2}} \cdot \frac{d\xi}{d\tau^A} + 1\right) \qquad (5.61)$$

where

$$\gamma \stackrel{\text{def}}{=} \frac{\theta^A \cdot \xi}{B}$$

denotes the revenue share of the capital tax in total tax proceeds. This condition is qualitatively very similar to condition (4.95) derived for the Goulder concept in the small-economy case and only national external-ities in Chapter 4. The additional component again is the strategic impact represented by the first term within brackets. A negative sign of multiplier (5.41) $d\xi/d\tau^A$ (i.e. a positive strategic effect) increases the probability of a positive fiscal dividend. It might then compensate for a fiscally bad performance of the environmental tax, possibly even in cases where the tax is on the decreasing branch of the Laffer curve (i.e. $\eta_{(B,\tau^A)} < 0$). In the case of a small open economy in Chapter 4, the result, in contrast, was that $\eta_{(B,\tau^A)} > 0$ is necessary for a positive fiscal dividend according to the Goulder concept.

Alternatively, turning to the decomposition method according to Schöb, definitions (5.46) and (5.53) lead to

$$(\text{MCF}_{\theta^A} - \text{MCF}_{\tau^A}) = \frac{1}{\frac{dB}{d\tau^A}} \cdot \left(\frac{\mp \xi \frac{\partial^2 r}{\partial k \partial \varepsilon^A} H^B - \varepsilon^A |D|}{|D|} \right.$$

$$\left. + \frac{\xi \frac{\partial^2 R}{\partial (\varepsilon^B)^2} H^A}{|D|} \cdot \frac{\frac{dB}{d\tau^A}}{\frac{dB}{d\theta^A}} \right) \quad (5.62)$$

from which it follows as necessary and sufficient conditions for Goulder's fiscal dividend to be positive that

$$(\text{MCF}_{\theta^A} - \text{MCF}_{\tau^A}) \cdot \frac{dB}{d\tau^A} \overset{!}{>} 0$$

$$\Longleftrightarrow \quad \frac{\frac{dB}{d\tau^A}}{\frac{dB}{d\theta^A}} \overset{!}{>} \frac{\mp \xi \frac{\partial^2 r}{\partial k \partial \varepsilon^A} H^B - \varepsilon^A |D|}{-\xi \frac{\partial^2 R}{\partial (\varepsilon^B)^2} H^A} \quad (5.63)$$

Since the RHS of condition (5.63) is positive for a capital-exporting coun-try and multiplier $dB/d\theta^A$ is positive, the pollution tax must be on the increasing branch of the Laffer curve, i.e. multiplier $dB/d\tau^A$ is positive. Therefore, the above result that $dB/d\tau^A$ might become negative is only possible for a capital-importing country. Consequently, condition (5.63) for a positive fiscal dividend is less strict for a capital-importing country.

Condition for positive environmental dividend

The net environmental effect resulting from an ecological tax reform can be determined from (5.48) and (5.57) as

$$(\mathrm{MEI}_{\tau^A} - \mathrm{MEI}_{\theta^A}) =$$

$$\frac{1}{\frac{dB}{d\tau^A}} \cdot \frac{\partial e}{\partial \varepsilon} \left(\frac{-\dfrac{\partial \varepsilon}{\partial \varepsilon^A}\left(\dfrac{\partial^2 r}{\partial k^2}\dfrac{\partial^2 R}{\partial \left(\varepsilon^B\right)^2} + H^B\right) + \dfrac{\partial \varepsilon}{\partial \varepsilon^B}\dfrac{\partial^2 r}{\partial k \partial \varepsilon^A}\dfrac{\partial^2 R}{\partial \varepsilon^B \partial K}}{|D|} \right.$$

$$\left. \pm \frac{\dfrac{\partial \varepsilon}{\partial \varepsilon^A}\dfrac{\partial^2 r}{\partial \varepsilon^A \partial k}\dfrac{\partial^2 R}{\partial \left(\varepsilon^B\right)^2} - \dfrac{\partial \varepsilon}{\partial \varepsilon^B}\dfrac{\partial^2 r}{\partial \left(\varepsilon^A\right)^2}\dfrac{\partial^2 R}{\partial \varepsilon^B \partial K}}{|D|} \cdot \frac{\frac{dB}{d\tau^A}}{\frac{dB}{d\theta^A}} \right) \quad (5.64)$$

For the net environmental effect to be positive, the necessary and sufficient conditions are

$$(\mathrm{MEI}_{\tau^A} - \mathrm{MEI}_{\theta^A}) \cdot \frac{dB}{d\tau^A} \overset{!}{>} 0$$

$$\Longleftrightarrow \quad \frac{\frac{dB}{d\tau^A}}{\frac{dB}{d\theta^A}} \overset{!}{\underset{<}{\gtrless}} \frac{-\dfrac{\partial \varepsilon}{\partial \varepsilon^A}\left(\dfrac{\partial^2 r}{\partial k^2}\dfrac{\partial^2 R}{\partial \left(\varepsilon^B\right)^2} + H^B\right) + \dfrac{\partial \varepsilon}{\partial \varepsilon^B}\dfrac{\partial^2 r}{\partial k \partial \varepsilon^A}\dfrac{\partial^2 R}{\partial \varepsilon^B \partial K}}{\pm \dfrac{\partial \varepsilon}{\partial \varepsilon^A}\dfrac{\partial^2 r}{\partial \varepsilon^A \partial k}\dfrac{\partial^2 R}{\partial \left(\varepsilon^B\right)^2} + \dfrac{\partial \varepsilon}{\partial \varepsilon^B}\dfrac{\partial^2 r}{\partial \left(\varepsilon^A\right)^2}\dfrac{\partial^2 R}{\partial \varepsilon^B \partial K}}$$

$$(5.65)$$

for denominator $\gtrless 0$ or, equivalently, the isolated environmental effect of the capital tax $\lessgtr 0$.

It can be seen from system (5.32) as well as multipliers (5.38) and (5.55) that the relative change in tax revenue on the LHS of condition (5.65) is the unweighted revenue-recycling effect known from decomposition (5.40)

$$\frac{\frac{dB}{d\tau^A}}{\frac{dB}{d\theta^A}} = -\frac{d\theta^A}{d\tau^A} \qquad (5.66)$$

From condition (5.65) it can be seen that if the foreign country effect on the global environmental situation induced by a domestic ecological tax reform is negligible compared to domestic effects (i.e. the second terms in both the numerator and the denominator on the RHS of condition (5.65) are close to zero), the reform is more probably advantagous for a capital-exporting than for a capital-importing country. If the foreign effect is not strong, according to definition (5.48) the MEI_{θ^A} for a capital-exporting country is negative. This implies that if the revenue-recycling effect of the tax reform is positive (i.e. that $d\theta^A/d\tau^A < 0$), the environmental effect resulting from the diminution of the capital tax is positive, too. Hence, for $dB/d\tau^A$ on the increasing branch of the Laffer curve, there is harmony between the environmental tax increase and the capital tax reduction with respect to the environmental objective. $dB/d\tau^A > 0$ is hence a sufficient condition for a positive environmental effect under the above-mentioned assumptions. For condition (5.65) to be fulfilled for a capital-importing country in the case that mainly domestic environmental depletion matters demands that either the fund-raising power (represented by $dB/d\tau^A$) of the environmental tax be rather low or that the (domestic) environmental effect of the pollution tax be significantly stronger than that of the capital tax.

If on the other hand a domestic ecological tax reform induces a strong foreign environmental effect that dominates the domestic effect by far (i.e. the first term in the numerator and in the denominator in (5.65) is close to zero), the condition can only be fulfilled for a capital-exporting country if the environmental tax is on the decreasing branch of its Laffer curve (i.e. $dB/d\tau^A < 0$). If the country is a capital importer, the condition demands that the environmental tax be on the increasing branch of its Laffer curve (i.e. $dB/d\tau^A > 0$). Furthermore, the revenue-recycling effect connected with the tax reform (represented by the LHS of condition (5.65)) must be quite strong, which means that the fund-raising power of the environmental tax must not be too small compared to that of the capital tax. This in turn implies that the environmental tax should not be very effective with respect to domestic pollution. The intuition behind this is that capital outflows resulting from the tax reform must not be too intensive.

What can be deduced from these findings is that the more weight is on the domestic effect of both tax changes resulting from an ecological tax reform in country A, the easier it is for a capital-exporting country to earn a positive environmental dividend according to the Goulder concept. But the stronger the environmental effects induced abroad, the more probable it is for a capital importing-country to realize a positive environmental dividend.

It has been demonstrated that a double dividend can be reached more easily for a capital-importing than for a capital-exporting country. This is especially true if the leakage effect of pollution migrating abroad is severe. With multiplier $dB/d\tau^A$ being negative, a double dividend cannot be realized for a capital-exporting country because it is not compatible with a positive fiscal dividend. For a capital-importing country a double dividend in the case of $dB/d\tau^A < 0$ is only possible if mainly domestic externality generation is responsible for the environmental situation. When the contribution of the pollution tax to the public budget is positive, i.e. $dB/d\tau^A > 0$, a double dividend is the more probable for a capital-exporting country the more domestic pollution generation is responsible for the country's environmental situation.

5.4.2 The Pearce Concept

The decomposition of the total welfare effect according to the Pearce concept which can likewise be derived from system (5.32) is

$$
\begin{aligned}
\frac{\partial e}{\partial u}\frac{du}{d\tau} =& \left(-\left(\frac{\partial e}{\partial \varepsilon}\frac{\partial \varepsilon}{\partial \varepsilon^A} - \tau^A \right) \cdot \frac{d\varepsilon^A}{d\tau^A} - \frac{\partial e}{\partial \varepsilon}\frac{\partial \varepsilon}{\partial \varepsilon^B} \cdot \frac{d\varepsilon^B}{d\tau^A} \right) \\
&- \left(\xi \cdot \frac{d\theta^A}{d\tau^A} + \varepsilon^A - \xi \frac{H^B}{\dfrac{\partial^2 R}{\partial\left(\varepsilon^B\right)^2}} \cdot \frac{d\xi}{d\tau^A} + \tau^A \frac{d\varepsilon^A}{d\tau^A} \right) \\
=& \left(-\left(\frac{\partial e}{\partial \varepsilon}\frac{\partial \varepsilon}{\partial \varepsilon^A} - \tau^A \right) \cdot \frac{d\varepsilon^A}{d\tau^A} - \frac{\partial e}{\partial \varepsilon}\frac{\partial \varepsilon}{\partial \varepsilon^B} \cdot \frac{d\varepsilon^B}{d\tau^A} \right)
\end{aligned}
\tag{5.67}
$$

$$+ \left(\theta^A + \xi \frac{H^B}{\dfrac{\partial^2 R}{\partial \left(\varepsilon^B \right)^2}} \right) \cdot \frac{d\xi}{d\tau^A} \tag{5.68}$$

The upper line again represents the first dividend consisting of the environmental effects in the home country as well as abroad. But this time, the domestic environmental effect is opposed to the general equilibrium tax base erosion effect which represents the DCI. The second line in equation (5.68) consists of the tax interaction effect ($\theta^A \cdot d\xi/d\tau^A$) and again the strategic component.

Condition for a positive second dividend

As a necessary and sufficient condition for a positive second dividend in the case of application of the Pearce concept leads to equation (5.67)

$$\xi \frac{H^B}{\dfrac{\partial^2 R}{\partial \left(\varepsilon^B \right)^2}} \cdot \frac{d\xi}{d\tau^A} - \left(\xi \cdot \frac{d\theta^A}{d\tau^A} + \varepsilon^A + \tau^A \frac{d\varepsilon^A}{d\tau^A} \right) \overset{!}{>} 0 \tag{5.69}$$

which can alternatively be written as

$$\frac{\eta_{(B,\tau^A)}}{\eta_{(B,\theta^A)}} \overset{!}{>} \frac{\beta}{\gamma} \left(-\frac{\xi}{\varepsilon^A} \frac{H^B}{\dfrac{\partial^2 R}{\partial \left(\varepsilon^B \right)^2}} \cdot \frac{d\xi}{d\tau^A} + \left(1 + \eta_{(\varepsilon^A,\tau^A)} \right) \right) \tag{5.70}$$

As in Chapter 4 the result is that for condition (5.70) to hold it is more unlikely the worse is the net effect of the ecological tax reform on domestic pollution. This is because a negative domestic environmental effect means that $\eta_{(\varepsilon^A,\tau^A)} > 0$. Apart from this, the interpretation of the condition is indentical to that of condition (5.61) for the Goulder concept.

Referring to presentation (5.68), the necessary and sufficient condition for a positive second dividend can alternatively be written as

$$\theta^A \gtrless -\xi \frac{H^B}{\dfrac{\partial^2 R}{\partial \left(\varepsilon^B \right)^2}} \quad \text{for} \quad \frac{d\xi}{d\tau^A} \gtrless 0 \tag{5.71}$$

which means that if the general equilibrium effect on the capital tax base, or equivalently the tax interaction effect, represented by the LHS of (5.71), is positive (i.e. $d\xi/d\tau^A > 0$), the strategic component is negative and must be smaller in absolute value. If, on the other hand, the ecological tax reform reduces cross-border capital flows (i.e. $d\xi/d\tau^A < 0$), the tax interaction effect is negative and must be smaller in absolute terms than the positive strategic effect. Therefore, even if the tax interaction effect $(\theta^A \cdot d\xi/d\tau^A)$ is negative, the second dividend according to the Pearce concept, in contrast to the framework in Chapter 4, might still be positive. The strategic component hence might increase the possibility for a positive second dividend according to both double-dividend concepts – a result which is more relevant for a capital-importing than for a capital-exporting country, however.

When turning to the decomposition of Schöb again and defining the net marginal cost of public funds (NMCF) of the respective tax instruments as the difference between the marginal cost of public funds (MCF) and the direct cost of internalization (DCI), the following definition is derived:

$$\text{NMCF}_i \overset{\text{def}}{=} \text{MCF}_i - \text{DCI}_i \, , \text{ with } i = \tau^A, \theta^A \qquad (5.72)$$

With the help of definitions (5.46), (5.50), (5.53) and (5.59), the second dividend according to the Pearce concept can be determined as

$$(\text{NMCF}_{\theta^A} - \text{NMCF}_{\tau^A}) =$$

$$\frac{1}{\frac{dB}{d\tau^A}} \cdot \left(\frac{\mp \xi \dfrac{\partial^2 r}{\partial k \partial \varepsilon^A} H^B - \varepsilon^A |D| - \tau^A \left(\dfrac{\partial^2 r}{\partial k^2} \dfrac{\partial^2 R}{\partial (\varepsilon^B)^2} + H^B \right)}{|D|} \right.$$

$$\left. + \frac{\xi \dfrac{\partial^2 R}{\partial (\varepsilon^B)^2} H^A \mp \tau^A \dfrac{\partial^2 r}{\partial \varepsilon^A \partial k} \dfrac{\partial^2 R}{\partial (\varepsilon^B)^2}}{|D|} \cdot \dfrac{\frac{dB}{d\tau^A}}{\frac{dB}{d\theta^A}} \right) \qquad (5.73)$$

The necessary and sufficient condition for a positive second dividend then is

$$(\text{NMCF}_{\theta^A} - \text{NMCF}_{\tau^A}) \cdot \frac{dB}{d\tau^A} \overset{!}{>} 0$$

$$\Longleftrightarrow \quad \frac{\frac{dB}{d\tau^A}}{\frac{dB}{d\theta^A}} \overset{!}{\gtrless} \frac{\mp \xi \dfrac{\partial^2 r}{\partial k \partial \varepsilon^A} H^B - \varepsilon^A |D| - \tau^A \left(\dfrac{\partial^2 r}{\partial k^2} \dfrac{\partial^2 R}{\partial (\varepsilon^B)^2} + H^B \right)}{-\xi \dfrac{\partial^2 R}{\partial (\varepsilon^B)^2} H^A \pm \tau^A \dfrac{\partial^2 r}{\partial \varepsilon^A \partial k} \dfrac{\partial^2 R}{\partial (\varepsilon^B)^2}}$$

$$(5.74)$$

for denominator of the RHS $\gtrless 0$.

For the case of country A as a capital exporter, it can be seen that condition (5.74) is less strict than condition (5.63) for the Goulder concept. Because of the additional effects which are the last terms in both the numerator and the denominator, the latter is smaller and the former is larger. The condition can hence also be met more easily if the fiscal performance of the environmental tax is poor, i.e. if $dB/d\tau^A$ is small. If country A is a capital importer, the impact of the adaptations of both the pollution tax and the capital tax on the pollution tax base are opposite: the rise in the pollution tax reduces domestic pollution generation; a reduction in the capital tax raises capital inflows and consequently domestic pollution generation. Whether the last terms in both the numerator and the denominator make condition (5.74) stricter or less strict depends on the sign of multiplier $dB/d\tau^A$. If it is positive, the condition is less strict.

Condition for positive first dividend

As defined in Chapter 4, the net marginal environmental impact (NMEI) of either tax instrument is reflected by the shadow price of the environment net of its DCI

$$\text{NMEI}_i \overset{\text{def}}{=} \text{MEI}_i - \text{DCI}_i \,, \text{ with } i = \tau^A, \theta^A \qquad (5.75)$$

With the help of definitions (5.48), (5.50), (5.57) and (5.59), the first dividend according to the Pearce concept can be determined as

$$(\text{NMEI}_{\tau^A} - \text{NMEI}_{\theta^A}) = \frac{1}{\dfrac{dB}{d\tau^A}}$$

$$\left(\frac{-\left(\dfrac{\partial e}{\partial \varepsilon} \dfrac{\partial \varepsilon}{\partial \varepsilon^A} - \tau^A \right) \left(\dfrac{\partial^2 r}{\partial k^2} \dfrac{\partial^2 R}{\partial (\varepsilon^B)^2} + H^B \right) + \dfrac{\partial e}{\partial \varepsilon} \dfrac{\partial \varepsilon}{\partial \varepsilon^B} \dfrac{\partial^2 r}{\partial k \partial \varepsilon^A} \dfrac{\partial^2 R}{\partial \varepsilon^B \partial K}}{|D|} \right.$$

$$\left. \mp \frac{\left(\dfrac{\partial e}{\partial \varepsilon} \dfrac{\partial \varepsilon}{\partial \varepsilon^A} - \tau^A \right) \dfrac{\partial^2 r}{\partial \varepsilon^A \partial k} \dfrac{\partial^2 R}{\partial (\varepsilon^B)^2} - \dfrac{\partial e}{\partial \varepsilon} \dfrac{\partial \varepsilon}{\partial \varepsilon^B} \dfrac{\partial^2 r}{\partial (\varepsilon^A)^2} \dfrac{\partial^2 R}{\partial \varepsilon^B \partial K}}{|D|} \cdot \frac{\dfrac{dB}{d\tau^A}}{\dfrac{dB}{d\theta^A}} \right)$$

$$(5.76)$$

The necessary and sufficient condition for a positive first dividend then is

$$(\text{NMEI}_{\tau^A} - \text{NMEI}_{\theta^A}) \cdot \frac{dB}{d\tau^A} \overset{!}{>} 0$$

$$\Longleftrightarrow \quad \frac{\dfrac{dB}{d\tau^A}}{\dfrac{dB}{d\theta^A}} \overset{!}{\gtreqless}$$

$$\frac{-\left(\dfrac{\partial e}{\partial \varepsilon} \dfrac{\partial \varepsilon}{\partial \varepsilon^A} - \tau^A \right) \left(\dfrac{\partial^2 r}{\partial k^2} \dfrac{\partial^2 R}{\partial (\varepsilon^B)^2} + H^B \right) + \dfrac{\partial e}{\partial \varepsilon} \dfrac{\partial \varepsilon}{\partial \varepsilon^B} \dfrac{\partial^2 r}{\partial k \partial \varepsilon^A} \dfrac{\partial^2 R}{\partial \varepsilon^B \partial K}}{\pm \left(\dfrac{\partial e}{\partial \varepsilon} \dfrac{\partial \varepsilon}{\partial \varepsilon^A} - \tau^A \right) \dfrac{\partial^2 r}{\partial \varepsilon^A \partial k} \dfrac{\partial^2 R}{\partial (\varepsilon^B)^2} \mp \dfrac{\partial e}{\partial \varepsilon} \dfrac{\partial \varepsilon}{\partial \varepsilon^B} \dfrac{\partial^2 r}{\partial (\varepsilon^A)^2} \dfrac{\partial^2 R}{\partial \varepsilon^B \partial K}}$$

$$(5.77)$$

for the denominator of the RHS $\gtreqless 0$.

The interpretation of condition (5.77) for $\partial e / \partial \varepsilon \cdot \partial \varepsilon / \partial \varepsilon^A - \tau^A > 0$ is similar to that of condition (5.65) for the Goulder concept. The main difference between the concepts is that environmental changes abroad have a stronger weight in the Pearce concept than in the Goulder concept. This in turn means that condition (5.77) can be fulfilled much more easily by a capital-importing than a capital-exporting country.

If the above conditions are analysed at the locus $\tau^A = \partial e/\partial \varepsilon \cdot \partial \varepsilon / \partial \varepsilon^A$, they reduce to

$$\left. (\text{NMEI}_{\tau^A} - \text{NMEI}_{\varrho^A}) \right|_{\tau^A = \partial e/\partial \varepsilon \cdot \partial \varepsilon / \partial \varepsilon^A} \cdot \frac{dB}{d\tau^A} \overset{!}{>} 0$$

$$\Longleftrightarrow \quad \frac{\dfrac{dB}{d\tau^A}}{\dfrac{dB}{d\theta^A}} \overset{!}{\gtrless} \frac{\dfrac{\partial^2 r}{\partial k \partial \varepsilon^A}}{\dfrac{\partial^2 r}{\mp \, \partial (\varepsilon^A)^2}} \quad \text{for denominator of the RHS} \gtrless 0$$

$$(5.78)$$

and in elasticity notation

$$\Longleftrightarrow \quad \frac{\eta_{(B,\tau^A)}}{\eta_{(B,\theta^A)}} \overset{!}{\gtrless} \frac{\beta}{\mp \, \gamma} \frac{\eta_{(\partial r/\partial \varepsilon^A;\xi)}}{\eta_{(\partial r/\partial \varepsilon^A;\varepsilon^A)}} \qquad (5.79)$$

for denominator of the RHS $\gtrless 0$.

The 'greater sign' and hence a positive denominator on the RHS of condition (5.79) applies to the importer case. Since in this case the numerator is positive as well, the LHS of condition (5.79) must be positive and greater than the RHS. The 'lower sign' and a negative denominator on the RHS of condition (5.79) are valid for the case that country A is a capital exporter. This condition to be fulfilled requires $\eta_{(B,\tau^A)} < 0$, which means that the environmental tax is on the decreasing branch of the Laffer curve. Consequently, a positive environmental or first dividend according to the Pearce concept is possible even if the tax rate is already as high as the marginal environmental damage in the initial equilibrium – a result that differs from those derived in Chapter 4. It is based on the fact that, although no environmental net effect according to the Pearce concept can be realized in the home country itself, positive environmental effects might occur abroad which are also perceived in the home country.

5.5 CONCLUSIONS

If public funds are raised with the help of lump-sum taxes, there is a similarity between the two national tax instruments, i.e. pollution tax and capital tax. Both are appropriate to simultaneously (i) manipulate prices on the world market and (ii) to internalize directly and indirectly externalities arising from domestic or foreign production. The targeting principle applies, which recommends that a government following two objectives should consequently employ two instruments: one policy aiming at improving the quality of the environment (i.e. the pollution tax) and the other at partly shifting the tax burden to foreigners (e.g. a tax on repatriated capital rents), thereby also influencing externality generation abroad. If, on the other hand, explicit taxes on international capital movements are excluded, pollution taxes might raise non-environmental national welfare by implicitly influencing factor rewards to capital.

Apart from these *national* considerations, *global* efficiency is only available through the introduction of environmental taxes in both countries, which account for the global damages.

Furthermore, in order to analyse the double-dividend character of environmental taxes in this extended model framework, the two concepts presented in Chapter 4 were applied. The ecological tax reform consisted of a rise in the pollution tax, the proceeds of which were then used partly to replace the distortionary capital tax. It was found that two additional effects modify the results of Chapter 4:

- First, leakage of pollution abroad counteracts domestic internalization efforts and might even worsen a unilaterally acting country's environmental situation. If mainly domestic externality generation determines environmental quality, the reform – from an environmental point of view – is more probably advantageous for a capital-exporting country. This is because both a pollution tax increase and a capital tax reduction have the same positive effect on domestic externality generation. The stronger the impact of foreign pollution on the environmental situation, the more easily the condition for a positive first dividend, according to both concepts, can be met by a capital-importing country. In the Pearce concept, environmental pollution abroad has a heavier weight within the first dividend compared to Goulder's concept. This strengthens the result that it is easier for a capital-importing country to realize a positive first dividend.

- Second, strategic considerations also influence the welfare of a country that unilaterally implements an ecological tax reform. The strategic manipulation of factor rewards to internationally mobile capital might then compensate for a poor fiscal performance of the pollution tax. It was found that a positive fiscal effect according to the Goulder concept is easier to reach for a capital-importing than for a capital-exporting country. The reason is that for a capital-importing country the outflow of capital due to internalization efforts is also in favour of its strategic ends. For the Pearce concept it was shown that there might be a positive second dividend even if the tax interaction effect was negative. This again is due to the strategic effects which are more probably positive for a capital-importing than for a capital-exporting country.

A double dividend – which, as demonstrated in Chapter 4, can only be realized if the tax system in the initial equilibrium is inefficient from a public finance point of view – was found to be more probable for a capital-importing than for a capital-exporting country. This holds especially if 'carbon leakage effects' are considerable.

An important difference from the double-dividend analysis in a closed or in a small open economy is that, from a public finance point of view, in the big-country case the nationally optimal tax rates of distortionary taxes are not equal to zero even if lump-sum taxes are available. This is due to strategic considerations.

The difference between introducing a capital tax and imposing a tariff, as in the trade models discussed in Chapter 3 and analysed in Chapter 4, consists of the fact that a capital tax generally cannot be levied selectively. If a model includes two or several goods and if pollution is not caused by production of all goods, influencing the international capital allocation is less effective for an indirect internalization. Because of the assumption of only one single composite good, the production of which is connected with pollution, this aspect remained unconsidered. If the environment is not modelled as a factor of production or if pollution does not result from production but is caused by capital used as a factor of production, the capital tax is the more effective instrument, however.

Chapter 6

Concluding remarks

The main objective of this book was an analysis and discussion of allocative effects that result from the implementation of an ecological tax reform. The attractiveness of green taxes is to earn a double dividend, i.e. to improve the environment and to reduce the excess burden of the tax system. The double-dividend issue has so far only been studied for closed and small open economies. Instead, this study has analysed the case of large open economies. In order to keep the analysis tractable, we concentrated on international capital mobility and transborder externalities, but omitted unemployment. International capital mobility is decisive for double-dividend considerations since the erosion of national tax bases constitutes an integral part of the problem.

From the main results the following fundamental suggestions for environmental policy can be deduced:

- **Double-dividend characteristic of environmental taxes**
  Whether there is a double dividend or not hinges crucially on (i) what concept underlies the analysis and (ii) the extent to which the tax system in the initial equilibrium is inefficient. An adequate strategy for national policy-making would be to improve the tax system's fiscal performance following optimal taxation guidelines and to introduce ecological tax components if required. Translated into the terms of the Goulder concept, this would mean: optimize the tax system so as to reach its second-best optimal shape from a

185

fiscal point of view – which requires using all tax bases including those for environmental taxes. Then introduce or further increase the ecological component in the tax system in order to earn an environmental dividend – this of course at the cost of sacrificing the fiscally optimal shape of the tax system (the second dividend becomes negative). This would mean altering the tax system towards its overall second-best optimal shape, incorporating fiscal and environmental effects. The conclusion hence is that environmental policy should be implemented in order to improve environmental quality and not the fiscal efficiency of the tax system.

- **The Goulder concept as a rule of thumb**

  Goulder, with his double-dividend concept, gives a guideline to policy-makers who do not have complete information. The aim is to make cost–benefit analyses dispensable before enacting an ecological tax reform. Such rules of thumb are comfortable and useful on the one hand, but dangerous on the other and must therefore be validated in general equilibrium analyses. By comparing Goulder's concept to the Pearce concept it was shown that the informational requirements for his concept are in fact not significantly lower. The possibility for a real no-regret policy in the case of a double dividend only arises if individuals are identical. But in this case a vote would even lead to the second-best optimum, whereas following the Goulder concept would mean leaving welfare potentials unexploited. If model assumptions are relaxed and individuals are not identical, Goulder's concept is no longer appropriate in guaranteeing a no-regret policy step.

- **Unilateral policy actions**

  The diverse interactions of unilateral environmental policies with other national objectives have to be carefully studied and evaluated. Even if strategic aspects or the influence of national policies on foreign transborder externality generation are not in the forefront of a country's considerations, these interactions are of great importance for national welfare. If they remain unconsidered when national policies are designed, unilateral ecopolitical actions may well lead to counter-productive effects on a country's income and environmental situation. Aspects such as international or global efficiency are irrelevant if international cooperation does not exist.

Possible extensions for future work in this field are to embed the different kinds of involuntary unemployment in a model structure that accounts for strategic aspects with regard to international mobility of goods and factors as well as for transborder externalities. Another interesting question is whether in a situation where countries have to rely on distorting taxes, global welfare is higher in the case of (i) cooperative actions when equiproportional emission reductions are most likely to be agreed upon or (ii) implementation of unilateral actions.

Bibliography

Althammer, Wilhelm and Wolfgang Buchholz (1993), 'Internationaler Umweltschutz als Koordinationsproblem', in Adolf Wagner, ed., *Dezentrale Entscheidungsfindung bei externen Effekten – Innovation, Integration und internationaler Handel*, Francke, Tübingen, ch. 5, 289–315.

Arnold, Volker (1984), 'Umweltschutz als international öffentliches Gut: Komparative Kostenvorteile und Verhandlungsgewinne', *Zeitschrift für Wirtschafts- und Sozialwissenschaften* 104, 111–29.

Bach, Stefan, Michael Kohlhaas and Barbara Praetorius (1995), 'Möglichkeiten einer ökologischen Steuerreform', *WSI-Mitteilungen* 4, 244–54.

Bach, Stefan, Michael Kohlhaas, Volker Meinhardt, Barbara Praetorius, Hans Wessels and Rudolf Zwiener (1994), *Ökosteuer – Sackgasse oder Königsweg? Wirtschaftliche Auswirkungen einer ökologischen Steuerreform*, Greenpeace, Hamburg.

Barrett, Scott (1992), 'International environmental agreements as games', in Rüdiger Pethig, ed., *Conflicts and Cooperation in Managing Environmental Resources*, Springer, Berlin, ch. 1, 11–36.

Baumol, William J. and D.F. Bradford (1972), 'Detrimental externalities and non-convexity of the production set', *Economica* 39, 160–76.

Baumol, William J. and Wallace E. Oates (1971), 'The use of standards and prices for protection of the environment', *Swedish Journal of Economics* 73, 42–54.

Baumol, William J. and Wallace E. Oates (1988), *The Theory of Environmental Policy*, 2nd edn, Cambridge University Press, Cambridge (UK).

BDI (Bundesverband der deutschen Industrie) (1994), *Umsteuern mit Ökosteuern?*, Vol. 278 of *BDI-Drucksache*, Bundesverband der deutschen Industrie e.V., Cologn.

Black, Jane, Maurice D. Levi and David de Meza (1993), 'Creating a good atmosphere: Minimum participation for tackling the "greenhouse effect" ', *Economica* 60, 281–93.

Boadway, Robin W. and Neil Bruce (1984), *Welfare Economics*, Blackwell, Oxford (UK).

Bohm, Peter (1993), 'Incomplete international cooperation to reduce CO_2 emissions: Alternative policies', *Journal of Environmental Economics and Management* 24(3), 258–71.

Böhringer, Christoph, Thomas F. Rutherford, Andreas Pahlke, Ulrich Fahl and Alfred Voß (1997), *Volkswirtschaftliche Effekte einer Umstrukturierung des deutschen Steuersystems unter besonderer Berücksichtigung von Umweltsteuern*, Vol. 37 of *Forschungsbericht*, Institut für Energiewirtschaft und Rationelle Energieanwendung, Universität Stuttgart, Stuttgart.

Böhringer, Christoph, Ulrich Fahl and Alfred Voß (1994), 'Ökologische Steuerreform – ein Königsweg?', *Energiewirtschaftliche Tagesfragen* 44(10), 622–4.

Bovenberg, A. Lans and Lawrence H. Goulder (1996), 'Optimal environmental taxation in the presence of other taxes: General-equilibrium analyses', *The American Economic Review* 86(4), 985–1000.

Bovenberg, A. Lans and Gilbert H.A. van Hagen (1999), 'How can we determine the truth about the double dividend?', in Howard Chernick, ed., *91st Annual Conference on Taxation*, Proceedings, National Tax Association, Washington DC, 35–9. Austin, Texas, November 8–10, 1998.

Bovenberg, A. Lans and Ruud A. de Mooij (1994*a*), 'Environmental levies and distortionary taxation', *The American Economic Review* 84(4), 1085–9.

Bovenberg, A. Lans and Ruud A. de Mooij (1994*b*), 'Environmental policy in a small open economy with distortionary labour taxes: A general equilibrium analysis', in Ekko C. van Ierland, ed., *International Environmental Economics. Theories, Models and Applications to Climate Change, International Trade and Acidification*, Vol. 4 of *Developments in Environmental Economics*, Elsevier, Amsterdam, ch. 10, 213–54.

Bovenberg, A. Lans and Ruud A. de Mooij (1994*c*), 'Environmental taxation and labor-market distortions', *European Journal of Political Economy* 10(4), 655–83.

Bovenberg, A. Lans and Ruud A. de Mooij (1996), 'Environmental taxation and the double-dividend: The role of factor substitution and capital mobility', in Carlo Carraro and Domenico Siniscalco, eds, *Environmental Fiscal Reform and Unemployment*, Vol. 7 of *Economics, Energy and Environment*, Kluwer Academic Publishers, Dordrecht, ch. 1, 3–52.

Bovenberg, A. Lans and Ruud A. de Mooij (1997), 'Environmental levies and distortionary taxation: Reply', *The American Economic Review* 87(1), 252–3.

Bovenberg, A. Lans and Frederick van der Ploeg (1994*a*), 'Environmental policy, public finance and the labour market in a second-best world', *Journal of Public Economics* 55(3), 349–90.

Bovenberg, A. Lans and Frederick van der Ploeg (1994*b*), 'Green policies and public finance in a small open economy', *The Scandinavian Journal of Economics* 96(3), 343–63.

Bovenberg, A. Lans and Frederick van der Ploeg (1996), 'Optimal taxation, public goods and environmental policy with involuntary unemployment', *Journal of Public Economics* 62(1–2), 59–83.

Buchanan, James M. (1969), 'External diseconomies, corrective taxes, and market structure', *The American Economic Review* 59, 174–7.

Carraro, Carlo and Domenico Siniscalco (1993), 'Strategies for the international protection of the environment', *Journal of Public Economics* 52(3), 309–28.

Cline, William R. (1992), *The Economics of Global Warming*, Institute for International Economics, Washington, DC.

Coase, Ronald H. (1960), 'The problem of social cost', *Journal of Law and Economics* 3, 1–44.

Copeland, Brian R. (1994), 'International trade and the environment: Policy reform in a polluted open economy', *Journal of Environmental Economics and Management* 26, 44–65.

Cornes, Richard C. (1992), *Duality and Modern Economics*, Cambridge University Press, Cambridge (UK).

Cornes, Richard C. and Todd Sandler (1986), *The Theory of Externalities, Public Goods, and Club Goods*, Cambridge University Press, Cambridge (UK).

Council of Economic Advisors (1994), *Den Aufschwung sichern – Arbeitsplätze schaffen*, Jahresgutachten, Metzler-Poeschel, Stuttgart.

Cropper, Maureen L. and Wallace E. Oates (1992), 'Environmental economics: A survey', *Journal of Economic Literature* 30, 675–740.

Dean, Judith M. (1992), 'Trade and the environment: A survey of the literature', in Patrick Low, ed., *International Trade and the Environment*, Vol. 159 of *World Bank Discussion Papers*, The World Bank, Washington, DC, ch. 2, 15–28.

Diamond, Peter A. (1973), 'Consumption externalities and imperfect corrective pricing', *The Bell Journal of Economics and Management Science* 4(2), 526–38.

DIW (1994), 'Ökologische Steuerreform auch im nationalen Alleingang!', *DIW Wochenbericht* 24, 395–404.

Dixit, Avinash K. (1975), 'Welfare effects of tax and price changes', *Journal of Public Economics* 4, 103–23.

Dixit, Avinash K. and Victor D. Norman (1980), *Theory of International Trade*, Cambridge Economic Handbooks, Cambridge University Press, Cambridge (UK).

Dockner, Engelbert J. and Ngo Van Long (1993), 'International pollution control: Cooperative versus non-cooperative strategies', *Journal of Environmental Economics and Management* 25, 13–29.

Endres, Alfred (1993), 'Internationale Vereinbarungen zum Schutz der globalen Umweltressourcen – Der Fall proportionaler Emissionsreduktion', *Aussenwirtschaft* 48, 51–76.

Endres, Alfred and Michael Finus (1998), 'Playing a better global emission game: Does it help to be green?', *Swiss Journal of Economics and Statistics* 134(1), 21–40.

Enquête Kommission 'Schutz der Erdatmosphäre' des Deutschen Bundestages (1992), *Klimaänderung gefährdet globale Entwicklung: Zukunft sichern – jetzt handeln*, Vol. 12,2400 of *Drucksache/Deutscher Bundestag*, Economica, Bonn.

Enquête Kommission 'Schutz der Erdatmosphäre' des Deutschen Bundestages (1993), *Erneuerbare Energien: der Weg zu einer nachhaltigen und klimaverträglichen Energieversorgung*, Vol. 12/20 (a–h) of *Kommissionsdrucksache (KD)*, Deutscher Bundestag, Bonn.

Enquête Kommission 'Vorsorge zum Schutz der Erdatmosphäre' des Deutschen Bundestages (1990), *Bericht der Enquête Kommission des 11. Deutschen Bundestages 'Vorsorge zum Schutz der Erdatmosphäre'*, Vol. 3 of *Drucksache/Deutscher Bundestag*, Economica, Bonn.

Felder, Stefan and Thomas F. Rutherford (1993), 'Unilateral CO_2 reductions and carbon leakage: The consequences of international trade in oil and basic materials', *Journal of Environmental Economics and Management* 25(2), 162–76.

Finus, Michael and Bianca Rundshagen (1998), 'Toward a positive theory of coalition formation and endogenous instrumental choice in global pollution control', *Public Choice* 96, 145–86.

Freeman, A. Myrick (1984), 'Depletable externalities and pigouvian taxation', *Journal of Environmental Economics and Management* 11, 173–9.

Fullerton, Don (1997), 'Environmental levies and distortionary taxation: Comment', *The American Economic Review* 87(1), 245–51.

Fullerton, Don and Jane G. Gravelle (1999), 'The irrelevance of the double dividend', in Howard Chernick, ed., *91st Annual Conference on Taxation*, Proceedings, National Tax Association, Washington DC, 75–80. Austin, Texas, November 8–10, 1998.

Fullerton, Don and Ann Wolverton (1997), *The case for a two-part instrument: presumptive tax and environmental subsidy*, Vol. 5993 of *NBER Working Papers*, National Bureau of Economic Research, Cambridge (MA).

Goulder, Lawrence (1995), 'Environmental taxation and the double dividend: A reader's guide', *International Tax and Public Finance* 2(2), 157–83.

Goulder, Lawrence H., Ian W.H. Parry and Dallas Burtraw (1997), 'Revenue-raising vs. other approaches to environmental protection: the critical significance of pre-existing tax distortions', *Rand Journal of Economics* 28(4), 708–31.

Heister, Johannes, Ernst Mohr, Wolf Plesmann, Frank Stähler, Tobias Stoll and Rüdiger Wolfrum (1995), 'Economic and legal aspects of international environmental agreements – the case of enforcing and stabilising an international CO_2 agreement', No. 711 of Kiel Working Papers, Kiel Institute of World Economics, Kiel.

Hettich, Frank (2000), *Economic Growth and Environmental Policy: A Theoretical Approach*, New Horizons in Environmental Economics, Edward Elgar, Cheltenham (UK). Forthcoming.

Hettich, Frank, Sebastian Killinger and Peter Winker (1997), 'Die ökologische Steuerreform auf dem Prüfstand – Zur Kritik am Gutachten des Deutschen Instituts für Wirtschaftsforschung', *Zeitschrift für Umweltpolitik & Umweltrecht* 20(2), 199–225.

Hoel, Michael (1991), 'Global environmental problems: The effect of unilateral actions taken by one country', *Journal of Environmental Economics and Management* 20, 55–70.

Hoel, Michael (1992), 'Carbon taxes: An international tax or harmonized domestic taxes?', *European Economic Review* 36, 400–6.

Hoel, Michael (1994), 'Efficient climate policy in the presence of free riders', *Journal of Environmental Economics and Management* 27(3), 259–74.

Hoel, Michael (1997a), 'Coordination of environmental policy for transboundary environmental problems?', *Journal of Public Economics* 66(2), 199–224.

Hoel, Michael (1997b), 'International coordination of environmental taxes', in Carlo Carraro and Domenico Siniscalco, eds, *New Directions in the Economic Theory of the Environment*, Cambridge University Press, Cambridge (UK), ch. 7, 193–238.

Kemp, Murray C. (1964), *The Pure Theory of International Trade*, Prentice-Hall, Englewood Cliffs (NJ).

Killinger, Sebastian (1996), 'Indirect internalization of international environmental externalities', *Finanzarchiv* 53(3+4), 332–68.

Killinger, Sebastian (1997), *A Note on the Double Dividend of Ecological Tax Reforms*, No. 54 of *IWÖ Discussion Papers*, Hochschule St. Gallen (HSG), St. Gallen.

Killinger, Sebastian and Carsten Schmidt (1998), 'Nationale Umweltpolitik und internationale Integration – theoretische Ansätze im Überblick', *Finanzarchiv* 55(2), 219–53.

Kox, Henk and Casper van der Tak (1996), 'Non-transboundary pollution and the efficiency of international environmental cooperation', *Energy Economics* 19, 247–59.

Kreps, David M., Paul Milgrom, John Roberts and Robert Wilson (1982), 'Rational cooperation in the finitely repeated prisoner's dilemma', *Journal of Economic Theory* 27, 245–52.

Krutilla, Kerry (1991), 'Environmental regulation in an open economy', *Journal of Environmental Economics and Management* 20, 127–42.

Laffont, Jean–Jaques (1988), *Fundamentals of Public Economics*, MIT Press, Cambridge (MA).

Larson, Bruce A. and James A. Tobey (1994), 'Uncertain climate change and the international policy response', *Ecological Economics* 11, 77–84.

Linscheidt, Bodo and Achim Truger (1994), 'Ökologische Steuerreform und Stabilität des Finanzsystems', *Vierteljahreshefte zur Wirtschaftsforschung* 63(4), 434–52.

Linscheidt, Bodo and Achim Truger (1995), *Beurteilung ökologischer Steuerreformvorschläge vor dem Hintergrund des bestehenden Steuersystems*, Vol. 62 of *Finanzwissenschaftliche Forschungsarbeiten*, Duncker & Humblot, Berlin.

Lipnowski, Irwin and Shlomo Maital (1983), 'Voluntary provision of a pure public good as the game of "chicken" ', *Journal of Public Economics* 20, 381–6.

Ludema, Rodney D. and Ian Wooton (1994), 'Cross-border externalities and trade liberalization: The strategic control of pollution', *Canadian Journal of Economics* 27(4), 950–66.

MacDougall, G.D.A. (1960), 'The benefit and cost of investment from abroad', *Economic Record* 36, 13–35.

Mäler, Karl-Göran (1989), 'The acid rain game', in Henk Folmer and Ekko C. van Ierland, eds, *Valuation Methods and Policy Making in Environmental Economics*, Vol. 36 of *Studies in Environmental Science*, Elsevier, Amsterdam, ch. 12, 231–52.

Mäler, Karl-Göran (1990), 'International environmental problems', *Oxford Economic Review* 6(1), 80–108.

Markusen, James R. (1975), 'International externalities and optimal tax structures', *Journal of International Economics* 5, 15–29.

Mauch, Samuel, Rolf Iten, Ernst Ulrich von Weizsäcker and Jochen Jesinghaus (1992), *Ökologische Steuerreform. Europäische Ebene und Fallbeispiel Schweiz*, Rüegger, Chur.

McGuire, Martin C. (1982), 'Regulation, factor rewards, and international trade', *Journal of Public Economics* 17, 335–54.

Meade, James E. (1952), *A Geometry of International Trade*, George Allen & Unwin, London.

Merrifield, John (1988), 'The impact of selected abatement strategies on transnational pollution, the terms of trade, and factor rewards: A general equilibrium approach', *Journal of Environmental Economics and Management* 15, 259–84.

Michaelis, Peter (1994*a*), 'On the economics of greenhouse gas accumulation: A simulation approach', *European Journal of Political Economy* 10, 707–26.

Michaelis, Peter (1994*b*), 'Sustainable greenhouse policies: The role of a comprehensive approach', University of Kiel, Kiel. Unpublished paper.

Misiolek, Walter S. and H.W. Elder (1989), 'Exclusionary manipulation of markets for pollution rights', *Journal of Environmental Economics and Management* 16, 156–66.

Münch, Rainer and Barbara Böttcher (1995), *Ökologische Steuerreform – Patentrezept oder Mogelpackung?*, Sonderbericht, Deutsche Bank Research, Frankfurt a.M.

Myles, Gareth D. (1995), *Public Economics*, Cambridge University Press, Cambridge (UK).

Nielsen, Søren Bo, Lars Haagen Pedersen and Peter Birch Sørensen (1995), 'Environmental policy, pollution unemployment, and endogenous growth', *International Tax and Public Finance* 2(2), 185–205.

Oates, Wallace E. (1993), 'Pollution charges as a source of public revenues', in Herbert Giersch, ed., *Economic Progress and Environmental Concerns*, Springer, Berlin, 135–52.

Oates, Wallace E. and Robert M. Schwab (1988), 'Economic competition among jurisdictions: Efficiency enhancing or distortion inducing?', *Journal of Public Economics* 35, 333–54.

OECD (1976), *Economics of Transfrontier Pollution*, OECD, Paris.

OECD (1994), *Trade and Pollution Linkages: Piecemeal Reform and Optimal Intervention*, Vol. 55 of *Working Papers*, OECD, Paris.

Oepping, Hardy (1995), *Ökologische Steuerreform: Eine mikroökonomisch fundierte Simulationsstudie*, Gabler Edition Wissenschaft, Deutscher Universitäts-Verlag, Wiesbaden.

Parry, Ian W.H. (1995), 'Pollution taxes and revenue recycling', *Journal of Environmental Economics and Management* 29(3), S-64 – S-77.

Pearce, David (1990), 'Economics and the global environmental challenge', *Journal of International Studies* 19(3), 365–87.

Pearce, David (1991), 'The role of carbon taxes in adjusting to global warming', *The Economic Journal* 101, 938–48.

Pezzey, John C.V. (1992), 'Analysis of unilateral CO_2 control in the European community and OECD', *The Energy Journal* 13, 159–71.

Pigou, Arthur Cecile (1932), *The Economics of Welfare*, Macmillan, London.

Ploeg, Frederick van der and Aart J. de Zeeuw (1992), 'International aspects of pollution control', *Environmental and Resource Economics* 2, 117–39.

Porter, Michael E. and Claas van der Linde (1995), 'Toward a new conception of the environment–competitiveness relationship', *Journal of Economic Perspectives* 9(4), 97–118.

Prognos (1991), *Die energiewirtschaftliche Entwicklung in der Bundesrepublik Deutschland bis zum Jahre 2010 unter Einbeziehung der fünf neuen Bundesländer*, Prognos, Basel.

Prognos (1993), *Prognos Deutschland Report. Die BRD 2000–2005–2010. Entwicklung von Wirtschaft und Gesellschaft*, Prognos, Basel.

Rauscher, Michael (1997), 'Environmental regulation and international capital allocation', in Carlo Carraro and Domenico Siniscalco, eds, *New Directions in the Economic Theory of the Environment*, Cambridge University Press, Cambridge (UK), ch. 7, 193–238.

Ruffin, Roy J. (1984), 'International factor movements', in Ronald W. Jones and Peter B. Kenen, eds, *Handbook of International Economics*, Vol. 1 of *Handbooks in Economics*, North-Holland, Amsterdam, ch. 5, 237–88.

Ruocco, Anna and Wolfgang Wiegard (1997), 'Green tax reforms: Understanding the double dividend hypothesis', *Zeitschrift für Umweltpolitik & Umweltrecht* 20(2), 171–98.

Sandler, Todd (1996), 'A game theoretic analysis of carbon emissions', in Roger D. Congleton, ed., *The Political Economy of Environmental Protection – Analysis and Evidence*, University of Michigan Press, Ann Arbor, ch. 11, 251–72.

Sandler, Todd (1997), *Global Challenges: An Approach to Environmental, Political, and Economic Problems*, Cambridge University Press, Cambridge (UK).

Sandmo, Agnar (1975), 'Optimal taxation in the presence of externalities', *Swedish Journal of Economics* 77, 86–98.

Schmidt, Carsten (2000), 'Designing International Environmental Agreements: Incentive Compatible Strategies for Cost-effective Cooperation', *New Horizons in Environmental Economics*, Edward Elgar, Cheltenham (UK). Forthcoming.

Schmidt, Carsten (2000), 'Incentives for international environmental cooperation: theoretic models and economic instruments', in Günther Schulze and Heinrich Ursprung, eds, *International Environmental Economics: A Survey of the Issues*, Oxford University Press, Oxford, ch. 6. Forthcoming.

Schneider, Kerstin (1997), 'Involuntary unemployment and environmental policy: The double dividend hypothesis', *The Scandinavian Journal of Economics* 99(1), 45–59.

Schöb, Ronnie (1996), 'Evaluating tax reforms in the presence of externalities', *Oxford Economic Papers* 48(4), 537–55.

Schöb, Ronnie (1997), 'Environmental taxes and pre-existing distortions: The normalization trap', *International Tax and Public Finance* 4, 167–76.

Schulze, Günther and Heinrich Ursprung (2000), 'Environmental policy in an integrated world economy: The political-economic view', in Günther Schulze and Heinrich Ursprung, eds, *International Environmental Economics: A Survey of the Issues*, Oxford University Press, Oxford, ch. 4. Forthcoming.

Smith, Stephen (1992), 'Taxation and the environment: A survey', *Fiscal Studies* 13(4), 21–57.

Smulders, Sjak A. (1995), 'Entropy, environment, and endogenous economic growth', *International Tax and Public Finance* 2(2), 319–40.

Snape, Richard H. (1992), 'The environment, international trade and competitiveness', in Kym Anderson and Richard Blackhurst, eds, *The Greening of World Trade Issues*, The University of Michigan Press, Ann Arbor, ch. 4, 73–92.

Tietenberg, Tom H. (1994), 'Implementation issues for globally trade-able carbon entitlements', in Ekko C. van Ierland, ed., *International Environmental Economics: Theories and Applications to Climate Change, International Trade and Acidification*, Elsevier, Amsterdam, 119–49.

Weitzman, Martin L. (1974), 'Prices vs. quantities', *The Review of Economic Studies* 41, 477–91.

Williamson, Oliver E. (1983), 'Credible commitments: Using hostages to support exchange', *The American Economic Review* 73, 519–40.

Winker, Peter (1996), *Kreditrationierung auf dem Markt für Unternehmerkredite*, Mohr & Siebeck, Tübingen.

Index